FLYING'S STRANGEST MOMENTS

Other titles in this series:

Boxing's Strangest Fights
Bridge's Strangest Games
Cinema's Strangest Moments
Cricket's Strangest Matches
Fishing's Strangest Days
Football's Strangest Matches
Gambling's Strangest Moments
Golf's Strangest Rounds
Horse-racing's Strangest Races
The Law's Strangest Cases
Medicine's Strangest Cases
The Military's Strangest Campaigns and Characters
Motor-racing's Strangest Races
The Olympics' Strangest Moments
Politics' Strangest Characters
Railways' Strangest Journeys
Rock 'n' Roll's Strangest Moments
Rugby's Strangest Matches
Sailing's Strangest Moments
Shooting's Strangest Days
Television's Strangest Moments
Tennis's Strangest Matches
Theatre's Strangest Acts
Science's Strangest Inventions
The World Cup's Strangest Moments

FLYING'S STRANGEST MOMENTS

Extraordinary but true stories from over
one thousand years of aviation history

John Harding

ROBSON BOOKS

Dedicated to
Flight Sgt. Lionel Harding, missing in action,
November 4th 1943.

First published in the United Kingdom in 2006 by
Robson Books
151 Freston Road
London W10 6TH

An imprint of Anova Books Company Ltd

ISBN 1 86105 934 5

A CIP catalogue record for this title is available from the British Library

Typeset by SX Composing D
Printed and bound by Creativ

This book can be ordered dire
Contact the marketing departr

www.anovabooks.com

Contents

Two from a Tower: Cordova, Spain (875)   1
The Flying Monk: Malmesbury, England (1010)   3
Flying's First Fatality: Istanbul, Turkey (1638)   5
Monsters from the Sky: Versailles, France (1783)   7
'The Balloon Swallowed Up': Paris, France (1784)   9
Taking London by Storm: London, England (1784)   11
'Up, Up and Away in my Beautiful Balloon . . .' Lyon,
    France (1784)   13
First Across the Channel: Dover to Calais (1785)   14
The First and Last Flight of the Aero-Montgolfiere:
    Boulogne, France (1785)   17
Zambeccari's Perilous Trip Across the Adriatic Sea:
    Bologna, Italy (1804)   19
The Doomed Conical Parachute: London,
    England (1817)   22
'The Flying Coachman' – a Reluctant Hero? Brompton,
    England (1853)   25
The Artificial Albatross: Trefeuntec, near Douarnenez,
    France (1856)   27
Earliest Flyer? Or is this just a Wind-Up? Luckenbach,
    USA (1865)   30
Ira Allen and his Daredevil Flying Brothers:
    Dansville, USA (1877)   32
The Eagle has Landed: North Pole (1896)   35
The Mystery Airship: Sacramento, USA (1896)   39
'The Incomparable Lincoln Beachey': Washington,
    DC, USA (1906)   42
A Brazilian Flying Nut: Paris, France (1906)   44
Grapefruit: Brooklyn, USA (1908)   46

The Remarkable 'Colonel' Cody: Farnborough
  Common, England (1908)   48
The First Aircraft Fatality: Fort Myer, USA (1908)   51
'Beautifully Coloured Birds': London, England (1909)   53
Houdini Pulls it Off: Diggers Rest, Australia (1910)   55
It's Quicker by Rail! London to Manchester,
  England (1910)   58
Higher, Always Higher! Switzerland to Milan (1910)   61
Flight Deck to Flight Deck: Willoughby Spit, USA
  (1910)   63
Looping the Loop: Juvisy, near Paris, France (1913)   65
Barrage Balloonatics! Western Front (1917)   67
Who Killed the Red Baron? Sailley-le-Sac, France
  (1918)   69
As I Flew Lying: Toronto, Canada (1918)   71
The Fox in the Box: Ploegsteert, Belgium (1918)   73
Hollywood Skywayman Crashes out of the Picture:
  Los Angeles, USA (1920)   75
God 'elp All of Us! London, England (1920)   77
Semprini's Last Serenade: Lake Maggiore,
  Italy/Switzerland (1921)   79
Wes, the 'Flying Tanker': Long Beach, USA (1921)   81
Byrd's North Pole Fraud: Spitsbergen, Norway (1926)   83
North Pole Again – and Tragedy: Spitsbergen,
  Norway (1926)   87
Dick Grace, Stuntman: Hollywood, USA (1926)   90
Angels from the Sky: Los Angeles, USA (1930)   92
The Flying Carpet: Los Angeles, USA (1930)   96
Hijacked! Lima, Peru (1931)   100
Shepperton's Ghost Plane: London, England (1932)   101
Death Aloft: Toronto, Canada (1935)   103
Amelia Earhart's Mysterious Disappearance:
  New Guinea (1937)   105
The Tragedy of Guernica: Guernica, Spain (1937)   107
Hindenburg Ablaze: New York, USA (1937)   109
'Wrong Way' Corrigan: Atlantic Ocean (1938)   112
Amy Johnson: Thames Estuary, England (1941)   115
The Rudolf Hess Mystery: Eaglesham, Scotland (1941)   119

UFO: Los Angeles, USA (1942)   122
The Plane from Nowhere: California, USA (1942)   124
Air Raid on America: Oregon, USA (1942)   126
Amazing Magee Brings the Roof Down! St Nazaire,
    France (1943)   129
'The Curse of the *Lady Be Good*': Soluch, Libya (1943)   131
'Après Moi le Déluge': Ruhr River, Germany (1943)   133
Death on the Rock: Gibraltar (1943)   136
Mussolini Rescued: Gran Sasso, Italy (1943)   139
The Mystery of the Unexplained Fall:
    Pennsylvania, USA (1943)   141
Divine Wind of the Kamikaze: Leyte Island, Philippines
    (1944)   143
Friday the 13th: Cambrai, France (1944)   146
The Desert Fox – Outfoxed! Normandy, France (1944)   148
Joe Kennedy Junior Dies: Blythburgh, England (1944)   151
The Colditz 'Cock' Glider: Colditz, Germany (1944)   153
Clarke Gable's War: The Ruhr, Germany (1944)   156
The Little Prince Falls to Earth: Lyon, France (1944)   159
Flossy's Fury: Toulon, France (1944)   161
Did Glenn Miller Die in a French Brothel? English
    Channel (1944)   164
'Where there's Foo, there's Fire': Northern France
    (1945)   167
The *Lady Lynn*: Nancy, France (1945)   170
Hanna Reitsch's Daring Flight: Berlin, Germany (1945)   173
Bricks Away! Burma, India (1945)   176
Little Boy: Hiroshima, Japan (1945)   177
Falling Down the Empire State: New York, USA (1945)   180
Morse Code Mystery: Santiago, Chile (1947)   182
The Goose has Lifted! Long Beach, USA (1947)   185
The Host with a Ghost: Dalkeith, Scotland (1947)   187
Croydon Ghosts: London, England (1947)   189
Flying Saucers Arrive: Mount Ranier, USA (1947)   191
The Disappearance of Flight 19: Fort Lauderdale,
    USA (1947)   193
The Candy Bomber: Berlin, Germany (1948)   197
Chasing Balloons? Kentucky, USA (1948)   199

Glass Coffin: Collinsville, USA (1948) 202
The Murder of Stanley Setty: Essex Marshes,
   England (1949) 204
A Murder in the Family: Quebec, Canada (1949) 206
Unlucky 13th Again! Northolt, England (1950) 208
One Lucky Man: Korea (1952) 211
Nevil Shute and the Prophecy of the Comets (1953) 213
The Mad Major Flies Under a Bridge Too Far:
   London, England (1953) 215
Bomb Kills Mother: Denver, USA (1955) 217
Newlywed Takes a Fatal Step: North Carolina, USA
   (1956) 219
The Day the Music Died: Clear Lake, USA (1959) 221
The Spy from the Sky: Sverdlovsk, USSR (1960) 224
The Right Stuff: Edwards Air Force Base, USA (1963) 226
Alfalfa Landing: Norfolk, USA (1966) 228
Air Con: Miami, USA (1966) 230
Cooper – or the real McCoy? Seattle, USA (1971) 233
Wings of Hope: Amazon River (1971) 236
Vesna Vulovic: Ceska, Czechoslovakia (1972) 238
Flight 401: Miami, USA (1972) 241
Croatian Hijack: La Guardia, USA (1976) 243
Pedalling across the Channel: English Channel (1979) 247
Death in the Desert: Tehran, Iran (1979) 249
A Haunted Hangar: Cosford, England (1980) 252
Flying High Again: Leesburg, USA (1982) 254
Couch Potato Takes Off: Los Angeles, USA (1982) 257
Gimli Glider: Gimli, Canada (1983) 259
South African Death Flights: KwaZulu/Natal,
   South Africa (1983) 262
Time Slip: Grand Turk, Bahamas (1983) 264
Round the World in Nine Days (1986) 266
Have a Nice Day! Templeton, USA (1987) 268
Matthias Rust Lands his Plane in Red Square:
   Moscow, USSR (1987) 270
Modern-day Daedalus: Crete (1988) 272
Pilot Sucked Out: Birmingham, England (1990) 274
Cuba Libre! Cuba (1992) 277

Bladder Bomb: Fort Lauderdale, USA (1993)   280
Attack on the White House: Washington, DC, USA
   (1994)   282
Ghost Planes: Longdendale, England (1995)   285
From Sea to Shining Sea: Pescadero, USA (1996)   286
The Exploding Toilet: Cincinnati, USA (1996)   289
Payne Stewart: Florida, USA (1999)   292
'A Very Nasty Man has Just Tried to Kill us All':
   Gatwick, England (2000)   295
The Da Vinci Cone: Mpumalanga, South Africa (2000)   297
A Warm Welcome: Gander, Canada (2001)   300
Now the drugs don't work . . . Tampa, USA (2002)   303
Fossett Hangs up his Balloon: Yamma Yamma,
   Australia (2002)   305
Glacier Girl: Greenland (2002)   307
A Dedicated Ghost: Randolph Air Base, USA (2003)   310
Lucky Skydiver: Johannesburg, South Africa (2004)   312
Unlucky Skydiver: Vologda, Russia (2005)   314
Dumped Upon From a Great Height: Leominster,
   USA (2005)   316
Someone Just Dropped in: Long Island, USA (2005)   318
Dinner and Dive: Bath, England (2005)   319

TWO FROM A TOWER

CORDOVA, SPAIN 875

In 852, a young astronomer poet named Abbas Ibn Firnas watched what might have been the first attempt at human-powered flight. A young daredevil jumped from a tower using only a huge winglike cloak to break his fall; he apparently survived, sustaining only minor injuries. This prompted Firnas to undertake his own, more sophisticated, attempt at flight.

He had arrived in the Caliphate of Cordoba, Spain, during a period of great creative turmoil, encouraged by its enlightened ruler. Firnas was employed to work on a huge variety of enterprises, which included, among other things, various forms of astronomical invention. It provided an ideal opportunity for him to design and build a flying machine capable of carrying a human being.

After experimenting with certain prototypes, he settled on a primitive version of a glider. With great excitement he invited the people of Cordova (capital of the Caliphate) to come and witness his – and mankind's – inaugural 'heavier-than-air' flight.

The crowds gathered on a nearby hillside and held their breath as he launched himself fearlessly from a tower – just as his predecessor had done. He had flown quite a distance – to the crowd's astonishment – when disaster suddenly struck and he was unceremoniously dashed to the ground. He survived, but badly injured his back.

Although Firnas did not leave any flight instructions, or diagrams, it is believed that his influence eventually reached other areas in Europe and word of his flight was brought to a monk named Eilmer of Malmesbury – possibly via returning Crusaders, or Anglo-Saxons making pilgrimages. Eilmer eventually succeeded in flying the length of two modern-day football fields using an apparatus similar to that of Firnas.

In the summer of 2003, American troops found themselves fighting at the Ibn Firnas Airport, just north of Baghdad. They probably gave no particular attention to that name, or the question of why it was attached to an airport.

THE FLYING MONK

MALMESBURY, ENGLAND 1010

In 1010, Eilmer, a young Benedictine monk, fastened wings to his arms and his feet and climbed to the top of the tower of Malmesbury Abbey. Eilmer typified the inquisitive spirit of medieval engineering enthusiasts, who delighted in developing gadgets such as small drawstring toy helicopters, windmills and sophisticated sails for boats. At the same time, church artists' depictions of angels were featuring increasingly more accurate depictions of birdlike wings, detailing the wing's camber (curvature) that was a crucial element in generating the lifting forces that enable a bird – or an aeroplane – to fly. Such a climate of thought led to a general acceptance that air was something that could be 'worked' – flying was no longer regarded as magical, but as something that could be attained by physical effort and human reasoning. Eilmer would be the first Englishman to put this line of thought into practice.

At that time, Malmesbury Abbey had a typical Saxon high tower, probably about 80 feet tall. The abbey stands on a hill top with a sharp 50- to 60-foot drop to the river about 600 feet away to the north and west, and less sharply to the river 1,800 feet away to the south and east.

Eilmer's wings were constructed of ash or willow-wand, covered with a light cloth, and attached to pivots on either side of a back-brace, with handholds so he could – hopefully – flap the wings. He had reportedly observed jackdaws in flight, and had worked out how to make use of the currents of air to glide, rather than simply plummet to earth.

3

Eilmer was quite a small man, and as he was using wings with a total area of about 100 square feet, his main difficulty was in holding himself steady on top of the tower in a wind strong enough for his purpose. Finally, however, he deemed the moment had come, and he leaped, passing over a city wall and descending into a small valley by the River Avon. The prevailing wind in that area is from the southwest, and leads to considerable uplift as it meets the hill and the abbey walls; local jackdaws delight in using this uplift to soar to considerable heights. Eilmer made use of it too, and was blown along the ridge by the wind.

However, it seems that it suddenly dawned on him what a risk he had taken, whereupon he panicked and came down with a bump – breaking both his legs. He had fallen into a marshy field (now known as St Aldhelm's Meadow) fully 150 feet lower than the point of his leap. In all, he managed to cover a distance of around 600 feet.

Given the geography of the abbey, Eilmer's landing site, and the account of his flight, he must have remained airborne for about fifteen seconds. At low altitude he apparently attempted to flap the wings, an action that made him lose control.

He subsequently decided, just like Firnas before him, that it was the lack of a tail that had led to his undignified landing and injury. He set about rectifying this shortcoming, and was making plans for a second flight when his abbot placed an embargo on any further attempts – and that was that. For more than half a century afterwards, the limping Eilmer was a familiar sight around the community of Malmesbury, where he eventually became a distinguished scholar.

In 1066, Eilmer saw Halley's Comet, which he had first seen as a young boy in 989. He declared prophetically, 'You've come, have you? . . . You've come, you source of tears to many mothers. It is long since I saw you; but as I see you now you are much more terrible, for I see you brandishing the downfall of my country.'

The Abbey features a stained-glass window of Brother Eilmer, and a local pub was named The Flying Monk in his honour – though, alas, a shopping centre now stands in its place.

FLYING'S FIRST FATALITY

ISTANBUL, TURKEY 1010

Hezarfen Ahmet Celebi was a Turkish scientist who was inspired to invent a viable flying machine by the unfortunate experiences of a series of earlier 'flying Turks'.

In 1010, another scientist, Ismail Cevheri, had launched himself into space from the 183-foot-tall Galata Tower, which rose 460 feet above the Golden Horn near the Bosphorus, equipped with odd-shaped wings that failed to work at all. He plunged to his death, to become the first person to die because of flight.

In 1159 an even more foolhardy attempt was made by one Siracettin who, during festivities in Istanbul, climbed the very same tower wearing nothing more than a voluminous, loose-fitting dress. As soon as he jumped his dress filled with air and he too plummeted to his death. Richard Knolles, a seventeenth-century historian, wrote, 'In steed of mounting aloft, this foolish Icarus came tumbling downe headlong with such violence, that he brake his necke, his armes and legs, with almost all the bones of his bodie.'

A third attempt was more sophisticated – spectacularly so, in fact. Lagari Hasan Çelebi (a contemporary of but no relation to Hezarfen) is reported to have constructed a seven-pronged rocket powered by around nine pounds of gunpowder. After lighting the fuse, he rose high in the sky off Sarayburnu before landing in the sea by means of a primitive parachute. After the event he was received by the Sultan and rewarded with seventy silver coins.

Hezarfen Ahmet Celebi, however, resumed research into winged apparatus and after making meticulous study of bird flight, undertook a series of experimental attempts. Eventually, he achieved his goal and flew right across the Bosphorus, landing on the slopes of Anatolia. He was personally congratulated by the Sultan, who had been among the many onlookers, and he was rewarded with a thousand gold pieces.

However, his celebrity status played against him. Religious leaders and palace advisers, sensing a threat to their influence, persuaded the Sultan that Celebi was dangerous. He was sent into exile in Algeria where he died brokenhearted at the age of 31.

Hezarfen Airfield, one of the three airports in Istanbul, remains a testament to this pioneer of flight.

MONSTERS FROM THE SKY

VERSAILLES, FRANCE 1783

The Montgolfier brothers, though acknowledged as pioneers in the history of human flight, based their startling success upon a total misunderstanding of the physics involved. They believed that it was smoke that provided the lift for the light fabric balloon constructions they had been experimenting with since boyhood. Only later did they realise that it was the hot air beneath the balloon that mattered.

After an inaugural unmanned flight from Annonay on 4 June 1783, the brothers were confident enough to mount a royal demonstration in Versailles. On 19 September 1783, a sheep, a duck and a rooster became the first hot-air balloon passengers! Despite the stench of the dense smoke created by a curious mix of straw, wool and old shoes, onlookers (including King Louis XVI) were impressed to see the balloon rise to a height of 1,640 feet and travel nearly 2 miles.

In November of the same year, the same balloon carried the first human air travellers – Pilatre des Roziers (a science teacher) and the Marquis d'Arlandes (an infantry officer) – on the first free flight not tethered to the ground. The balloon, measuring 77,692 cubic feet, was propelled by an iron furnace which, high over Paris, started a fire that burned holes in the balloon fabric and threatened the cords that attached the balloon to the gallery in which the two men rode. D'Arlandes quickly grabbed a sponge and a bucket of water brought along for just such an emergency, and extinguished the flames. After that, whenever the aeronauts found themselves dropping uncomfortably close to the Paris rooftops, they threw more straw on the brazier and rose to a more comfortable altitude. Twenty-five minutes after take-off they allowed the fire to subside and landed gently between two mill houses.

They had travelled more than 5 miles across Paris and reached a height of 3,000 feet, with D'Arlandes doffing his hat to the open-mouthed spectators below. He later wrote of his surprise at the silence and absence of movement among the spectators below. People were clearly stunned by the sight. Some were terrified.

Earlier in the year, on 27 August, the French physicist Jacques Charles's hydrogen balloon was carried away from Paris by a storm to the village of Gonesse some fifteen miles away, where the superstitious peasants of the village, believing the balloon to be a monster that was attacking them from the sky, proceeded to rip it to shreds with scythes and pitchforks!

'THE BALLOON SWALLOWED UP'

PARIS, FRANCE 1784

French abbots Miolan and Janninet had a novel scheme. They proposed to propel their balloon through the air by means of the forcible expulsion of hot air from an opening halfway up the balloon itself. Buoyancy would, they claimed, be maintained by a pan of combustible material burning below in the passenger carriage. Sadly, their claims were to prove little more than . . . hot air.

Their immense balloon was constructed at great expense, and on Sunday, 11 July 1784, thousands of people, each of whom had paid dearly for his or her ticket, started to assemble at the Jardin de Luxembourg in Paris from six in the morning for what promised to be an amazing spectacle.

Most of the morning, however, would be taken up with transporting the balloon from the observatory to the place of ascent; it was only at midday that, finally, the job of inflating it began. The spectators thus had to endure hours of waiting around in the hot July sun. By four in the afternoon, the balloon had still not risen from the ground and the crowd were becoming impatient.

Murmurs of discontent rapidly developed into a clamour, as suspicions arose that the much-vaunted ascent was not going to happen at all. Finally, wild with disappointment, a section of the audience threw themselves upon the barricades separating balloon from audience, broke it down and attacked the carriage of the balloon, smashing the instrument and the apparatus and trampling them underfoot.

They then set on the balloon itself. In the general melee, people struggled to seize and carry off a bit of the balloon to preserve as a relic until, finally, someone set the remaining material on fire. Meanwhile, the two abbots escaped as they best could under protection of a number of friends, but the damage to their reputations was irreparable.

In Parisian newspapers and popular prints, the two men were lampooned and caricatured mercilessly – Abbé Miolan was represented as a cat with a band round his neck, while Janninet appeared as a donkey. In a popular coloured print of the time, the cat and the donkey are shown arriving in triumph in their famous balloon at the Academy of Montmartre, to be received by a solemn assembly of turkey cocks and geese.

Numerous songs and epigrams with the unfortunate abbés as their subjects also appeared at the time, while someone discovered that the letters that composed the words 'l'Abbé Miolan' was an anagram of 'ballon abime' – 'the balloon swallowed up'.

TAKING LONDON BY STORM

LONDON, ENGLAND 1784

The handsome and charming 22-year-old Vincenzo 'Vincent' Lunardi, secretary to the Neapolitan ambassador at the English court, is thought to be Britain's first aeronaut.

His first machine was a hydrogen balloon, made of oiled silk, with a diameter of 33 feet and a volume of 18,200 cubic feet. His first flight took place on 15 September 1784, in the presence of the Prince of Wales and other distinguished personages, from the grounds of the Honourable Artillery Park at Moorfields in London.

At 1 p.m., before a crowd of more than 150,000, he shook hands with the Prince, lifted his dog and cat into the carriage of his red-and-blue-striped balloon, climbed in and launched his aerostatic *ménage à trois* into the sky, rising to a height of four miles. He eventually landed near North Mimms, where he left his cat (said to be not best pleased with the experience) in the care of a local woman, before taking off again, finally touching down safely in a field near Ware, in Hertfordshire.

This success spurred Lunardi on to greater feats. He decorated his next balloon with the British Union Jack, and in homage to the beauty of a society belle, Mrs Sage, asked for the honour of taking her into the 'blue Paradisian skies'. Thrilled, she accepted.

For the flight from London, on 29 June 1785, he announced that he would also carry a certain Colonel Hastings and George Biggin (a distinguished Etonian, amateur chemist and inventor of a coffee percolator). The good lady, however, weighed in at some fourteen stone and, fearing his balloon might be unequal to the task, Lunardi along with Colonel Hastings gallantly stepped down.

With British flags waving and throngs cheering, the balloon rose and was soon floating over St James's Park and Piccadilly, whereupon Mrs Sage and Mr Biggin settled down to a lunch of chicken, ham and Italian wine, nonchalantly tossing the remnants over the side. An hour later, they landed in a field near Harrow, where a furious farmer, 'abusive to a savage degree', accused the couple of damaging his crops. They were rescued by a group of boys from Harrow school.

London, however, had been taken by storm. Lunardi's audacious aeronautical adventures had captured everyone's imagination. Soon there was the 'Lunardi' bonnet – a balloon-shaped hat about two feet high – and 'Lunardi' skirts, decorated with balloon motifs; they became some of the most sought-after fashion accessories of the time. Mrs Sage duly recorded all these events and published an account of her experiences as 'England's First Female Aeronaut'.

'UP, UP AND AWAY IN MY BEAUTIFUL BALLOON . . .'

LYON, FRANCE 1784

Although the first flight of any significant length in any sort of machine was achieved on 21 November 1783 by two men (Dr Pilatre des Roziers and the Marquis d'Arlandes), a woman soon managed to fly higher – and for longer. On 4 June 1784, Madame Elisabeth Thible, a French opera singer, became the first woman to fly when she went up in a Montgolfier balloon.

Madame Thible's balloon, named Le Gustave (after Sweden's King Gustav III, who viewed the ascent), rose 8,500 feet and her flight lasted 45 minutes. This was 20 minutes longer than the flying trip her male counterparts had undertaken some six months earlier, and her altitude was three times higher.

She was guided in her quest by pilot and artist Monsieur Fleurant. Madame Thible didn't waste her time while floating on high. She proceeded to sing an operatic selection as she rose higher and higher, thus becoming the first person to broadcast music from the air! Fleurant later told reporters that the opera singer 'sang like a bird' while she drifted across the rooftops of Lyon.

FIRST ACROSS THE CHANNEL

DOVER TO CALAIS 1785

Jean Pierre François Blanchard was a French scientist who invented a variety of elaborate feats of engineering, including a hydraulic pump system that raised water 400 feet from the Seine river to the Château Gaillard. In the 1770s, he became attracted by the problems of flight and worked on designing heavier-than-air flying machines, including one based on a theory of rowing in the air currents with oars and a tiller. Before long, he had built a birdlike aerial bicycle with flapping wings – though this never did fly. The achievements of the Montgolfier brothers then inspired him to try a combination of the lifting power of the balloon with flapping wings for propulsion. His highly original contraption took its first flight on 2 March 1784.

Like many inventors, Blanchard depended on the generosity of benefactors, although he was often loath to acknowledge them. In 1784, an American doctor named Jeffries, who had an interest in meteorology, offered to pay Blanchard the costs of taking his new balloon across the English Channel to France. Such generosity was to be no guarantee that the doctor would actually be able to take part in the flight, and share the glory, however! Blanchard insisted on travelling alone.

In December 1784, he took the balloon to Dover, then barricaded himself inside Dover Castle, locking Jeffries out. Jeffries recruited a squad of sailors and then enlisted the services of the castle governor to negotiate an agreement between the two men. To no avail, however, as Blanchard persisted in trying to leave his sponsor behind!

When the inflated balloon (carrying a gondola packed with Blanchard's own steering gear, consisting of wing paddles and a hand-turned fan to act as a propeller) was tested for lift-off with the two men aboard, it was found to be too heavy. Blanchard again suggested he should make the flight alone, but Jeffries was suspicious enough to inspect the Frenchman's clothing – to find he was wearing a leather belt under his coat, fitted with a set of heavy lead weights!

The flight was postponed. At last, however, on 7 January 1785, with both men on board, the balloon took off in good conditions from the cliffs of Dover, heading towards Boulogne. They carried only 30 pounds of ballast with Blanchard still doubtful of the balloon's capacity to carry two passengers. Apparently, Dr Jeffries had only been permitted to go on the understanding that he would jump overboard if necessary!

Although the pair had eventually dropped all their ballast overboard with the French coast still some miles away, the balloon never managed to climb to a safe altitude, and it seemed they would come down in the sea. Frantically, the two men began jettisoning everything they could. First to go were the extravagant gondola decorations, followed by Blanchard's useless steering gear. Then followed the anchors and the two men's coats, followed by their trousers! The remedy worked and the balloon climbed to a safe height, finally arriving at the French coast at 3 p.m. to land just outside Calais.

On the following day a splendid fete was celebrated in their honour at Calais. Blanchard was presented with the freedom of the city in a golden casket. The municipal body purchased the balloon, with the intention of placing it in one of the churches as a memorial of the experiment, and also resolved to erect a marble monument on the spot where the famous aeronauts landed.

Blanchard's career continued apace. Later that year he carried out the first successful parachute experiment when he dropped an animal in a small basket from an air balloon. On 9 January 1793, he made the first-ever balloon ascent from Pennsylvania in North America, carrying a letter from George Washington all the way to New Jersey, and creating the idea of

THE FIRST AND LAST FLIGHT OF
THE AERO-MONTGOLFIERE

BOULOGNE, FRANCE 1785

In 1785, Pilatre des Roziers, who two years earlier had made the first-ever human ascent in a Montgolfier balloon, set out to fly from France to England. Des Roziers claimed he had devised a new balloon that was secure and which, he thought, would remain in the air for an unusually long time.

His novel construction consisted of not one but two balloons: one filled with hydrogen gas, beneath which he suspended a second Montgolfier balloon filled with hot air from a fire. The addition of the Montgolfier would, he hoped, free him from the necessity of having to throw over ballast when he wished to ascend and to let off gas when he wished to descend. The fire of the Montgolfier, he calculated, could be regulated to enable him to rise or fall at will.

It was an untried machine, and he was setting out under unfavourable conditions. What's more, while in storage the balloon had been gnawed by rats and was full of holes. Despite warnings as to the dangers involved, however, he pressed on. His financial backers were insisting he make good his claims but, most of all, he wanted to equal the achievement of Jean Pierre Blanchard, the first person to cross the Channel, on 7 January 1785 – in the opposite direction.

For some weeks he was grounded at Boulogne by strong winds but, on 15 June at four in the morning, the conditions seemed perfect and seven hours later des Roziers, accompanied by his brother Romain, climbed into the carriage. A nobleman

17

made an offer of 200 louis to join them, and was preparing to climb aboard when des Roziers stepped forward to prevent him, admitting that the experiment was too unsafe to endanger the life of another person.

Finally the Aero-Montgolfiere, as it was dubbed, rose to the sound of cannon fire, and the brothers waved the cheering crowds below goodbye. It would be a short and fatal flight. The balloon, after travelling some half a mile or so out to sea and reaching a height of 700 feet above sea level, met a westerly wind that began to drive it back toward the shore.

In order to descend and seek a more favourable current of air to take them out to sea again, des Roziers tried to open the valve of the gas balloon; but the cord attached to the valve was at the end of a long rope and difficult to work – and des Roziers' exertions only succeeded in dislodging it. This caused a tear to open in the balloon material itself. After a fissure of some several yards' width opened up, the valve seemed to disappear into the balloon, which rapidly started to deflate.

As it did so, the watching crowd beneath saw a violet flame appear at the top of the construction, which swiftly spread over the whole globe, before enveloping both the Montgolfiere and the brothers. Still clinging to the balloon carriage, the men were then hurled to the earth, landing in front of the Tour de Croy, three miles from Boulogne, and 300 feet from the sea.

When onlookers reached the pair, des Roziers was found dead and badly burned in the carriage. His brother was still breathing, but was unable to speak, and died a few minutes later. By sad chance, they had died only a few feet from the monument that marked the spot where the successful Blanchard had descended.

Eight days after the catastrophe, a young Englishwoman who lived at a convent in Boulogne, and whom des Roziers had met a few days prior to his last ascent, belatedly became so overcome with shock at his sudden death that she was seized with convulsions and also died.

ZAMBECCARI'S PERILOUS TRIP ACROSS THE ADRIATIC SEA

BOLOGNA, ITALY 1804

By the time the enthusiastic but impractical Comte Zambeccari set off to cross the Adriatic Sea by balloon he had suffered many misadventures – due largely to his own incompetence.

This particular trip, however, seemed doomed from the start. On 7 October, after enduring 48 hours of steady rain, and having been let down by various colleagues who'd been expected to help fill the balloon, he completed the task with the help of two flying companions, Andreoli and Grassetti, and at midnight they rose over the town of Bologna to begin their quest.

Weather conditions were severe and their equipment soon began to fail them. They could not see their barometer clearly because the wax light in the lantern would not burn in such a rarefied atmosphere. Soon the intense cold prevailing at the altitude they'd rapidly reached, added to their general weariness, combined to produce a state of almost total prostration. Zambeccari and Grassetti fell into a deep sleep. Andreoli only remained awake because of a large quantity of rum he'd ingested while working on the balloon. After some time, however, he succeeded in getting a bemused and confused Zambeccari to his feet.

It was two o'clock in the morning, their compass had been broken and, as they descended slowly through a thick layer of whitish clouds, they heard a muffled sound, which they immediately recognised as the breaking of waves.

Suddenly, Zambeccari saw the surface of the sea just below them. He seized a large sack of sand, but before he could throw it over they hit the water. They proceeded to throw everything that would lighten the balloon into the sea – ballast, instruments, much of their clothing, their money, the oars. The balloon then unexpectedly proceeded to rise with such rapidity and to such a great height that the three men had difficulty in hearing each other speak. Zambeccari became ill and was sick, while Grassetti started bleeding from the nose; all were breathing with great difficulty.

Having been thrown on their backs as the balloon took its sudden start upwards, a low and deadly atmospheric temperature then seized them and they found themselves covered with a coating of ice! After half an hour, at a great height, the balloon began to slowly descend and, once again, they ditched into the sea. It was now four in the morning on a moonless night and the sea was rolling heavily. Unable to make observations, they guessed they must be in the middle of the Adriatic.

The carriage was now being regularly submerged and the balloon, being no more than half full, started to act like a sail in the wind, so the wretched trio were dragged along at the mercy of the storm and the waves until daybreak, when they found themselves opposite Pesaro, four miles from the shore. Just as they began to comfort themselves with the prospect of a safe landing, a wind from the shore proceeded to drive them rapidly out to open sea again!

Unfortunately, boats coming within sight no sooner saw the balloon bouncing and rolling on the water than they rapidly made sail to get away from it. However, fate at last directed them towards a boat whose skipper recognised the 'infernal machine' to be a balloon and quickly sent his longboat to the rescue.

The sailors threw out a cable by means of which they rescued the three men, who were by then completely exhausted. The balloon proceeded to rise out of the water in spite of the efforts of the sailors who wanted to capture it. The longboat, however, suddenly received a severe jolt from the rope still attached and the men quickly cut themselves free. The balloon immediately rose with incredible rapidity and was lost in the clouds, never to be seen again.

It was eight in the morning when they finally got on board. Grassetti was comatose, his hands mutilated, while the combination of cold, hunger and fear had completely exhausted Zambeccari, who later commented, 'The brave captain of the vessel did everything in his power to restore us. He conducted us safely to Ferrara, whence we were carried to Pola, where we were received with the greatest kindness, and where I was compelled to have my fingers amputated.'

THE DOOMED CONICAL PARACHUTE

LONDON, ENGLAND 1817

Robert Cocking was a professional watercolourist and amateur scientist who spent many years developing an improved design for a parachute.

The great defect of the then standard umbrella-shaped parachute was its violent swinging during descent. Cocking calculated that if the parachute were made conical (vortex downwards), this oscillation could be avoided; and if it were made of sufficient size, there would be resistance enough to check too rapid a descent.

It was not until 1817 that Cocking had an opportunity to make his jump. He convinced the owners of a balloon, the Royal Nassau, that a parachute jump was just the sort of publicity they needed; it did not seem to bother them that Cocking had no experience whatever in parachuting or that he was 61 years old at the time. He built a parachute in a funnel shape and attached a basket underneath in which he could ride.

The trial was planned for take-off from Vauxhall Gardens. There were worries about the safety of Cocking's contraption, however, and as the hour approached, the proprietors of the Gardens did their best to dissuade the inventor, offering to take the consequences of any public disappointment. He was undeterred and, at around six in the evening, Mr Green the balloonist, accompanied by a Mr Spencer, a solicitor, entered the balloon car, which was then let up about forty feet so that the parachute could be fixed below.

22

A little later, Mr Cocking, casting aside his heavy coat and cheerfully downing a glass of wine, entered his parachute amid loud cheers with the band playing the national anthem. The balloon and aeronauts above, and himself in his parachute swinging below, rose in the gathering dusk out of view of the Gardens.

The aeronauts experienced a good deal of difficulty in rising to a suitable height, partly due to the resistance to the air offered by the expanded parachute, and partly to its weight. Cocking had planned on reaching 8,000 feet but when the balloon reached 5,000 feet, over Greenwich, Green called out that he would be unable to ascend to the requisite height if the parachute was to descend in daylight.

Green said later, 'I asked him if he felt quite comfortable, and if the practical trial bore out his calculation. Mr Cocking replied, "Yes, I never felt more comfortable or more delighted in my life," presently adding, "Well, now I think I shall leave you." I answered, "I wish you a very 'Good Night!' and a safe descent if you are determined to make it and not use the tackle" [a contrivance for enabling him to climb up into the balloon if he desired]. Mr Cocking's only reply was, "Good-night, Spencer; Good-night, Green!" Mr Cocking then pulled the rope that was to liberate himself, but too feebly, and a moment afterwards more violently, and in an instant the balloon shot upwards with the velocity of a sky rocket.'

As soon as it was released, it was obvious that Cocking had neglected to take one thing into account: the weight of the parachute. The entire apparatus weighed 250 pounds, roughly ten times the weight of the modern parachute.

Cocking's parachute descended swiftly for a few seconds, but still evenly, until suddenly the upper rim seemed to give way, and the whole apparatus collapsed (taking the form of an umbrella turned inside out, and nearly closed). The machine then descended with great rapidity, oscillating wildly. Two or three hundred feet from the ground, the basket became disengaged from the remnant of the parachute, and Cocking was doomed. His broken body was found in a nearby field.

Meanwhile, Green and Spencer had a narrow escape of their own. At the moment the parachute disengaged they had crouched down in the carriage, Green clinging to the valve-line to permit the escape of gas. The balloon shot upwards, the gas pouring from both the upper and lower valves. The two men were then forced to put their mouths to tubes attached to an air bag that they had had the foresight to provide for themselves, otherwise they would have been suffocated. The gas still managed to deprive them of sight for four or five minutes.

When they came to, they found they were at a great height but descending rapidly. They managed a safe descent near Maidstone, Kent, still unaware of the fate of their late companion.

'THE FLYING COACHMAN' – A RELUCTANT HERO?

BROMPTON, ENGLAND 1853

In the early 1840s, a man called William Henson began searching for investors in his Aerial Transit Company. He'd patented a flying machine consisting of a steam locomotive, tied to canvas wings, which supposedly would take letters, goods and packages across the skies. Henson figured it would take £5,000 to get his business up and running and asked Sir George Cayley to become an investor.

Cayley, the Sixth Baronet of Brompton, northeastern Yorkshire, had always been a man of diverse interests. Over the years he'd come up with the idea for the tension wheel, still used in bicycles today. He had invented and patented the forerunner to the modern tank tread, designed an artificial hand for one of his tenants' sons, designed new drainage systems for local farmlands, and became a champion for railway safety after witnessing one of the first railway accidents, in 1830.

He had known for years that aircraft wouldn't fly consistently unless a powerful engine could supply the flight's thrust. He'd tried to build engines based on hot air and gunpowder but they hadn't worked, and he knew Henson's wouldn't, either. But Henson inspired Cayley to renew his aeronautical experiments and, because Cayley knew the engine problem couldn't be solved yet, he turned to gliders.

By 1840, his model constructions were becoming increasingly advanced – indeed, they appear uncannily similar

25

to modern aircraft: a pair of large monoplane wings towards the front, with a smaller tailplane at the back comprising horizontal stabilisers and a vertical fin. And in 1849, his 'governable parachute' as he called it – a triple-winged craft with a cage to hold a pilot – carried the ten-year-old son of one of Cayley's servants into the air for several yards.

Within a few years, he designed one large enough to, he hoped, carry a pilot and, after he'd demonstrated that animals could fly in it safely, in late June or early July 1853 the glider construction was ready for a fully grown man. There was just one problem – no one was willing to volunteer to be the pilot!

Undaunted, Cayley proceeded to arrange a test flight and, just before the glider began rolling down a hillside on his estate, Cayley told his unsuspecting coachman, John Appleby, to jump inside. Local youngsters then began pulling the craft, faster and faster, and it rolled forward on its tricycle undercarriage until the bewildered coachman found himself hurtling swiftly down the slope toward a narrow valley. The ground then dropped away beneath him – and he was alone in the sky, crouching in a boatlike shell suspended from a billowing set of cloth wings with the 79-year-old Cayley chasing after him below! In that moment, Appleby became the world's first pilot of a heavier-than-air machine.

The glider proceeded to sail 900 feet across Brompton Dale, fortunately for all concerned landing safely in a meadow on the other side. Excited onlookers rushed to the scene as the shaken coachman pulled himself free. He was anything but ecstatic. According to family legend, he blurted out, 'Please, Sir George, I wish to give notice. I was hired to drive, not to fly!'

THE ARTIFICIAL ALBATROSS

TREFEUNTEC, NEAR DOUARNENEZ, FRANCE
1856

Captain Le Bris was a French mariner who had in his younger days made several voyages around the Cape of Good Hope and Cape Horn, and whose imagination had been fired by the sight of the albatross. He was fascinated to see the bird wheeling and floating without any apparent exertion, its wings seemingly held rigid. Having apparently never read 'The Rime of the Ancient Mariner', he killed one of the birds, and claimed to have observed a very remarkable phenomenon. In his own words, as quoted by M. de la Landelle: 'I took the wing of the albatross and exposed it to the breeze; and lo! in spite of me it drew forward into the wind; notwithstanding my resistance it tended to rise. Thus I had discovered the secret of the bird! I comprehended the whole mystery of flight.'

Le Bris thought he had detected a quality to the wing's interaction with the air that he termed 'aspiration'. By December of 1856, he had constructed the first of two large relatively lightweight gliders based closely on the proportions and configuration of the albatross, which he designated, not surprisingly, *The Artificial Albatross*.

It consisted of a canoe-shaped body, the front portion being decked over, provided with two flexible wings and a tail. It was 13½ feet long and 4 feet wide at its broadest point, made of light ash ribs, well stayed, and covered on the outside with impermeable cloth, so that it could float if need be.

The wings were each 23 feet long, so that the whole apparatus was 50 feet across, and spread about 215 square feet of supporting surface; the total weight, without the operator, was 92 pounds. It was fitted with hand-operated levers to change the angle of incidence of the wings and with foot-operated devices to alter the relative position of the tail.

The idea was that Le Bris would stand upright in the canoe, his hands on the levers and cords, and his feet on the pedal to work the tail. His expectation was that, with a strong wind, he would rise into the air and reproduce all the evolutions of the soaring albatross, without any flapping whatever.

Le Bris's first experiment was conducted on a public road at Trefeuntec, near Douarnenez. Believing that it was necessary that the apparatus should have an initial velocity of its own, in addition to that of the wind, he chose a Sunday morning when there was a good ten-knot breeze and, placing his artificial albatross horizontally on a cart, he started down the road against the brisk wind, the cart being driven by a handy peasant.

The Albatross was held down by a rope passing under the rails of the cart and terminating in a slipknot fastened to Le Bris's wrist, so that with one jerk he could loosen the attachment and allow the rope to run. He stood upright in the canoe, his hands on the levers and depressing the front edge of the wings, so that the wind should press upon the top only and hold them down, their position being temporarily maintained by assistants walking along on each side.

When they came to the right turn in the road the assistants were directed to let go, and the driver was told to put his horse into a trot.

After a momentary glitch when the restraining rope was caught by a nail on the cart, *The Artificial Albatross* finally broke free – one report relating that the driver of the cart was snared in the line and was taken aloft as well! Le Bris and the glider rose to a height of about 300 feet, with the cart driver dangling below, sailed about 600 feet, and then came to a controlled and gentle landing, only damaging a wing; the cart driver made a soft landing and was unhurt.

Whatever the truth about the altitude reached, the distance flown, or whether there was an unwilling cart driver hanging from a rope beneath, it seems entirely credible that Le Bris did manage to make a gliding flight in his machine.

After repairing the damage, he made a second attempt, this time dispensing with the cart, the horse and the driver. Instead, he built a large nautical mast and yardarm from which the repaired Artificial Albatross was suspended – 10 feet above a nearby quarry.

The yardarm was swung out so that the apparatus should face both the wind and the quarry, while Le Bris adjusted his levers so that only the top surfaces of the wings should receive the wind. When he felt a sufficiently strong wind, he raised the front edge of the wings upward, brought the tail into action through the pedal and 'aspired forward into the breeze'. He then tripped the hook suspending the apparatus, and the *Albatross* glided off and sailed off down into the quarry.

Unfortunately, erratic upward gusts of winds rising over the lip of the quarry caught Le Bris's machine and he lost control, the *Artificial Albatross* plunging to the bottom and breaking into fragments. Fortunately, Le Bris came away with just a broken leg.

Undaunted, a few years later in late 1867, or early 1868, he built a second *Artificial Albatross* at Brest – almost a duplicate of the first with the exception that it was somewhat lighter and carried a weight meant to provide some additional stability. This time he launched from a stationary cart, caught a rising wind by adjusting the incidence of the wings and managed to lift to about 35 feet and glide forward about 70 feet. Subsequent attempts, however, resulted in terminal damage to the machine and Le Bris's career as a 'sailor of the air' ended.

A contemporary wrote, 'His means and his credit were exhausted, his friends forsook him, and perhaps his own courage weakened, for he did not try again. He retired to his native place, where, after serving with honour in the war of 1870, he became a special constable, and was killed in 1872 by some ruffians whose enmity he had incurred.'

EARLIEST FLYER? OR IS THIS JUST A WIND-UP?

LUCKENBACH, USA 1865

German-born Jacob Brodbeck, a local schoolteacher in Gillespie County, Texas, had always had an interest in mechanics and inventing; in Germany he had attempted to build a self-winding clock, and in 1869 he would design an ice-making machine. His most cherished project, however, was his 'air-ship', which he worked on for twenty years. His main problem – common to all would-be flyers – was how to get an adequate power source aboard his craft that would not be too heavy to lift a plane. The internal combustion engine had not yet been invented and the steam engine weighed too much to be able to lift itself, let alone any plane in which it might be housed.

So Brodbeck, relying on his knowledge of spring-driven clocks, built a small model with a rudder, wings and a propeller powered by coiled springs. To his delight, it actually flew.

Encouraged, he set about raising funds to build a full-sized version – one capable of carrying a man. His theory was simple: whereas his spring-powered toys fell to earth after the spring unwound itself, his projected airship would have a pilot who could rewind the spring, thus providing, so he thought, a continuous source of power for the propeller.

He managed to persuade a number of local men to buy shares in his project, promising to repay them within six months of selling the patent rights to his machine and, on 20 September 1865, made his first flight in a field about three miles east of Luckenbach. His airship, for which Brodbeck predicted speeds between 30 and 100 miles per hour, featured an enclosed space for the aeronaut, a water propeller in case of accidental landings on water, a compass and a barometer. It was said to have risen 12 feet in the air and to have travelled about 100 feet before the springs unwound completely and the machine crashed to the ground. Brodbeck had failed to take into consideration one small but vital factor – it is impossible to rewind a spring while it is unwinding!

There are disagreements as to exactly where and when this 'flight' took place. The most intriguing version claims that Brodbeck crated his plane and took it to Washington, DC, where he flew it off a three-storey building. It was also reported to have had a steam engine, not a coiled spring. The airship supposedly hung in the air and maintained an even flight for a few seconds, then gradually settled to the ground. The wings folded over and severely crushed Brodbeck, who was said to have spent several months in a Washington hospital as a result.

Understandably, after this considerable setback Brodbeck's backers refused to put up money for a second attempt. Undaunted, he went on a fundraising tour of the United States but failed to find anyone brave (or foolish) enough to risk their money on him. Some of his blueprints and plans were then said to have been stolen and his disgusted wife is supposed to have thrown some of his designs into a local creek! Brodbeck finally returned to Texas to live on his ranch near Luckenbach, where he tinkered with his ice-making machine until his death in 1910, seven years after the Wright brothers' first flight in Kitty Hawk, NC.

IRA ALLEN AND HIS DAREDEVIL FLYING BROTHERS

DANSVILLE, USA 1877

In the late 1930s, the name of the Flying Allens first began to appear in big, bold letters on equipment and in publicity wherever this renowned family of acrobats and balloonists were featured attractions. Their beginnings, sixty years earlier, however, were rudimentary to say the least...

Ira, the youngest of three brothers, first became interested in ballooning when, serving with the Union Army during the American Civil War, he had the opportunity to watch the observation balloon Intrepid, operated by Professor Thaddeus Sobieski Coulincourt Lowe.

After discharge in 1866, Ira returned to his home in Dansville in upper New York State, where his enthusiasm for balloons had a contagious effect on brothers Comfort and Martin. Already well known locally for tightrope-walking stunts, they decided to construct a balloon of their own and try to incorporate it into their act.

At this point, the embryo flyers lacked two essentials: money and a knowledge of the basics of construction. Because gas generators, such as those used by Professor Lowe, were far beyond their reach financially, the Allens opted for hot air to provide lift. Construction of the balloon would be a trial-and-error, do-it-yourself process.

The arrival in town of Pullman and Hamilton's Travelling Circus unexpectedly speeded things up. One of their most popular attractions, the balloon ascension with trapeze,

32

appeared to be in jeopardy as their balloonist languished in jail for indiscreet activity while under the influence of alcohol. Ira Allen thus stepped forward, ready and willing to make the trip aloft.

He had never done any ballooning in his life before, but he was used to high altitudes as a tightrope walker. On the designated day the balloon took off and ascended slowly while Ira performed daring feats on the trapeze rope attached underneath. Fifteen minutes later it descended into nearby fields.

More significantly, the Allen brothers were able to inspect Pullman and Hamilton's balloon carefully. They noted its scale and made measurements with a cloth tape as they scribbled figures on scraps of paper. When the show moved on, cutting and stitching began, on the lawn of Comfort's home in Dansville. Possessing an ingenious ability to invent, improvise, construct and adapt, the brothers slowly but surely developed a viable balloon.

Now they had to create the hot air. In the spring of 1878, in a field on the south side of lower Ossian Street, Dansville, the brothers dug a trench running east and west. By covering it with sheet metal except for openings at each end, they created a fire-box and flue. As straw, wood, leaves and anything else combustible burned in the trench, their balloon, suspended between poles over the downwind opening, began to fill with hot air and liberal quantities of smoke! It was ready, almost, to take off!

A dozen or so men grasped the fabric to keep it earthbound. Finally, when the balloon bulged and became restless, tugging at restraining hands, one of the assembled shouted, 'Let 'er go!' Away it soared into the blue skies over the hills with Ira clinging to a rope harness underneath, making only his second balloon ride.

At this stage of the art, balloonists had no flight control. Altitude depended upon temperature aloft but, more important to the flyer, the balloon descended whenever, and wherever, air inside cooled to the point at which the pull of gravity exceeded lift.

On this initial flight, Ira had no parachute rigging – he simply sailed away at the mercy of the elements and laws of physical science, eventually returning to earth about seven air miles from launch point.

This practice of riding a balloon to earth, however, did not meet with the wholehearted approval of the 'ground crew'. They had to hunt for the downed flyer via horse and wagon, then haul the equipment a long way back to Dansville. The Allens thus began experimenting with a parachute.

Panels of strong material were cut to dimensions scaled up from an ordinary umbrella. They developed the rigging and a device by means of which the contraption could be securely attached beneath the balloon yet released at the will of the flyer. In a half-dozen test flights, inflated balloons ascended with parachutes dangling below and carrying only a sack of sand weighing about the same as a man. Eventually, after minor modifications and reassuring test results, Martin Allen took off at a carnival in Weedsport, NY, then drifted back to earth beneath an Allen-made parachute.

One nagging problem remained unsolved. The parachutist now landed close to the base of operations, true, but the balloon still drifted along for miles. The tiresome retrieval process had not been eliminated. The Allens' knack for problem-solving went to work again. A rope, rigged from top centre of the balloon, dangled just below its widest part when inflated. At the rope's end, they tied a cloth sack of sand weighing five to ten pounds. Once the parachutist had cut loose, the sandbag came into operation, tipping the balloon over. As hot air and smoke poured from the inverted balloon, it plummeted earthward reasonably close to launching point.

The Allens then perfected a high-wire balloon exhibition of the most exacting standards. Demands for performances came from far and wide and for the next half-century they would thrill audiences across the USA. In the 1980s, a fourth-generation member of the Allen family was still carrying on the family traditions with 'Magical Mystery Flights' operating out of West Chester, Pennsylvania, while the Allens' home town of Dansville still hosts the New York State Festival of Balloons every September.

THE EAGLE HAS LANDED

NORTH POLE 1896

In 1895, a Swede named Salomon Andrée planned to reach the North Pole aboard the *Oern* (*'Eagle'*), a gigantic balloon 97 feet high and 67 feet in diameter and which held 160,000 cubic feet of hydrogen; underneath was suspended a gondola equipped with a kitchenette and bedroom. Andrée planned to cover the 745 miles separating Spitsbergen and the North Pole in under two days.

He told friends that if successful, and if he found a good station near the North Pole, he might remain there from three to five years. All would depend upon his ability to get supplies.

His scheme was a wild one, but nevertheless he succeeded in interesting some important people. The Tsar of Russia gave liberally to his project; Alfred Nobel subscribed $17,750 to the enterprise; Captain Windran, the celebrated explorer, gave $1,000; the Rothschilds donated a large sum; and geographical societies and those interested in Arctic exploration from a variety of countries also contributed generously. Even King Christian of Denmark added to the subscription fund.

In early 1896, the balloon completed, Andrée chartered the steamship Virgo to transport his expedition to Danes Island near Spitsbergen in the Arctic. Arriving in early summer, he built an enormous hangar to house the *Eagle*. The hangar contained a hydrogen generator, which he used to inflate the balloon. He then fitted it with ropes and sails, loaded it with provisions, and readied it for flight.

To accompany him to the Pole, Andrée had chosen Dr Nils

Ekholm, a meteorologist, and Dr Nils Strindberg, a physicist (and cousin of the well-known playwright of the same name). However, bad weather foiled the attempt and Andrée returned to Sweden. Before they left for home, Ekholm resigned from the expedition because he discovered that the *Eagle* was plagued by constant leaks. Andrée replaced him with Knut Fraenkel, a young lieutenant in the Swedish Corps of Engineers.

Andrée returned to Danes Island in early June 1897 and was prepared to set off by 1 July, but winds and storms again intervened. Although doubtful about proceeding, however, he was persuaded by Strindberg and Fraenkel to begin the journey. At 1.45 a.m. on 11 July 1897, spectators on Danes Island cheered as the *Eagle* disappeared over the horizon. They were the last people to see the men alive.

In the years that followed there were many theories put forward as to the balloonists' fate and whereabouts. Andrée's mother advanced the theory that her son might have found the open Polar Sea and remained there. 'He is just the boy to stay,' said she, 'because he knows his old mother would willingly spare him to his work.'

Then, in 1930, sailors from a Norwegian sealing vessel discovered Andrée's last camp and the skeletons of the balloonists on White Island, east of Spitsbergen Island. They also found Andrée's journal, which told the story of the doomed expedition.

Apparently, after leaving Danes Island, Andrée's balloon had floated northward, but, just as Ekholm had feared, serious gas leaks caused the *Eagle* to lose altitude. By day two, it was leaving its marks in the ice every 160 feet or so. Even though they threw all their ballast overboard, the carriage began to strike the polar ice cap. The next day, this bumpy ride became a crawl and the craft ground to a halt with two-thirds of the route still to be completed.

The stranded explorers salvaged supplies and sleds from the *Eagle* and began walking south. For two and a half months they trekked towards Spitsbergen Island, but the flowing ice kept carrying them eastward, away from their goal. Andrée eventually shot a polar bear – however, though the fresh meat was a welcome treat, they had trouble cooking it and had to eat it half-raw. ('Raw bear with salt tastes like oysters,' he wrote.) Finally, in October, 1897, they reached White Island, but died soon afterward. Andrée's last, incoherent journal entry was dated 17 October – a day before his 43rd birthday. Since they had plenty of food and clothing, however, it was clear that they had not starved or frozen to death. In fact, for another twenty years the cause of their deaths remained unknown.

Then, in 1949 a Danish doctor, reading Andrée's description of the illness they suffered guessed the cause of death. He scraped meat from a bearskin that had been found in Andrée's camp and had it analysed. The meat was infected with trichinae. Andrée, the first airborne Arctic explorer, and his two companions appeared to have died of trichinosis, caused by eating improperly cooked polar-bear meat.

However, in 2000 Dr Mark Personne, director of the Swedish Poisons Information Centre, made a close study of the disposition of the bodies when they were eventually found and concluded that they must all have died within a few hours of each other. Only one (Strindberg) had been interred, so he must have been the first to die. Yet the journals of Andrée and Fraenkel make no mention of his death, suggesting that they themselves died before they had time to record it. They were not in their sleeping bags, indicating they did not even have time to consider themselves ill and retire to bed.

Trichinosis is rarely fatal and so, even with weakened victims, is very unlikely to have killed all three within such a short space of time. Personne suggests that the most probable cause was straightforward, if virulent, bacterial food poisoning: botulism, ingested from the infected carcass of a seal they had shot on the ice, brought with them and inadequately heated during food preparation.

Among the exotic items recovered from the exhibition were quantities of Russian and US money in silver and gold, a white dress tie, an expensive porcelain bowl, the heavy silver base for a German vase, a white shirt in its original wrappings, a large collection of heavy towels, old newspapers, packets of personal letters, and two tickets to the Stockholm Exposition of 1897.

THE MYSTERY AIRSHIP

SACRAMENTO, USA 1896

The excitement started on 17 November 1896, in Sacramento, California, on a dismal, rainy night. Through the dark clouds, there appeared a bright light moving slowly west, and apparently about a thousand feet above the rooftops. Among the hundreds of people who saw it was George Scott, an assistant to the Secretary of State of California. Scott persuaded some friends to join him on the observation deck above the capitol dome and from there they thought they could see three lights, not one. Above the lights was a dark, oblong shape.

Elsewhere, there were more detailed sightings. R L Lowery, a former street railway employee, said he heard a voice from above call, 'Throw her up higher; she'll hit the steeple.' When he looked up, he saw two men seated on a bicycle-like frame, pedalling. Above them was a 'cigar-shaped body of some length'. Lowery said that the thing also had 'wheels at the side like the side wheels on Fulton's old steam boat'.

Newspapers were cautious and reported merely a 'mysterious light' or 'wandering apparition', while some suggested the whole thing had been a hoax or the result of a natural effect, like glowing swamp gas. Then, five days after its first appearance, the 'airship' came back.

It was Sunday night and weather conditions were as before: dark and overcast. This time the light appeared from the northwest and went straight over the town, running against the wind. One witness with a small telescope reported that the lamp was 'an electric arc light of intense power'. He also observed that the light didn't move in a straight line, but seemed to bob up and down in the wind. Another witness with field glasses reported seeing a dark body above the light.

It took just thirty minutes for the thing to cross the city and disappear to the southwest. During this time thousands of people observed it, including the city's deputy sheriff and a district attorney.

That same night the 'airship' also appeared above San Francisco some ninety miles away, where hundreds more observed it, including the mayor. It cruised as far as the Pacific Ocean, where its searchlight, a beam that stretched out over 500 feet, reportedly frightened the seals on Seal Rock, sending them plunging into the safety of the sea.

Over the next few days airship sightings were made not just in California, but from as far away as Washington State and Canada. It was suggested that the airship was the work of a mysterious inventor who was testing his device at night lest his ideas be stolen. After all, balloons capable of carrying people had been around for almost a hundred years by now, and the key to powered flight might soon be discovered.

One San Francisco attorney, nicknamed 'Airship' Collins, claimed that he was representing the eccentric and wealthy inventor who had constructed the thing at a secret location in Oroville, just 60 miles north of Sacramento. According to Collins the airship was 150 feet long, and could carry 15 passengers. It had two canvas wings 18 feet wide and a rudder shaped like a bird's tail, he alleged. When the mysterious inventor failed to appear, however, Collins found himself the object of ridicule and backed off from his earlier claims.

Another San Francisco attorney claimed that there was not one airship, but two, and that they would be used to bomb Havana. William Henry Hart, a former attorney general, asserted that it could carry four men and 1,000 pounds of dynamite. Hart's airship never was made public either, however, and by early December the lawyer, as well as the lights in the sky, had disappeared.

Everything was quiet for two months until, on 2 February 1897, the 'airship' appeared over the town of Hastings,

Nebraska. On 5 February it was seen 40 miles farther south near the town of Invale. Reports started to flow in from all over the state. On 16 February it was sighted over Omaha. One farmer claimed he'd encountered the airship on the ground, under repair, describing it as cigar shaped, about 200 feet long and 50 feet across at the widest point, gradually narrowing to a point at both ends.

Soon the airship had been sighted all over the Midwest, including reports from Texas, Kansas, Iowa and Missouri. Stories about encounters with the crew on the ground appeared. Finally, in April, the excitement reached its zenith when the 'airship' arrived in Chicago. On 11 April a photograph of the thing was produced, though experts later pronounced the image to be fake.

On 15 April, near Kalamazoo, Michigan, there were reports that the airship had crashed and exploded. Despite this, airship sightings continued for a few more days, but by the end of April the excitement was over.

Nothing resembling the various descriptions of the craft had yet been invented. Some have suggested people had been seeing the planet Venus, which was prominent in the sky at the time the sightings started. When the sightings stopped, it was becoming increasingly less visible.

Perhaps there really was a mysterious inventor who secretly built an airship and flew it around the country. If he did exist he certainly was successful in hiding his secret. It remains undiscovered even today.

'THE INCOMPARABLE LINCOLN BEACHEY'

WASHINGTON, DC, USA 1906

Lincoln Beachey was America's most famous and most skilled stunt flyer of the pre-World War I era. He was the first to fly inside a building, the first to point his machine straight down and drop vertically until maximum velocity was reached, the first to pick a handkerchief from the ground with his wingtip. He dived his primitive biplane – in which he sat in the open air in front of the lower wing – over Niagara Falls into the mists and emerged still flying. He even flew through the skyscraper 'canyons' of downtown Chicago, dressed as a woman, dancing his biplane wheels across car tops and cobblestones.

He was also a passionate man who worked tirelessly to promote aviation in the USA, passing out millions of brochures urging readers to write to their congressmen to facilitate investment in aviation. He personally and publicly petitioned the government to let him give them a demonstration but, when the time came and only two cabinet members arrived for the exhibition, Beachey knew he must break the rules if he was to get everyone to watch.

It had only been a couple of years since the Wright brothers had made their epic flight in a heavier-than-air aircraft, so Beachey at this early stage of his career was still flying a lighter-than-air controlled balloon craft (called a dirigible) consisting of a gas-filled bag with a framework carrying the motor, controls and pilot suspended underneath it. He took off in just such a craft from Washington's Luna Park on 10 September

1906. Within minutes of his clearing the treetops and heading toward the Capitol Mall, the news of a 'flying ship' was on the wires. People appeared at windows and on rooftops, crowds gathered in thousands, business ceased, and shoppers, merchants and deliverymen watched open-mouthed as Beachey floated over the summer streets.

President Wilson was working in the Oval Office when he heard what he thought was a fly. But the buzzing got louder and appeared to be coming from outside. Looking out his window he saw, heading for the windows of the Oval Office, an 800-pound biplane! The plane did not waver from its course until the last possible moment, when Lincoln pulled his machine straight up and spun, flashing his name written across the wings, B-E-A-C-H-E-Y. He then climbed above the White House, looped back and dived at it again and again as if on a bombing run.

He then headed straight for the Capitol. Congress adjourned to witness the spectacle as Beachey 'attacked' the building, ending his flight by waving his wings to Congress. He then flew back to the polo field across from the White House and, after quickly refuelling, he climbed to 3,000 feet and performed another aerial ballet. Suddenly, he appeared to be stuck upside down, his motor seemed to have failed and he began to fall and spin! He dropped out of the sky in a deadly upside-down spiral and, from a distance, did not seem to pull out of it. Personnel at the Army hospital saw the aviator fall and rushed out with ambulances. However, Beachey had landed safely.

The editors of *Aero and Hydro*, the country's leading voice of American aviation, lauded his aerial demonstration as an heroic act that had forced the government to recognise the necessity of their involvement in the new technology of aviation. Soon afterwards, Congress finally began appropriating significant amounts of money for the creation of an air force.

Unfortunately, Beachey's luck – and his life – came to an end on 14 March 1915 while performing a stunt at the Panama Pacific International Exposition in San Francisco. He was diving over San Francisco Bay in a new plane built especially for aerobatics, but the wings broke away and he crashed into the bay at full speed.

A BRAZILIAN FLYING NUT

PARIS, FRANCE 1906

The eccentric Brazilian Santos-Dumont was just 5 feet 4 inches tall, and always flew in a dapper suit, red tie and a Panama hat. He became a worldwide household name after circling the Eiffel Tower on 19 October 1901, in a small cylindrical hot-air balloon called a 'dirigible', controlled by a rudder he'd invented. The event drew a crowd of more than five thousand people. He later took to flying around Paris to dinner parties in his dirigible, tying it on hitching posts used for horses!

Santos-Dumont was the man of the hour. Men imitated his fashion style, turning down the brims of their hats and rolling up their trouser legs in just the way he did. While perfecting the dirigible, he grew tired of having to retrieve his pocket watch in flight and designed what today is the common wristwatch. The famed Paris jeweller Louis Cartier made the first one for him.

He also pre-empted the pioneering Wright brothers when he turned his attention to powered flight. At the Bagatelle cavalry grounds in Paris on 23 October 1906, he flew the first powered flight of 60 metres (197 feet) before a group of formal observers from the Aero Club de France. For this he was awarded the Archdeacon prize of 3,000 francs for the first flyer to cover 25 metres (82 feet).

He bettered this performance twice on 12 November, first with a distance of 82.6 metres (271 feet) in 7.2 seconds and then with a wavering flight of 220 metres (722 feet) in 21.4 seconds, gaining a further reward from the Aero Club of 1,500 francs. The instability of the plane's design, however, led to its abandonment the following year.

It was two full years after Santos-Dumont's 1906 flight that the Wright brothers would publicly demonstrate one of their planes, achieving much better results than he had up to that time, but still not managing to realise a complete flight as the aeroplanes of today do. For machines had at that point still not managed to carry out an important part of aeroplane flying: the take-off. Would-be flyers launched their constructions from a pillar, the forward impulse being provided by a weight connected to the aeroplane by a wire. On falling, the weight caused the aeroplane to leave the rails and project itself into space. Santos-Dumont, by contrast, was the first to actually take off and fly under his own power.

Dumont never patented his inventions, however, entering instead into a gentlemen's agreement with the French government that his planes be used for the public good. His end was a tragic one: he hanged himself in a Brazilian hotel room on 23 July 1932, depressed that aeroplanes he had pioneered and made fashionable were being used to bomb and rain down fire on civilians in both his native land and abroad.

GRAPEFRUIT

BROOKLYN, USA 1908

Ruth Law Oliver was the first woman to loop the loop in an aeroplane, setting a non-stop distance record in 1916 for both men and women by performing sixteen consecutive loops! She was also the first to make a night flight and the one-time holder of the Chicago to New York aerial speed record. In fact, she enjoyed one of the longest and most colourful careers of early female aviators – so successful that, in 1917, she could earn as much as $9,000 a week for exhibition flights. After World War
· I, she formed 'Ruth Law's Flying Circus', a three-plane troupe that amazed spectators at state and county fairs by racing against cars, flying through fireworks and setting altitude and distance records.

However, she first hit the headlines with a bizarre stunt involving a baseball player and a grapefruit!

Wilbert Robinson was a famous player and manager from baseball's early period, one of the 'old Orioles' of the 1890s, a rough-and-tumble team that played hard and lived the same way. He went on to become manager of the Brooklyn Dodgers in an era when they were sometimes known as the 'daffy Dodgers' for their antics on the field. Robinson endeared himself to the Brooklyn fans and became a kind of baseball icon.

In 1908, Washington Senators catcher Gabby Street had caught a baseball dropped from the Washington Monument – a distance of 555 feet. The ball was estimated to be travelling at 280 miles an hour when Gabby grabbed it. It was the thirteenth ball dropped in the experiment. Robinson, however

46

scoffed that this wasn't all that difficult a feat and enlisted Ruth Law to fly a plane higher than the Washington Monument and drop a ball for him to catch!

There are several versions of what happened next – one of which put Dodger batter Casey Stengel in the plane to make the drop. But Law actually flew alone. When Robbie, 53 years old at the time, caught the object he saw falling from the plane, he was splattered with warm juice – from a grapefruit!

The impact knocked him to the ground, whereupon he exclaimed: 'Help me, lads, I'm covered with my own blood.'

Law explained in 1957 that she had forgotten the baseball back in her hotel room and when she discovered the situation it was too late to retrieve the ball. So she took a grapefruit from the lunch of one of the ground crew and dropped that instead!

THE REMARKABLE 'COLONEL' CODY

FARNBOROUGH COMMON, ENGLAND 1908

On 16 October 1908, the peace of Farnborough Common in Hampshire was broken by a four-cylinder engine stuttering into life. Before a small audience of farmers, soldiers and reporters, the engine powered an ungainly construction of bamboo, canvas and piano wire along the bumpy heath and up into the morning air.

The flight of British Army Aeroplane No.1 was brief. Just 27 seconds after leaving the ground, having covered a mere 1,390 feet, the plane clipped trees and crashed to earth. Yet it marked Britain's inaugural powered flight. The event also established the legend of the aeroplane's charismatic and controversial pilot, the American cowboy 'Colonel' Samuel Franklin Cody.

Since arriving in England in the 1890s, Cody had become a popular hero, first as a vaudeville entertainer, then as a pioneer aviator and inventor. Yet his life was shrouded in myth and rumour. In his cowboy clothes and a stetson hat, with shoulder-length hair and an extravagant moustache, the big Texan cut an outlandish figure. It was not hard to believe he had at one time been a performer in a travelling Wild West show called 'The Klondyke Nugget' (as he had in the 1890s). While in England, his company, including several members of his family, toured the music halls, which were very popular at the time, giving demonstrations of his horse riding, shooting and lassoing skills. Important to his success was the fact that many people believed they were watching the 'real' Buffalo Bill Cody, whose surname he took when young – something that, as his Wild West appearance suggests, he did nothing to discourage.

It was around this time that Cody's son Leon became interested in kites. This sparked a similar obsession within Cody and the two of them competed to make the largest kites capable of flying at ever-increasing heights. After a great deal of experimentation, financed by his show, Cody patented his famous kite design in 1901, a winged variation of an earlier double-cell box kite. He offered this to the British War Office in December 1901 for use as a 'spotter' in the Boer War, and made several demonstration flights of up to 2,000 feet in various places around London.

A large exhibition of the Cody Kites took place at Alexandra Place in 1903 and Cody later actually succeeded in crossing the English Channel in a canoe towed by one of his kites. His exploits even came to the attention of the admiralty, who hired him to look into the military possibilities of using kites for observation posts. He produced a pioneering man-carrying kite, capable of raising a passenger to 1,000 feet, that proved so useful for reconnaissance that he was employed at the Aldershot Balloon Factory in 1905. Finally, in 1908, with France, America and Germany apparently racing ahead in aviation technology, the British Army asked Cody to build a prototype aeroplane.

Officially named 'British Army Aeroplane No.1' Samuel Cody's 1908 design was always known as the Cathedral, a name derived, perhaps, from either the machine's cavernous hangar or a contraction of the word 'catahedral', a term referring to the wing style. The Cathedral was a larger machine than those developed by the Wright brothers and was notable for its use of ailerons (a part along the back edge of an aircraft's wing that can be moved to help the aircraft turn or to keep it level) fitted between the wings.

Following the brief but sustained flight at Farnborough in 1908, a year later, with a larger engine, the Cathedral made flights that lasted for over an hour. It was announced as the first official flight of a heavier-than-air machine in the British Isles. Oddly, however, the War Office subsequently decided that there was no future in aeroplanes, and Cody's contract with the Army ended – they didn't even provide him with funds to repair his historic machine.

Cody continued undaunted, however. On 7 June 1909, he received a Royal Aero Club certificate and, on 14 August, carried passengers for the first time in the world – first, his old workmate Colonel Capper, and then his wife, Lela Cody. Then, on 5 September, he made a world-record cross-country flight of 1 hour 3 minutes.

Cody continued to build ever more sophisticated machines, entered international competitions and won many prizes. His finest hour came in 1912, however, when he entered a version of his original Army plane fitted with a new 120-horsepower engine for the War Office's first military trials. In the face of opposition from Europe's biggest aeroplane builders, Cody won the two first prizes. The War Office thus had to buy a plane remarkably similar to the one he had first built them in 1908 – this time for £5,000!

His only stroke of bad luck came when one of the machines he had hoped to enter, his Cody IV (a monoplane), was involved in a collision with a cow. During the ensuing court case the owner of the cow claimed for damages. The judge, ignoring the defence's plea that the cow had committed suicide, awarded the sum of £18 to the farmer.

On 7 August 1913, Cody was out for a joyride in his latest – and last – design, a seaplane, built to compete in the *Daily Mail*'s 'Seaplane Race around Britain'. This was Cody's largest machine, with a wingspan of nearly 60 feet, fitted with a 100-horsepower engine, a single rear rudder, a four-bladed propeller, a large central float and two wing floats. At an altitude of 500 feet, however, the plane broke up and Cody and his passenger were both killed. He was buried with full military honours in the Aldershot Military Cemetery – the first civilian to be afforded such an honour, and certainly the only Wild West cowboy – alongside the great heroes of Britain's military past. The funeral procession drew an estimated crowd of 100,000.

THE FIRST AIRCRAFT FATALITY

FORT MYER, USA 1908

On 17 September 1908, one of the famous Wright brothers, Orville, was preparing to demonstrate his flying machine to Army officials at Fort Myer, Virginia, when a fellow officer urged Lieutenant Thomas Selfridge, a West Point graduate and the army's foremost aeronautical expert, to go along for the ride. Selfridge had been assigned to a board conducting the first trials of the Wright aeroplane to see if it could fly 40 miles an hour, carry two persons aloft, and be portable enough to be transported by a mule-drawn wagon. When Orville had made the first flight at Fort Myer, the crowd had gasped in astonishment and for the next two weeks, record after record was broken as the aeroplane proved its capabilities.

Selfridge climbed into the passenger seat to fly with Orville, who followed him, giving him specific instructions as to how to sit during the flight. 'I don't have to tell you to keep your nerve,' said the aviator. 'You've been up often enough to know how to do that. Just sit tight, and don't move around any more than you actually have to.' The pair then took off.

Not long into the flight, they were in a slow turn during the fourth round when Wright heard a tapping sound. Then came two big thumps. A new, elongated propeller, never before tested, had been installed on the aircraft prior to the flight, but excessive vibration had caused the propeller to strike a guy wire on the aircraft, tearing it from its fastening in the rudder and breaking the propeller off about two feet from the end.

The aeroplane shook violently, making a sudden turn to the

right. The engine was shut off but the plane nosed straight downward, headed for the ground. In an almost inaudible voice, Selfridge exclaimed 'Oh! Oh!' as he hung desperately to the wing struts.

When the plane was about 25 feet from the ground it began to level out. A few more feet and it would have landed safely. Instead there was a terrifying sound of splintered wood as it crashed into the ground.

For a moment there was silence as a noiseless cloud of dust rose around the wreckage. Then a chorus of human voices gasped, and there was the trampling of running feet as a human wave rushed toward the wreckage. Men raised the crumpled plane and found both men pinned beneath the wreckage.

Once extricated they were carried on stretchers to the post hospital, where Wright was found to have sustained a fractured thigh and several broken ribs on his right side. Although his injuries were serious, he recovered after a long convalescence. Selfridge wasn't so lucky. A combination of a fractured skull and internal injuries proved fatal. He died that afternoon, and so America's first military pilot had become the first man killed in a heavier-than-air flying machine.

In France, Wilbur was shocked at the news and tortured by guilt. As the older brother, he felt that he was somehow responsible. 'I cannot help thinking over and over again "If I had been there, it would not have happened",' he commented later.

The oddest aspect of the event, however, was that Orville had been distinctly unhappy about flying with Selfridge. 'I don't trust him an inch,' he wrote to brother Wilbur. 'He is intensely interested in the subject, and plans to meet me often at dinners, etc. where he can pump me. He has a good education and a clear mind. I understand that he does a good deal of knocking behind my back.'

Orville Wright was absolved of any blame, however, and a week later, Selfridge was buried with full military honours in Section 3 of Arlington National Cemetery, near the very spot that he fell to his death. One year on, the Signal Corps purchased a Wright machine for $30,000. It was the world's first military aeroplane.

'BEAUTIFULLY COLOURED BIRDS'

LONDON, ENGLAND 1909

In 1908, the suffragette Muriel Matters of the Women's Freedom League distinguished herself by being one of three women involved in a disturbance at the House of Commons; two protestors, including Matters herself, were found chained to the grille of the Ladies' Gallery. The removal of the grille, which was necessary to free Matters, she saw as a 'symbol of the breaking down of one of the barriers that are between us women and liberty'.

As a result of this, on 18 February 1909, she was entrusted with a unique aerial demonstration aimed to coincide with the state opening of Parliament. To support the attempt by her suffragette associates to petition the prime minister for votes for women, Matters would fly over London and shower leaflets upon those below. It was the first use of the air for political lobbying and publicity.

Early that morning she joined a Mr Henry Spencer and his yellow torpedo-shaped 80-foot-long balloon at the Welsh Harp, Hendon. Written in large letters on one side were the words, 'Votes For Women'; on the other side, 'Women's Freedom League'.

They started at 1.30 p.m., with the intention of arriving at Westminster just as the procession was passing. Matters was reported to have been dancing around in circles, 'to keep her feet warm' before she was lifted into the balloon, smiling bravely. After half an hour's delay in starting the engine, she and Spencer set off towards Cricklewood.

In fact, the wind prevented the balloon from following the royal procession's golden coach carrying the king and queen and air currents took her up to about 3,500 feet, so that she was unable to use her megaphone to address the parliamentarians. She did, however, scatter the 56 pounds of handbills she had taken with her.

The balloon was eventually carried by the wind to Coulsdon in Surrey via Wormwood Scrubs, Kensington and Tooting. On reaching the suburbs the mechanism was stopped and the airship drifted over a field, where a descent was made after a trip of about one and a half hours. A rope was thrown out to a farmer, who guided the balloon to a safe spot. The airship had been pursued from Hendon by members of the League in a car and the handbills she'd thrown out along the way enabled the car to track them.

The *Daily Mirror*'s headline sniffed: 'Suffragette Airship Plot Fails! Airship Fiasco!', but on landing Muriel told a *Mirror* reporter, 'It was like nothing on earth! It was quite wonderful. We could see Westminster but of course the people in the streets couldn't see us. We were throwing down bills all the time, yellow, green and white [the colours of the Women's Freedom League] – they floated down to the people below like beautifully coloured birds.'

HOUDINI PULLS IT OFF

DIGGERS REST, AUSTRALIA 1910

In 1910, when Australia's 'Aerial League' heard that Harry Houdini, the celebrated escapologist, was to visit the country on a theatrical tour, it invited him to bring his Voisin biplane along, mindful of the publicity such a flight would generate in their attempts to promote aviation.

Houdini's aircraft resembled an enlarged version of a box kite. Powered by a 60-horsepower engine, the Voisin, while not as advanced as its contemporary, the Blériot monoplane, was certainly capable of sustained flight in the hands of an experienced pilot.

Houdini's attempt to become the first person to fly over Australian soil soon encouraged opposition. Ralph Banks, an American who had brought a Wright Flyer down from Sydney, was determined to beat Houdini into the air and attempted a flight on 1 March, only to have a sharp gust of wind cause his aircraft to dive into the ground after take-off, smashing it completely; Banks escaped with minor injuries.

Houdini's other competitor was one Mr Jones, an Adelaide businessman who had visited Europe and England in the hope of finding an aircraft capable of being demonstrated and sold in Australia. The machine, a Blériot monoplane, was assembled and displayed in John Martin's store in Rundle Street, Adelaide.

From there it was moved to Bolivar, a country town outside Adelaide, where on 13 March the first attempts at flying it were to be made. The aircraft was run around a paddock but it struck a clump of grass, lurched into the air and, after travelling about 50 feet, landed without damage.

On 17 March 1910, another attempt resulted in the aircraft stalling and crashing, causing extensive damage to the propeller, undercarriage and wheels. It was returned to Adelaide for repairs and was later destroyed by fire while in storage for the winter.

Little publicity attended these efforts in South Australia, but those of Harry Houdini, now at Diggers Rest, received wide reporting. Houdini knew the value of publicity and there were plenty of observers present to witness his initial flights.

Following the advice of his mechanic, Houdini waited until 18 March, when weather conditions were perfect, and then taxied the aircraft to test the engine and controls. He then opened the throttle, the engine roared and the aircraft surged toward a clump of trees before soaring skyward and stayed aloft for about a minute. He landed safely and went on to fly on two or more occasions that day.

A description of the third successful flight on 18 March 1910 appeared in the *Argus*:

> The third flight lasted 3½ min. and was unmarred by any fault. Houdini swept boldly away from the flying field, confident of his control of the plane, and passing over rocky rises and stone fences, described a great circle, which was, at the lowest estimate, well over two miles. The machine, in rounding curves, leaned over, as one sees a seagull lean sideways to the wind, but the aviator felt that he was no longer a 'fledgling', and, the curve negotiated, straightened the plane with a turn of the wheel. The descent was faultless, and the plane came to rest within 20 ft. of the starting point, where the little knot of witnesses were standing.

Houdini went on to give further demonstrations at Rose Hill in Sydney and a monument to his inaugural flight is located on the Old Calder Highway in Diggers Rest.

Interestingly, he taught himself how to drive a car during

that time he was learning to fly – so that he could get out to the airfield! After his Australian tour, Houdini abandoned the plane and never drove again.

IT'S QUICKER BY RAIL!

LONDON TO MANCHESTER, ENGLAND 1910

In 1906, the London *Daily Mail* offered a prize of £10,000 for the first aviator to fly from London to Manchester within 24 hours. No more than two landings were allowed en route and the aviator had to start and finish within five miles of the *Daily Mail*'s London and Manchester offices. When the offer was made, the newspaper's money seemed safe. At that time the leading aviator in Europe could only stay in the air for seconds at a time and had flown a mere 200 metres (656 feet); the distance between the two cities was 298 kilometres (185 miles).

Claud Grahame-White was a successful car dealer in London's exclusive Mayfair district. With his new Gnôme-engined Farman III plane he planned to follow the London & North Western Railway all the way north and persuaded the company to whitewash its sleepers for 100 yards to the north of every junction, to ensure he stayed on the right line!

On Saturday, 23 April 1910, he took off in the dark from Park Royal, in north London. All along the route people thronged the railway bridges and vantage points to cheer him on. His was probably the first aeroplane ever seen in some of the counties he crossed.

Unfortunately, engine problems and bad weather saw him abandon this first attempt just outside Lichfield in Staffordshire. He arrived back in London to find a competitor, Frenchman Louis Paulhan, had arrived on the scene. Similarly equipped with a Gnôme-engined Farman a head-to-head race between Frenchman and Englishman created a great deal of patriotic excitement in both countries. Grahame-White even received a telegram saying, 'Every Englishman is watching you. Win the competition and preserve the honour of Old England!'

On Wednesday, 27 April 1910, having carried out a test flight at 2 p.m., Grahame-White felt the wind was too strong for an attempt and so went back to his hotel. At 5.30 p.m on the same afternoon, Louis Paulhan, realising that Grahame-White expected him to start the following morning, seized the moment. Eschewing a test flight, he took off, banked round over 4,000 cheering spectators and headed north.

It would be another half an hour before Grahame-White realised his rival was in the air. Only a few hundred stragglers from the crowd of thousands remained on the ground to witness him take off at 6.30 p.m.

By the time night fell, he'd travelled 60 miles to Roade, in Northamptonshire, while Paulhan had reached Lichfield, a good 117 miles from London. At Roade, after having a cup of tea in a signal box, Grahame-White returned to his aeroplane to find the field full of well-wishers. He was carried shoulder high and then made to sign autographs by the light of a bicycle lamp.

He expected to fly through the night. By means of moonlight and the headlamps of his friends' automobiles, he took off once again and was making good progress when disaster struck. He was only about twenty miles from Lichfield when the Gnôme's engine began to fail. A head wind picked up as dawn approached, his ground speed dropped to a crawl and he was forced to land at the village of Polesworth, about ten miles from Lichfield and still well behind his rival.

Up ahead, Paulhan was making good progress, passing Stafford at 4.45 a.m. and Crewe at 5.20 a.m. At the official finishing post at Burnage, near Didsbury on the outskirts of Manchester, the official time-taker and other Royal Aero Club members were waiting, having slept at a nearby inn on chairs. By 5 a.m., a crowd of several thousand had gathered, made up of workers, tradesmen, farmers and country gents. The roads were full of cars and the platform of the nearby elevated station was packed. At 5.25 a.m. a buzz went round the crowd as they learned that a signalman had phoned up the line to say an aeroplane was only 5 miles away.

Paulhan finally landed at 5.32 a.m. and climbed stiffly down from his seat and vowed never to undertake such a flight again, 'Even for twice £10,000!' He was mobbed by the crowd and had to be escorted by two policemen to the station, where his train had just pulled in, He had succeeded in flying from London to Manchester in just over 12 hours – 4 hours 12 minutes of which had been spent in the air.

Louis Paulhan was duly certified by a committee of the Royal Aero Club as having abided by the rules and on Saturday, 30 April, he drove straight from the Club in Piccadilly to the luncheon given in his honour at the Savoy Hotel in the Strand. Claude Grahame-White was also present, and he received a 100-guinea cup as consolation.

HIGHER, ALWAYS HIGHER!

SWITZERLAND TO MILAN 1910

Georges Chavez was a Peruvian born in Paris. A popular and skilful pilot, in 1910 he was one of five men who took up the challenge of making a flight from Switzerland, through the Simplon Pass, to Milan, where an aviation meeting was being held.

Two weeks previously, he had set a new altitude record of 8,840 feet (2,652 metres) in his Blériot XI. He would need all the height he could get to make it safely through the Simplon Pass. To the west, the mountains towered to 13,000 feet (3,900 metres) while at its peak the pass touched 6,600 feet (2,000 metres) The total distance to Milan was 94 miles (151 kilometres), but the rules of the competition allowed flyers to make the journey in stages. The first leg, and the most difficult of all, was through the mountains and was 25 miles (40 kilometres) long.

In the late summer, a number of competitors gathered on the Swiss side of the pass at the town of Brig, where the railway to Italy disappeared into the Simplon Tunnel, to attempt the dangerous flight.

On 23 September 1910, after Chavez had made several unsuccessful attempts, the weather on the Swiss side of the pass was deemed perfect, with a clear blue sky and no wind at the take-off field. The smoke from a marker-fire at the mouth of the pass, which showed competitors the wind strength there, was also rising vertically. At 1.30 p.m., Chavez took off in his Blériot, made two great climbing circles of the town and headed into the pass. He successfully reached the Simplon Hospice, situated at the head of the pass, his plane passing over the refuge before beginning its descent.

There was more wind on the Italian side, though, and Chavez was forced to fly down a steep ravine to the east, the Gorges du Gondo, rather than carry on in the face of the wind. By going this way he was adding several miles to the journey. With black peaks towering above the tiny wooden monoplane, he pressed on in splendid isolation, struggling with the controls to keep his plane level in the cold, turbulent mountain air.

At times the Blériot would gain or drop dramatically up to 60 feet as it hit a particularly strong current. Occasionally it came within feet of the great rock faces. However, 41 minutes after take-off he was sighted by excited spectators waiting on the landing field at Domodosola on the Italian side of the pass. He cut the engine and glided down to land. He had made it through the Pass!

But with the Blériot a mere 30 feet from the ground, tragedy struck. To the horror of the watching spectators, Chavez and his plane suddenly plunged to earth. Gravely injured, he was taken to hospital, where he died four days later.

The accident has never been satisfactorily explained. Some eyewitnesses claimed the Blériot had suffered structural failure, but it seems more likely that Chavez, numb with cold and fatigue, had let the aircraft lose airspeed and stall where there was no room for recovery. His dying words were reported to be 'Arriba, siempre arriba' ('Higher, always higher'), which is now the motto of the Peruvian Air Force.

FLIGHT DECK TO FLIGHT DECK

WILLOUGHBY SPIT, USA 1910

For some time, pioneer aviator Glenn Curtiss had been trying to convince the US Navy that an aeroplane could take off and land on board a ship. When the Navy finally agreed to a trial, a young pilot, Eugene Ely, whom Curtiss had signed up for his air show some six months earlier, was assigned the task of flying from a special platform built on the cruiser Birmingham. His machine, the Hudson Flyer, was brought aboard by crane.

On the gloomy morning of Monday, 14 November 1910, an entourage of Navy officials and onlookers awaited the big show. The weather was bad but, with about an hour of light left, at 3.00 p.m., clouds lifted enough for Ely to feel confident enough to make the attempt. He cranked up his motor, a restraining line was cut and the plane trundled down the gently sloping deck.

Wearing a padded football helmet and bicycle tubes as a survival vest (for he couldn't swim) Ely broke free from the deck. Barely gaining the necessary speed, he briefly sank low enough to shatter his propeller tips on the waves. He flew on with the entire plane vibrating badly and managed to make a credible landing on the sandy beach called Willoughby Spit – but short of the intended target, the US Navy yard.

Ely figured that in not making the yard, he had failed, and his colleagues spent the evening trying to convince him that he had, in fact, succeeded. His particular landing place was unimportant. It would soon be forgotten. The world would remember that he had shown that a plane could fly from a ship, and that navies could no longer ignore aeroplanes. Ely did not cheer up until he was promised a chance to do it again. 'I could land aboard, too,' was his comment.

The next morning the splintered propeller was wrapped in a bathrobe and carried to Ely's Pullman train drawing room, where he and his friends held a champagne party. The Navy also presented Ely with a cheque for $500 to pay for the damaged propeller, and made him a lieutenant in his US Aeronautical Reserve.

Two months later, on 18 January 1911, Curtiss and Ely were busy making arrangements to demonstrate that an aeroplane could land, as well as take off, from a ship at anchor. It was arranged for a large 'deck' to be built on the cruiser USS Pennsylvania at Mare Island Navy Yard near San Francisco. The platform was 130 feet long and 30 feet wide. Twenty-two manila rope-lines 3 feet apart, and propped up to a foot high with 50-pound sandbags tied to each end, were strung across it. This would serve to arrest the incoming plane.

When the plane landed, hooklike skis devised by Curtiss and fitted on the undercarriage caught the ropes and rapidly brought the machine to a stop. It took only ten sandbags to stop Ely and the Hudson Flyer. Pandemonium broke loose on board and from the surrounding vessels, which roared out blasts of 'Welcome Aboard'. After completing interviews and posing for photographs, Eugene Ely was escorted to the captain's cabin, where he was honoured guest at an officers' lunch. One hour later, he made a perfect take-off from the platform.

Nine months later, on 19 October, Ely was flying a routine demonstration at the Georgia State Fair. While diving from several hundred feet, he was seen to be fighting to maintain control, but the plane crashed near the grandstand. Ely died of a broken neck after being thrown from his seat; he was 25. A notable flying career, which had lasted only eighteen months, had ended. Sadly, an unruly crowd rushed to the wreckage to strip souvenirs from the aeroplane and even pieces of clothing from Ely's body.

LOOPING THE LOOP

JUVISY, NEAR PARIS, FRANCE 1913

Despite having only got his pilot's licence six months previously, a young Frenchman named Adolph Pégoud made headlines on 19 August 1913. He performed only the second parachute jump in history from an aeroplane – piloted by himself! It was thought that the change in balance as a man jumped out could render a plane out of control. So, at a considerable risk to himself (not to mention those below) he jumped from his own single-seater Blériot XI. The plane made a spectacular crash landing and he landed safely in a tree after a perfect parachute jump.

The feat brought Adolphe Pégoud to the notice of the famous aeroplane designer Louis Blériot himself, who decided that he was just the man he needed to demonstrate the aerobatic qualities of his new Blériot design. Blériot was keen to prove that his aeroplanes were safer than his competitors' because they could be recovered to level flight from almost any altitude, however extreme. Pégoud was thus employed as a rudimentary test pilot and on 1 September 1913 he made a series of experiments at Juvisy, near Paris, on a modified 50-horsepower machine, which included making 90-degree banked turns.

These culminated with the world's first inverted flight, confounding critics who said that an aeroplane could not possibly fly upside down. Pégoud was held in by a strong shoulder harness. Once back on the ground, he told how it had not been an entirely pleasant experience as petrol had started to drizzle out of the air hole in the 'top' of his petrol tank and blow back over him in the airstream while he was upside down!

A few weeks later, he went up again ready to experiment with different ways of getting back to level flight. He attempted 'flick turns', tail slides, a vertical figure 'S' and, finally, a brand new trick. Instead of rolling over, he would put the Blériot's nose down to vertical and then continue to pull back on the control stick until he came out of his dive flying in the opposite direction. Pégoud had also realised he could improve on this trick by making a full circle in the air rather than just a half-circle.

Starting the right way up and in a moderate dive to gain speed, he pulled back on the stick to bring the nose up to vertical and then kept the stick back toward his stomach until he was inverted. The horizon appeared upside down. Pégoud held his nerve and kept the stick back until the ground was below again and he was back in level flight. He had looped the loop!

Although credited with having achieved the first loop in the world, it emerged later that he had been beaten to it by a matter of days. On 9 September, Lieutenant Petr Nikolaevich Nesterov had looped his Russian Army 70-horsepower Nieuport monoplane at Kiev in the Ukraine. At the time he was placed under arrest by his commanding officer for risking army property, but after it emerged that he was a hero, he was promoted to the rank of captain!

BARRAGE BALLOONATICS!

WESTERN FRONT 1917

Belgian-born Willy Coppens joined the Compagnie des Aviateurs in 1914 and, at his own expense, he enrolled in a civilian flying school at Hendon, England, along with 39 of his fellow countrymen. After additional training in France, Coppens began flying two-seaters in combat during 1916. The following year, he was assigned to single-seat fighters and soon became an expert at shooting down enemy observation balloons.

After downing a balloon, Coppens would often perform aerial acrobatic displays above the enemy. However, on one occasion, the balloon he was attacking shot upward and Coppens actually landed his cobalt-blue Hanriot HD1 fighter plane on top of it! He then performed probably his most ingenious trick, completely impromptu. Switching off his engine to protect the propeller, he waited until his aircraft slid off the top of the balloon, then restarted the engine – and watched as the German balloon burst into flames and sank to the ground!

However, German pilots were just as adept at balloon acrobatics. Indeed, one of the most remarkable escapes from a balloon 'strike' happened on Monday, 22 July 1940 over Plymouth. In trying to avoid a barrage balloon, Junkers Ju 88 pilot Hauptmann Hajo Hermann actually stalled on top of it! With unbelievable luck and no little skill, he was able to gain control of his plane again by allowing it to slide off the balloon upside down.

WHO KILLED THE RED BARON?

SAILLEY-LE-SAC, FRANCE 1918

The death of Manfred von Richthofen – aka the 'Red Baron', the highest-scoring fighter pilot of World War I – has been a matter of controversy since that April morning in 1918 when he made what was probably one of the few mistakes in his long and illustrious career. Quite simply, no one is quite sure who finally shot the Red Baron.

Allied pilots had ample reason to dread the sudden appearance of the Baron's bright-red fighter sweeping towards them out of the sun. In twenty months of combat, he officially shot down 80 enemy aircraft, including 21 planes in the month of April 1917 alone!

On the morning of Sunday, 21 April 1918, he led his flight of Fokker triplanes to search for British observation aircraft, eventually jumping on a pair of lumbering RE8 observation planes of the No.3 Australian Squadron. Canadian Captain Roy Brown, leading a flight of eight Sopwith Camels far above, dived into the fray along with some Albatross Scouts and a second group of Fokkers.

Among the Allied group was a young Canadian, Wilford May, flying his first combat patrol. Although told by Brown to stay above any fight, should one develop, May couldn't resist the temptation, but he quickly became overwhelmed in the aerial tangle of thirty or more planes. He was forced to break away, but was spotted by Richthofen, who sensed his next victim.

As the panicking May lost altitude, trying every manoeuvre he could think of to stay out of the Baron's sights, Brown dived to help his fellow airman. It was then, with Brown closing from behind, that Richthofen, usually a meticulous and disciplined fighter pilot, made a crucial error. He broke one of his own rules by following May for too long, too far and too low into enemy territory. In fact, he was two miles behind the Allied lines when Brown finally caught up with him and fired. Brown claimed it was his fire that downed the Red Baron.

This is where the subsequent confusion begins, however. The chase had passed over the machine-gun nests of the 53rd Battery, Australian Field Artillery, from where Sergeant C B Popkin opened fire with his Vickers gun, followed by gunners William Evans and Robert Buie, plus a number of riflemen.

Whether hit from the air or the ground, Richthofen was mortally wounded. He tore off his goggles, opened the throttle briefly, then cut off the engine and dipped down for a crash landing. His plane bounced once, breaking the propeller, and settled in a beet field alongside the Bray–Corbie road near Sailley-le-Sac. He died moments later. It was 10.50 a.m.

The Royal Air Force swiftly gave official credit for the Baron's death to Captain Roy Brown, who was rewarded for his efforts that morning with an extra Bar to his Distinguished Flying Cross. Upon viewing Richthofen's body on the following day, Brown wrote that, 'there was a lump in my throat. If he had been my dearest friend, I could not have felt greater sorrow.'

After the war, however, articles appeared in the press to question the official attribution of the Baron's destruction to Brown. One article claimed that Richthofen had landed unscathed and that Canadian soldiers had jumped from their trenches and killed the Baron before he could climb out of his triplane.

In a later book in 1969, a Lieutenant R A Wood of the 51st Battalion asserted that an unknown gunner from his own unit had brought down the Baron, a claim supported in detail in 1975 by Private V J Emery of the 40th Battalion. Emery believed that the 'unknown rifleman' from Wood's platoon was in a better position to have fired the fatal shot than any of the other gunners in the area.

AS I FLEW LYING

TORONTO, CANADA 1918

After a disappointment in love, the writer William Faulkner (originally spelled 'Falkner') left his home town of Oxford Mississippi and headed for Canada. The United States had entered the war in 1917 and he tried to enlist in the Army Air Corps as a pilot. When he was rejected for being too short he decided instead to try and enlist with the RAF in Canada as a British citizen. He changed the spelling of his name to its present form, believing this would look more British; he affected a British accent and adopted what he thought was a British persona. In his RAF application he also lied about numerous facts, including his birth date and birthplace.

He was accepted and reported for duty in Toronto on 9 July 1917. He began training at the School of Military Aeronautics in Toronto, but when the war ended on 11 November 1918, Cadet Faulkner was still in the third and final phase of pre-flight training.

He received an honourable discharge and afterwards bought an officer's dress uniform and a set of wings for the breast pocket – even though, during his period with the RAF, he never left North America, and never flew in combat. However, that did not stop him from spinning yarns about his 'distinguished' flying career, one of which concerned a mysterious injury that required a plate to be surgically implanted in his head, causing lingering pain. When listeners assumed that he had incurred his 'injuries' in the skies over France, Faulkner did little to dissuade them.

71

Some of his tales of 'injuries' even made it into later biographical notes accompanying his novels.

His brief service in the RAF would serve him well in his written fiction, particularly in his first published novel, *Soldiers' Pay*, in 1926. Faulkner's tall tales about his flying career came back to haunt him later, however, especially when Malcolm Cowley was assembling *The Portable Faulkner*, a collection of his work. When Cowley requested biographical information about Faulkner's RAF career, Faulkner suggested that Cowley write only a brief 'Who's Who' account: 'Was a member of the RAF in 1918.' He added, 'You're going to bugger up a fine dignified distinguished book with that war business.'

THE FOX IN THE BOX

PLOEGSTEERT, BELGIUM 1918

Major William Avery 'Billy' Bishop was the leader of newly formed Royal Air Force Squadron, the 'Flying Foxes'. In less than six months of actual flying time, he downed 67 enemy planes, but the morning of 19 June 1918 was to mark his last combat flight. It would prove to be an interesting one.

Flying a few miles over the lines in enemy territory, Bishop dropped out of the clouds to check his position. It was 9.58 a.m. He recognised the landmark of the Ploegsteert Wood, south of Ypres, and he also immediately identified the three aircraft flying away from him to his left at about 300 yards – German Pfalz D.IIIa scouts. This solidly constructed German single-seater carried two Spandau guns internally in the front fuselage and had proved to be a steady platform, capable of absorbing a great deal of battle damage. It had played a large part in the revival of German air superiority in the early spring of 1918 and three Pfalzes together were not a threat to be taken lightly.

Having spotted Bishop, the German scouts began to turn, and Bishop followed them. By the time he had drawn a bead on one of the three, they had come halfway around the circle. Suddenly they dived on him, guns blazing. Bishop saw the tracers tear through his lower left wingtip as he got in a short burst himself. The three fighters slipped beneath him. Banking to the left to bring his machine to bear again, Bishop took a quick look behind him. Two more Pfalz scouts were diving on him at high speed. This instinctive glance had probably saved his life.

73

Now time was of the essence. Deciding to make a quick attack on the original three before the other two could enter the fray, Bishop opened fire quickly from what was for him an unusually long range. One of the three aircraft was struck instantly and its pilot killed. It fell away, out of control. The other two began to climb while the two newcomers, still diving and finally in range, opened fired on Bishop, who pulled up into a steep turn. The two German scouts passed beneath him. Then the two that had been climbing toward the cloud layer collided. Both aircraft disintegrated in a shower of wood, metal and fabric.

Turning his attention to the remaining two Pfalzes now climbing toward the safety of the clouds, Bishop sent tracers into one of them at 200 yards, starting the enemy aircraft spiralling toward the ground, only 1,000 feet below. The fifth Pfalz escaped into the clouds.

With the ceiling down to 900 feet, Bishop continued his patrol somewhere between Neuve Eglise and Ploegsteert. He was beginning to think of returning to base when out of the misty drizzle appeared an outline with which he had become very familiar in recent months – a German two-seater. Without being spotted, he slipped into the blind spot beneath and behind the reconnaissance aircraft and, raising his nose, sent a short burst from both guns into its belly. It shuddered, seemed to hesitate in the air and then fell toward the ground. With the pilot struggling desperately to regain control of the aircraft and the observer slumped lifeless in the rear seat, the two-seater smashed into the ground and went up in flames.

Then, as suddenly as it had begun, it was over. Bishop was alone in the sky again. He hardly realised it at the time, but this had indeed been his finest achievement in the air. During his final sortie he had downed five aircraft in the space of fifteen minutes. It was a fitting way to end a remarkable combat flying career.

HOLLYWOOD SKYWAYMAN
CRASHES OUT OF THE PICTURE

LOS ANGELES, USA 1920

Wing-walking was not new in 1918; it was not unheard of for a pilot or passenger (if absolutely necessary) to climb out onto a wing and make a timely repair or pry loose a stubborn control surface. But flyer Ormer Leslie Locklear took the practice to new levels, devising stunts that tempted fate to its limits.

When Locklear met the promoter William Pickens in 1919, the latter already had a great deal of experience promoting flying barnstormers like Lincoln Beachey and other post-war flyers, but from the very beginning Pickens knew he was going to have his greatest success with Locklear. Jumping from one plane to another was Locklear's trademark stunt; then, when the public tired of that, he worked on jumping from a car to a plane and from a plane to car. Locklear was severely injured in some of the earlier attempts of this stunt, but Pickens used that (and the exaggerated use of bandages) to heighten the drama and stir public interest

One stunt carried out by Locklear, along with a second pilot – the 'Dance of Death' – is still difficult to believe, and is probably the most thrilling aerial stunt ever performed. Locklear would pilot one plane and fly right next to a second plane, with the two aircraft almost touching wings. At a signal, with the controls locked in place, the two pilots would change places, passing each other as they scampered across the wings!

Locklear and Pickens went from strength to strength and became very wealthy. They lived in high style, in contrast to the poverty of most other barnstormers. They became even more successful when they brought the act to Los Angeles and came to the attention of the movie-making community. After several highly publicised exhibitions at an airfield owned by Sydney Chaplin, Charlie Chaplin's brother, Pickens arranged for Locklear to appear as a stuntman in Universal Films' *The Great Air Robbery* in 1919. This enabled him to perform many of his signature moves, and to develop even more. Near the end of the film he climbs down from a plane to a speeding car, fights with the villain, then grabs the undercarriage of the plane above him and climbs back into it just as the car overturns and crashes.

The following year, 20th Century-Fox made him an offer for a feature film, *The Skywayman*, in which he starred with his fellow pilot Milton 'Skeets' Elliot. They performed a variety of hair-raising stunts including a train-to-plane transfer and wing-walking. They even performed at night, illuminated by searchlights and foregoing the usual much safer device of using camera filters to make daytime scenes appear as though shot at night. This was to prove to be their undoing.

On 2 August 1920, he and Elliot were to execute the film's final aerial stunt, a spiralling dive at night over oilfields near Los Angeles from 5,000 feet with phosphorus flares glowing on the wings to give the impression the plane was on fire. Locklear had told the director to kill the searchlights illuminating the dive to signal when it was time for the pilots to pull out. But for some reason the lights were never turned off, and when Locklear and Elliot finally realised how low they had fallen, it was too late. The plane crashed into the pool of an oil well, killing both occupants.

Not one to sacrifice exciting film footage, producer Fox took advantage of the publicity and rushed the film into release – including the final, fatal plunge. To his credit, however, the moviemaker did earmark 10 per cent of the film's profits for the families of the men who had died and Locklear received a gala Hollywood funeral.

GOD 'ELP ALL OF US!

LONDON, ENGLAND 1920

In 1919 the Australian prime minister, the Rt Hon Billy Hughes, impressed by the potential for aviation in Australia, offered on behalf of the Commonwealth Government a prize of £10,000 for the first Australians to fly an aircraft from England to Australia. The race was to be conducted under the supervision of, and under rules drawn up by, the Royal Aero Club. The rules stipulated, *inter alia*, that the flight had to be conducted within a period of thirty consecutive days and concluded before midnight on 31 December 1920.

The pilots who signed on to compete for the prize were all young men who were fresh out of military service and hungry for the zest, glory and adrenaline fix that only a great adventure could provide.

Among the six entries, the two most promising crews were those of Captain Douglas and Lieutenant Ross and brothers Captain Ross Smith and Lieutenant Keith Smith. The Smith brothers set out first in their converted Vickers-Vimy bomber, whose registration number was G-EAOU (God 'Elp All Of Us!), which they had painted on its side, reflecting the significant dangers that they all faced.

Douglas and Ross were to fly in a magnificent Alliance aircraft fitted with the latest Rolls-Royce engines – both crews, in fact, were backed to the limit with machines, engines and equipment provided by the powerful companies whose reputations were at stake. The Vickers-Vimy crew took off on the morning of 12 November. The Alliance crew planned to start the following day from Hounslow aerodrome, ten minutes south-west of London and the official starting point.

Captain Douglas viewed the competition with confidence. The one-day start of the Vickers-Vimy combination did not trouble him. The 'Dodger', as he was known in Queensland boxing circles, was a believer in 'big jumps'. He spoke happily, confidently, of 'reaching Australia in ten flights'. What, then, was a day here or there? And, had the unexpected not happened, 'Dodger' would probably have been right. But it was the unexpected, the almost unbelievable, that happened.

Most people following the race were prepared for an accident or two, or even for a disaster, possibly, on the deserts of Syria or the ocean stretch between Java and Australia. But none anticipated, or could even have dreamed of, what did actually happen.

At Surbiton, six miles from the starting point, with the cheering crowds at Hounslow scarcely out of sight, the huge Alliance machine, flying low, nose-dipped and crashed with terrific force into an orchard. Lieutenant Ross was killed outright. Captain Douglas died shortly afterwards. Thus did this 'world' flight end – almost before it had begun.

Ross Smith, the main pilot of the Vickers-Vimy that eventually won the race, commented after only the first leg of the journey that, 'this sort of flying is a rotten game. The cold is hell, and I am a silly ass for ever having embarked on the flight.'

It took them 27 days 20 hours.

SEMPRINI'S LAST SERENADE

LAKE MAGGIORE, ITALY/SWITZERLAND 1921

Italy's Count Caproni, famous for designing large World War I aeroplanes, decided that he wanted to construct an aeroplane that would cross the Atlantic Ocean to New York. With this in mind, he attached three sets of 98-foot triplane wings to a 77-foot-long houseboat! Described as a Triple Hydro-Triplane, this machine was as amazing as it was ridiculous. The naïve philosophy behind it was that the more wings the better; moreover, the plane was powered by no less than eight 400-horsepower American Liberty engines, providing ten times as much power as the average passenger aircraft was using at the time. The aircraft-boat hybrid, which was called *Capronisimo*, weighed in at 55,000 pounds and led one Italian historian to remark that it 'would not have looked out of place sailing up the English Channel with the Spanish Armada'.

In January 1921, Caproni enlisted a pilot named Signor Semprini to test his Ca 90. Despite Semprini's objections, Caproni ordered him to take off with a ballast load equivalent to sixty passengers. Crowds gathered on 4 March 1921 around Lake Maggiore to enjoy the spectacle.

The air was soon filled with the roar of the beast's 3,200-horsepower engines as it began to move across the lake. Shortly after lift-off, however, its nose dipped, causing the ballast to roll toward to the front of the plane. It had climbed only 60 feet out of the water before the centre wing section crumbled and the aeroplane plunged back into the water, killing Semprini.

There were speculations at the time that the pilot had

crashed deliberately so as to save the lives of future passengers from certain death. It would seem much more likely that the pilot was the unfortunate victim of gross incompetence. Possibly to save Count Caproni's credibility, the insane invention was mysteriously destroyed in a fire while undergoing repairs.

WES, THE 'FLYING TANKER'

LONG BEACH, USA 1921

In November 1921, over Long Beach, California, US barn-stormer Earl Daugherty, trying to draw the attention of paying passengers, decided to introduce a new wing-walking stunt. It was a balmy day as two planes took off – one piloted by Frank Hawkes, the other by Daugherty. When the appropriate height was reached and the planes were barely six feet apart, the crowd was aghast to see Wesley May get out of Hawkes's plane, and swing himself pendulum-like along one of his wings. Miraculously, he then jumped on to the wing of the second plane!

To make things even more hair-raising, he was carrying a heavy 50-pounds can of fuel on his back, which dangerously affected his balance. He made it to the fuselage, however, then managed to unstrap his can, uncap it and, with one hand clutching the plane, he tipped the contents of the can at the opening of the gas tank. Some went in. Most poured into the slipstream, soaking May. But he had achieved what he had, unbelievably, set out to do.

A nearby plane took photographs, because in 1921 this was definitely newsworthy, despite a growing sense of public cynicism that this was just another barnstorming prank by misplaced youngsters who could not forget the war.

Both pilots were elated – it was a giant leap into the future! Wes, the 'Flying Tanker', proved gasoline could be transferred in mid-flight. In fact, it was the beginning of one of the most important engineering concepts in the history of aviation, one that would keep planes in the sky for longer and longer trips.

Daugherty and May never lived to see the refinement of their act, however. May died shortly afterwards, following a freak parachute accident, and Daugherty plunged to his death when his plane disintegrated over Long Beach some seven years later.

BYRD'S NORTH POLE FRAUD

SPITSBERGEN, NORWAY 1926

Standing proudly today in the Henry Ford Museum, in Dearborn, Michigan, is the Fokker Tri-motor the *Josephine Ford*, in which Richard Byrd and pilot Floyd Bennett made the inaugural flight over the North Pole in 1926. They took off on 9 May, from Kings Bay, Spitsbergen, and completed the historic mission in just 8 hours and 25 minutes. Once there, Bennett apparently swung the plane to the right to confirm their position on the sextant, circled and then confirmed it twice more. Of his impressions of that historic moment, Byrd wrote: 'We felt no larger than a pinpoint and as lonely as a tomb; as remote and detached as a star.'

Sixteen hours after take-off, the *Josephine Ford* arrived back at King's Bay where they were greeted with delight. Boat whistles sounded and a Norwegian band struck up 'The Star-Spangled Banner' as cheering men hoisted the two American aviators to their shoulders and paraded them around the base camp.

In fact, exploring the Arctic by air was not exactly a new idea by 1926. In 1897, Swedish balloonist Saloman Andrée had perished in an attempt to fly across the North Pole. Another abortive quest was made in 1909 by American Walter Wellman in a dirigible. A 1925 expedition by Roald Amundsen and Lincoln Ellsworth, using Dornier-Wal twin-engine flying boats, nearly ended in disaster barely 160 miles from their goal.

Among the dangers flyers had to contend with were powerful Arctic winds that could easily throw a plane off course.

Navigating from the air was also hazardous, since the dazzling white of ice and snow or the Arctic fog made the land seem horizonless against the sky. Landing to take bearings meant setting a craft down on unknown terrain – or no terrain at all, but instead treacherously deceptive sea ice.

Richard Byrd and his crew later received a hero's welcome in London and on 23 June 1926, a ticker-tape parade down New York City's Broadway. In Washington, the US Congress promoted Byrd to Commander and Bennett to Warrant Officer, and awarded both men rare peacetime Medals of Honor.

Byrd's logbook, records and calculations were hurried to a select panel of scientists at the National Geographic Society. After checking and rechecking the data, the committee confirmed that Richard Byrd and Floyd Bennett had indeed been the first men to fly over the North Pole. The National Geographic Society awarded Byrd the coveted Hubbard Gold Medal and Bennett with another gold medal.

The trip earned Byrd widespread acclaim, enabling him to secure funding for subsequent attempts on the South Pole. He later wrote in a 1928 autobiography, 'If the expedition had failed, which it might well have done with all hope centred in just one plane, I should still be trying to pay back my obligations.'

But was Byrd's great achievement all that it seemed? Or was the historic flight, in fact, a complete fraud?

There were several reasonable grounds to doubt the claim that he had reached the North Pole. Among the simplest was his failure to drop more than a hundred US flags intended to mark the Pole so that explorer Roald Amundsen's dirigible, the *Norge*, could verify the claim on reaching the North Pole a few days later. (In fact, Amundsen's achievement was robbed of its significance by Byrd's flight.)

More damning, however, was the evidence from the two men's diaries and a mechanical analysis of their plane carried out by the Norwegian-American aviator and explorer Bernt Balchen.

In October 1926, Floyd Bennett and Balchen started a tour around the States in the *Josephine Ford* sponsored by the

Guggenheim Foundation in an effort to boost interest in aviation among the American public. The flight took the two pilots from coast to coast and when they finally returned to Washington, DC, they were told by Byrd to take the plane to Detroit, where it would be put on permanent exhibit in the Ford Museum. (It sits there today.)

However, it was on the coast-to-coast tour that Balchen first became suspicious about Byrd's North Pole data. During his 'historic' trip, Byrd had logged an average of 70 miles an hour, the same as Bennett did on the publicity tour. Balchen figured that, with ski landing gear, the best the *Josephine Ford* could have managed would have been 68 mph.

What's more, the distance from Spitsbergen to the Pole is roughly 1,550 miles; in order to make it in the 15½ hours that Byrd and Bennett were away, and even allowing for tailwinds en route, the plane would have to have averaged better than 100 miles an hour!

It was thus a physical impossibility for the *Josephine Ford* to have made it to the Pole and back during the time Byrd claimed. How far north they flew is anyone's guess; that they did not reach the Pole is not guesswork, it is a simple question of mathematics.

By the time Byrd died on 12 March 1957, he had amassed 22 citations and special commendations, nine of which were for bravery and two for extraordinary heroism in saving the lives of others. In addition, he earned the Medal of Honor, the Congressional Life Saving Medal, the Distinguished Service Medal, the Flying Cross, the Navy Cross and three ticker-tape parades.

Over the years, Governor – later, Senator – Byrd, who became a powerful figure in US military circles – ferociously attacked anyone who dared suggest that his North Pole claims were fraudulent. He made Balchan's life particularly difficult, as he suspected that he knew the truth about the flight and could ruin him. There was intense pressure put on Balchan by Byrd when Balchan's autobiography was to be published. Balchan later commented: 'I had not written anything derogatory about Byrd, I had simply stated what I know to be a fact, that he had not reached the North Pole on his flight in 1926. I know this for two reasons, first, because the plane was incapable of making this flight in the 15½ hours claimed, and secondly, because Floyd Bennett told me so.'

Indeed, before he died of pneumonia a few years after the flight, Floyd Bennett admitted to an air-force officer friend that he and Byrd never made it to the North Pole. In revenge, Byrd blocked the award of the Congressional Medal of Honor and promotion to one of Bennett's friends.

Byrd's subsequent explorations in the Antarctic established him as a courageous and ground-breaking explorer. It also achieved his second great wish – to be the first person ever to fly over the South Pole when on 29 November 1929, he and three others crossed the South Pole in a plane called, ironically, the *Floyd Bennett*.

When he died at his home in Boston in 1957, Byrd was acclaimed an international hero. In the years following his death, however, further close, scientific analysis has only added to the doubts about his first great claim to fame.

NORTH POLE AGAIN – AND TRAGEDY

SPITSBERGEN, NORWAY 1926

It is now accepted that the first flight over the North Pole took place a few days after the Byrd 'record' and was a joint Norwegian-American-Italian venture. Strangely, it also created a furore – and had a tragic conclusion.

The co-leaders were the great Norwegian explorer Roald Amundsen, American adventurer Lincoln Ellsworth and Italian Umberto Nobile, the designer and pilot of the airship the *Norge* in which they flew.

They departed from King's Bay, Spitsbergen on 11 May and flew by way of the North Pole to Teller, Alaska. It was the first undisputed attainment of the North Pole by air and the first crossing of the polar sea from Europe to North America. Additionally, it gave Amundsen, who led the first expedition to reach the South Pole (in 1911), the distinction of being the first person to travel to both poles of the earth.

However, following the *Norge* flight a bitter dispute broke out between Amundsen and Nobile over who should receive credit for leading the expedition. With no clear outcome, Nobile returned to King's Bay in 1928, as sole leader of his own expedition in the airship *Italia*. They departed from King's Bay on 22 May 1928 and successfully flew over the North Pole – but on the return trip the following day they crashed on the ice northeast of Spitsbergen.

The *Italia* carried a crew of sixteen. At the time of the crash, nine crew members – including Nobile – were in the main cabin and were thrown onto the ice. One additional crew member was in the rear cabin and was also thrown onto the ice, but was later found dead. Six other crew members were inside the balloon envelope, which disappeared when, relieved of the weight of the main cabin, it floated away in free flight. Their remains were never found.

Remarkably, a number of supplies, including a radio and a tent, were also thrown to the ice and the survivors were able to establish a camp. The radio eventually allowed them to establish contact with the outside world. They used a red dye to paint red stripes on the tent to make it more visible from the air and the site became known in the extensive press coverage as the 'Red Tent'.

The *Italia* crash sparked a massive search-and-rescue operation, the first in the far north, which included planes and ships from six countries. On 23 June 1928, Nobile was taken to the mainland from the ice floe but further rescue was made impossible by bad weather. He then damaged his plane when returning for more survivors and had to be rescued himself again. Ultimately, the Russian icebreaker *Krassin* reached the by then badly disintegrating ice floe and rescued the remaining survivors on 12 July, seven weeks after the *Italia* crashed.

A tragic irony was that Roald Amundsen – ostensibly the cause of the whole expedition – lost his life travelling by air in a French Latham seaplane from Norway to Spitsbergen to take part in the rescue mission. The idea that Amundsen lost his life searching for his bitter rival Nobile has a heroic ring, true, but is not entirely accurate.

By the time Amundsen finally departed Tromsø in northern Norway on 18 June bound for Spitsbergen, radio contact had already been established with the *Italia* survivors on the ice floe, their position was known and the rescue had started.

Amundsen probably intended to search for *Italia* crew members who had been left inside the envelope when it floated away and for the missing three-man party that had begun a trek to land from the Red Tent ice floe. One of the three was the renowned Swedish meteorologist Dr Finn Malmgren, who was a veteran not only of the 1926 *Norge* flight but also of Amundsen's Maud drift in the Arctic Ocean.

In fact, the icebreaker *Krassin* rescued two of the three from a small ice floe on 12 July before proceeding to the Red Tent ice floe, but Malmgren had died earlier under mysterious circumstances on an undetermined date.

The search for Amundsen and the Latham crew continued throughout the summer of 1928 but was discontinued in September when fishermen found a pontoon later identified as having come from the Latham. On 14 December 1928, Norway observed a national day of mourning for Amundsen and the Latham crew.

DICK GRACE, STUNTMAN

HOLLYWOOD, USA 1926

One of the top stunt flyers of his day, Dick Grace earned a reputation for skilful aerial work that spanned many years. William Wellman, himself a veteran World War I flyer, set out to make the war film *Wings* in 1926, starring Buddy Rogers, Richard Arlen and Clara Bow and including the first brief appearance of a young Gary Cooper. The movie featured aerial dogfights, bombing raids, spectacular crashes and a massive re-creation of the September 1918 Battle of Saint-Michel that involved 3,500 infantrymen and five dozen planes. There were, however, several major stunts that had to be carried out, and the always-in-demand Dick Grace was hired to execute them.

For one scene, the field he was to crash into had been set up with barbed wire, 6-foot cedar posts, trenches and shell craters – some as much as 12 feet deep. The terrain was meant to resemble No Man's Land. Director Wellman assured Grace that a 25-foot section would be rigged with flimsy balsa-wood posts and yarn instead of wire in case his crash landing went awry. But the stunt flyer would have to hit his mark travelling at almost 100 miles per hour – and also avoid hitting several cameramen on the field.

Grace had an entire emergency crew ready with an ambulance, equipment to extricate him from the wreck and another plane ready to rush him to a hospital if he was injured. In late September 1926, all was ready for the scene, and he executed the first crash with consummate skill, hitting the ground just 17 feet from the closest camera.

Grace himself later described the moment of collision as he roared in at 90 miles per hour: 'I jerked the stick over to the right, giving just a slight left rudder. The wing dipped and the fuselage swayed to the left. In this position I knew the ship would be a cinch to go on its back, but that's what Bill [Wellman] wanted. With a dull thud the wing hit and crumpled, then the landing carriage crashed. The poor ship tottered over to the other wing and broke that, and the thing started over on its back. As it did I ducked my head forward. It was my one measure of protection, but it happened to be just the right one. With a terrific crash something wedged between my flying coat and the back of the seat.'

When he examined the wreckage, Grace realised that he had missed the flimsy balsa posts and had hit the hardwood ones. As the plane turned over, two jagged pieces of cedar fence post had come through the fuselage, and one was just inches from where his head had been. Ducking his head had probably saved his life.

When Grace performed a second crash – with a Fokker D.VII – he was not so fortunate. As he hit the ground at 110 miles per hour, the impact caused the straps holding him to snap, and his head went into the instrument panel. He was pulled from the wreckage and seemed unhurt. But he later collapsed, and an examination revealed a broken neck: four cervical vertebrae were crushed, and a fifth was dislocated. He was told by doctors that he would have to remain in a cast for a year. Grace refused to follow their advice.

After eleven weeks, he took off the neck harness and jumped out of his second-floor hospital room to spend an evening with his girlfriend. Unfortunately, his appearance (a slight paralysis on the right side of his face had caused his features to become twisted out of shape) shocked the young lady. According to Grace, the next day she decided to become engaged to someone else!

ANGELS FROM THE SKY

SAN FRANCISCO, USA 1930

As air travel became more affordable and flights became longer, it was apparent that someone would have to tend to the comfort of the passengers. The stewardess team was the brainchild of Ellen Church of Iowa. A 26-year-old registered nurse with a pilot's licence, Church approached Boeing Air Transport with a proposal to include nurse-stewardesses on long flights.

BAT agreed to a three-month experiment, and Church arranged for seven other 'nurses' to serve as the original team of 'Sky Girls'. She also drew up a manual to guide the new staff. To highlight the professionalism of the so-called Original Eight, the women were given a uniform of a dark-green, double-breasted wool with silver buttons and a wool cape to keep them warm in the draughty, unheated cabins. The cape's pockets were required to be large enough to hold a spanner and a screwdriver to secure the passengers' wicker chairs to the floor of the cabin and a railway timetable to be consulted if a flight was delayed or abandoned and passengers had to be found other means of getting to their destination.

In addition to screwing down the seats and serving meals, Church's handbook instructed the stewardesses that they were also required to swat flies in the cabin, calm passengers and mop up any leaks from the lavatory. At the end of the flight, stewardesses were sometimes required to help push the plane into the hangar too!

Their maiden flight, at 8.00 a.m. on 15 May 1930, was between San Francisco and Chicago. That first flight on a 24-

passenger plane took 20 hours, with 13 stops. The dozen or so passengers flying from San Francisco to Chicago, Illinois, in a clattering Boeing 80A tri-motor plane owned and operated by Boeing were served a meal of chicken, fruit salad and bread rolls. And they were told not to dispose of their glowing cigarette butts through the open windows.

The requirements for stewardesses in the 1930s were strict. In addition to being registered nurses, the women had to be single, younger than 25 years old, weigh less than 115 pounds (so as to permit maximum capacity for mail), and stand less than 5 feet 4 inches tall.

For their services, the first group of BAT stewardesses earned $125 a month. Away from 'home port' they were allowed $6 per day expenses – $4 for a hotel and $2 for meals. They found they could not get a decent hotel for that price, nor three meals per day for that allowance; if they spent more it came out of their own pockets.

They were given strict instructions: should there be any passengers on the plane, they were not to talk to them. Instead, they were expected to just sit quietly and not move back and forth in the aisle. Also they were not allowed to have dinner, or dates, with a passenger or to go out with the pilots or co-pilots – just like hospital rules, in fact!

In a 1930 manual for stewardesses, entitled 'Dos and Don'ts', it is clear that some of these first requirements are a reflection of the elite, heroic image pilots held in the public's mind at the time. Directions to stewardesses included, 'A rigid military salute will be rendered the captain and co-pilot as they go aboard and deplane before the passengers. Check with the pilots regarding their personal luggage and place it onboard promptly.' They were also instructed that a 'ready smile' was essential.

Harriet Fry Eden, one of the first stewardesses, recalled her debut flight on 1 May 1930 when she and the 'Chicago girls' were flown to Cheyenne in order to meet up with the 'San Francisco girls'. The first stop was Iowa City to refuel and pick up mail, but no passengers. After take-off, the girls ate their lunch. At Omaha, the pilots changed and as they came through the cabin they did not speak to the girls – in fact, they simply glared at them; in fact, throughout the first leg of their trip, neither the pilot nor co-pilot spoke to them at all.

The chilly reception the first stewardesses got from pilots quickly evaporated. After flying for less than eighteen months, Harriet Fry explained that, on some segments, the pilots would invite her to the cockpit, where she sat on a sack of mail. She noted, 'The pilots sometimes did hedge-hopping around 500 feet from the ground. We would frighten the pigs and the farmers didn't like that.'

She also recalled: 'Our lavatory was very nice with hot and cold water but the toilet was a can set in a ring and a hole cut in the floor so when one opened the toilet seat, behold, open-air toilet! Soon chemical toilets made their debut. The only thing wrong with them was in rough weather and turbulence: I would often see the contents of the toilet running out into our cabin from under the door which meant a quick mop-up. That, I did not like.'

Marriage for stewardesses was taboo from the beginning. Ellis (Crawford) Podola was let go after two months of flying when her marital status was revealed. Steve Stimpson of Boeing Air Transport – sometimes called the father of stewardess service – touched on the origins of the no-marriage rules in a speech for the 25th anniversary of stewardesses. Stimpson related, 'As to married stewardesses: we hired only one – that we know of – and that was very early and when we were in a great hurry. Miss Crawford would be out on a trip and be delayed by bad weather and/or other causes, sometimes for several days, and her husband would phone me around three o'clock in the morning and say, "Mister, where is my wife?" '

Another member of the original group, Inez Keller Fuite, remembered that when the planes were forced to make emergency landings in farmers' fields, the stewardesses had to help knock down fences to enable the plane to take off again. 'The plane ran out of gas and had to make an emergency landing in a wheat field,' she once recalled. 'People from the surrounding area came in wagons and on horseback to see the plane. They'd never seen an aircraft before and they wanted to touch it and to touch me. One of them called me the Angel from the Sky.'

THE FLYING CARPET

LOS ANGELES, USA 1930

Travel writer Richard Halliburton's exploits made him a living legend and provided five best-sellers for his eager American audience. Yet he was destined to die, like a bright human comet, in a blaze of glory and mystery that has never been solved.

During the inter-war years, Richard Halliburton crossed the world while risking his life by performing stunts during the course of his travels. Before the advent of television, Americans in their millions sat glued to the radio, eagerly listening for news of what 'Dick' Halliburton had done next.

However, the Wall Street Crash of 1929 caught Halliburton with $100,000 in the stock market, of which he lost more than 80 per cent. There was nothing left for him to do but mount yet another trip and write yet another book. Without much enthusiasm, he decided to fly around the world in a light plane, stopping for adventures at any likely places.

Ladies' Home Journal tentatively agreed to buy a series of articles that would help fund the trip. The only problem with the plan was that Halliburton did not know how to fly and had no desire to learn! Thus, in 1930, he persuaded Moye W Stephens, one of TWA's original pilots, to embark with him on one of the most fantastic, extended air journeys ever recorded. It would provide him with material for probably his most famous and successful book, *The Flying Carpet*.

Halliburton told Stephens, 'I've just given myself an aeroplane and I want you to fly us to all the outlandish places in the world, Turkey, Persia, Paris and – Pasadena. We're going to fly across deserts, over mountains, rescue imprisoned princesses and fight dragons. We must have the world. We can have the world!'

The plane they chose was an open-cockpit Stearman C3B powered by a J-5 Wright 'Whirlwind' engine with a range of about 800 miles cruising at 120 miles per hour. They began their trek on Christmas Day, 1930, by flying from Los Angeles to New York City. The men and plane then went by ship to London, where their serious flying began.

From France they flew south via Spain to Gibraltar and thence to Fez, where they crossed the Atlas Mountains and began a 1,700-mile flight to cross the Sahara Desert to the legendary city of Timbuktu. Refuelling would be a major problem flying across the desert. Reluctantly, the French military authorities authorised them to use two fuel dumps maintained by Shell Oil for a fortnightly supply convoy to Gao. The first was at Adrar oasis, 400 miles south of Colomb-Béchar, which they reached the first day. The second, 500 miles farther south, was only an unattended tank beside the track.

Their only possible chance of rescue if they ran out of gas was a military truck that made the trip there every two weeks. Fighting a head wind on the second day, the pair were half an hour overdue in reaching the second dump. Halliburton kept recalling 'the morbid stories I'd heard in Colomb-Béchar about death on the Sahara'.

Finally, Stephens spotted several discarded gasoline tins beside the track. They landed and taxied over. 'We noted a curious-looking sand dune nearby,' Halliburton recalled. 'A pump handle was sticking out of it. There was our tank! A thousand eyes would never have seen it from above.'

Digging away a 'ton of sand', they unlocked the tank, then transferred the precious fluid a gallon at a time in 'annihilating heat'. Halliburton left a receipt for 100 gallons – at $4 a gallon – in the middle of the Sahara! In partial sponsorship, Shell would cancel his debt after his return.

They then re-crossed the Sahara back to Madrid before flying east to Angora, Cairo, Damascus, Baghdad and Tehran. They then took the west coast of the Arabian Sea to India.

When he felt in the mood, and this could last for several weeks, Halliburton would write chapters for his book, which was to be the main source of income upon his return. Unfortunately, halfway through his trip, the *Journal* backed out of its agreement to buy Richard's stories, leaving him with no immediate source of income. Too heavily committed to the enterprise, Halliburton couldn't back out now even if he wanted to.

This downturn of luck was compounded by a series of near-disasters. Halliburton acquired a sunburn so severe while swimming across the Sea of Galilee that he had to be hospitalised in Jerusalem for a week. In Nepal, Moye was demonstrating his acrobatic talent for the entertainment of local natives; he started a slow roll but suddenly stopped. Halliburton, who was in the front cockpit, hadn't fastened his seat belt and almost fell to his death! Flying high up the slopes of Mount Everest on his 32nd birthday, Halliburton nearly caused the plane to stall by standing up in the air stream to snap a picture of the summit, while in Singapore he almost got himself killed by catching an anchor line in the propeller of the now pontoon-equipped *Flying Carpet*.

Among other perils they encountered was fog over the Alps, snow and hail in Persia and having to fly through a swarm of locusts north of Mindanao. Italian police arrested Halliburton for swimming in a Venice canal. In Sumatra and Dutch Borneo they were welcomed by head-hunters. When they departed, Halliburton was carrying a gift from the tribal chief of 150 pounds of human heads! Besides the added weight, they smelled badly and Moye finally threw them overboard as they flew on to Manila – arriving there during the tail-end of a typhoon. In Manila the plane was loaded aboard the USS *McKinley* and the trio sailed for San Francisco where landing wheels were again installed for the final leg of their flight back to Los Angeles.

Stephens figured they had flown 33,660 miles in 374 flying

hours, making 178 landings on airfields, polo fields, pastures, rivers and creeks in 34 countries. Halliburton returned to the US not merely broke, but $2,000 in debt having spent $50,000 on the trip – not including a $14,000 gas bill from Shell Oil Company.

His publishers gave him five months to finish his book, and *The Flying Carpet* was published late that year. Royalties from the book netted him over $100,000 in the first year of issue alone.

Soon after finishing a fifth book, the intrepid traveller decided to ignore the warnings of seasoned sailors and set sail on the ship that would take him away from his book-hungry public and into the arms of a watery death. His boat, the *Sea Dragon*, put to sea from Hong Kong on 4 March 1939. It was last heard from, via radio, on 23 March 1939, when it reported encountering heavy weather near the International Dateline. Halliburton managed to get a radio message out to a friend as his boat was sinking.

In typical Halliburton style, he simply said: 'Wish You Were Here'.

HIJACKED!

Commercial flying wasn't very old before the first hijack occurred, on 21 February 1931. Pilot Byron Rickards took off from Lima, the capital of Peru, to fly to the southern city of Arequipa in the mountains of southern Peru. On landing, his Panagra Ford tri-motor plane was immediately surrounded by armed soldiers who told him it was to be detained for the use of would-be revolutionaries and that henceforth he was to fly according to their orders. Contravening every rule of modern pilot training, he refused. He continued to refuse until 2 March, when his captors informed him that their revolution had been successfully concluded, and that he was free to return to Lima – so long as he took one of the junta with him!

Incredibly, thirty years after he became the world's first hijacked pilot, it happened to Rickards again! This time he was the victim of a father-and-son team, who tried to hijack a Continental Boeing 707 that he was piloting from El Paso to Cuba. The hijackers were not politically motivated – they were hoping Castro would reward them for bringing him a $3.3 million airliner. This time, Rickards felt obliged to concur with the two men. However, as the aircraft set off down the runway, it was chased by four cars full of FBI agents and police, who shot the tyres off. Two hours later, the amateur hijackers were overpowered.

SHEPPERTON'S GHOST PLANE

LONDON, ENGLAND 1932

In 1929, a Vickers Vanguard aircraft broke up 4,000 feet in the air and crashed in a field near Shepperton. The pilot, Captain E R Scholefield, and his mechanic, Mr F W Cherrett, were killed instantly.

Three years later, in 1932, strange noises were heard at night, which suggested that the whole tragic incident was being re-enacted again in chilling ghostly fashion. On hearing the phantom crash people dashed out of their homes to look for a wrecked plane, only to find nothing.

Captain W J Gibson and his wife, whose bungalow was situated only a few hundred yards from the scene of the real crash, heard the phantom aeroplane not once, but four or five times, on successive nights, always shortly before midnight. As Captain Gibson had served with the Royal Air Force in the 1914–18 war and seen many crashes, there could hardly have been a more authoritative witness.

Mrs Gibson described how, on the first occasion, she was sitting at home with her husband when he remarked that there was an aeroplane close by that was obviously in difficulties. He had hardly spoken before there was the sound of a massive crash, and a huge vibratory aftermath was felt. It sounded so real that they both went to look for the wreck, but found nothing. Next morning they made inquiries and found that other people had heard the sound of the approaching aeroplane, followed by the crash.

Their neighbour, Mrs Harding, was equally emphatic about

101

the ghost machine. She stated that she had been on a boat on the Thames when the plane came down. One wing came off and crashed into the river near her. She therefore had a vivid recollection of it and the sounds the Gibsons heard were very similar to those that she experienced. She was quite sceptical about ghosts, but this eventually occurred so many times that she became quite unnerved.

Not only was the phantom plane heard, but some residents actually saw it, claiming that it was surrounded with a leadenish blue light. Another resident, on looking out one night just before the ghostly crash, saw a white and misty aeroplane, and heard the droning of its engine. Her dogs began to howl.

It was strongly suggested by the beleaguered community that in order to lay the ghost to rest, a church service should be held at the scene of the crash. However, after making a few more visits, the phantom plane suddenly stopped its visits and was not seen again.

DEATH ALOFT

TORONTO, CANADA 1935

When John McGraw, manager of baseball's New York Giants, bought minor-league star Len Koenecke from Indianapolis for $75,000 and four players in 1931, he immediately predicted the young outfielder 'will be a bright star in the National League'. But Koenecke lasted just one season with McGraw's Giants. In 1932, he joined the Brooklyn Dodgers and, in 1934, had his best-ever season hitting .320, 14 home runs and setting a NL fielding record. However, his off-field behaviour had begun to deteriorate: he broke training rules and he bagan to drink. After being frequently disciplined by manager Casey Stengel, Koenecke was finally released from his contract on 17 September 1935. By the end of that day, he was dead.

Completely at a loss, the troubled player had boarded an American Airlines plane in St Louis heading for Buffalo where he had played in the minors earlier in his career and still had friends.

He started to drink on board and his behaviour became extremely erratic – so much so that, during an argument with a passenger, stewardess Eleanor Woodward came to investigate the fracas. Koenecke floored her with one punch, and was ordered off the plane when it landed in Detroit.

There the almost deranged traveller chartered a small three-seater to complete the journey to Buffalo. There were three men on board – Koenecke, pilot William Joseph Mulqueeney and Irwin Davis, a friend of the pilot.

Koenecke sat beside the pilot, and somewhere over

Canadian territory began playing with the controls. Although ordered to stop, Koenecke continued to behave dangerously, and was told to get out of the seat and move to the rear. Soon the paying passenger and Davis were wrestling on the floor. At a later hearing, Mulqueeney commented, 'It was either a case of the three of us crashing or doing something to Koenecke.'

Pilot Mulqueeney was still flying the plane, but was able to grab a fire extinguisher and vigorously hit Koenecke in the head several times. Finally the ballplayer was down and quiet. The fight had damaged the inside of the aeroplane, there was blood in the compartment, an unconscious man was on the floor, but Mulqueeney was able to land on a Toronto racetrack. By the time the officials arrived, however, Koenecke had died of a brain haemorrhage; the two men were arrested for manslaughter and jailed.

At the trial the two accused told their story, and when it was determined that the deceased had alcohol in his body, the jury delivered a ruling of self-defence and the men were released. A lawyer representing Mulqueeney and Davis said that they believed Koenecke was going to force the plane into a suicide dive for a 'spectacular death'.

Stengel was shocked to hear of Koenecke's death, but refused to talk to the media about the incident. The Dodgers decided that silence from the organisation would be perceived as indifference, and convinced newspaperman Roscoe McGowen to call the Associated Press, posing as Stengel, and give a short statement. McGowen/Stengel's sympathetic remarks were duly reported the following day. Thereafter, Koenecke's name drifted away into oblivion.

AMELIA EARHART'S MYSTERIOUS DISAPPEARANCE

NEW GUINEA 1937

In 1937, celebrated female aviator Amelia Earhart attempted to fly around the world, along with co-pilot Frederick J Noonan. On the most difficult leg of her attempt, she and Noonan vanished in the central Pacific. Her loss was mourned by an American public enamoured of a daring and modest young pilot who'd already flown solo, nonstop across the Atlantic Ocean and had been awarded a Distinguished Flying Cross by the US Congress.

Despite a tremendous search effort, personally ordered by then US President Roosevelt, no physical evidence of the aviators or their plane was ever found. The question of what really happened has fuelled a debate over the real intention of Earhart's flight. Did she simply get lost and just disappear, or was there an ulterior motive to her flight?

One theory was that Earhart was on an intelligence flight to study military activities of the Japanese in the Pacific. Maps, charts and other documents, apparently from Earhart's Electra, were allegedly discovered in a locked safe that later disappeared.

There was also said to be an aerial photo taken by the USAAF in 1944 over the island of Taroa – the second largest island on Maloelap Atoll, some 35 minutes' flight north of Majuro in the Pacific Marshall Islands – that showed what appeared to be a twin-tail Electra, with a broken left wing. The island was occupied at the time by the Japanese.

The possible scenario suggests that Earhart ran out of fuel, was picked up by the Japanese, and taken to Saipan. Forty years after her disappearance, four Chamorro women were interviewed by a Catholic priest on Saipan. All the women stated that when they were young girls, sometime around 1937, a foreign woman, thin in stature with brown hair, cut short, was present on Saipan. They described her as looking 'sickly', with one side of her body and one hand burned.

One of the Chamorro women remembered hearing that a plane had crashed 'southwest of us' and that the pilot had been a woman. She recalled that the Japanese were 'very startled' because she was piloting the plane. Later, two of the girls were asked to make two wreaths for the 'American', who had died of amoebic dysentery.

Yet another story concerns that of a bottle, its cork sealed with wax, which washed ashore on the coast of France in October 1938 with a note inside. The French language message stated that the writer had been a prisoner of the Japanese on Jaluit, where he claimed to have seen Amelia Earhart and a male individual, both of whom were being held on the atoll for alleged spying on Japanese installations. The writer of the note stated he had been placed on a Japanese vessel bound for Europe, and would throw the bottle overboard when the ship neared port. (This message is in the US National Archives in Washington, after having been given to American authorities at the US Embassy in Paris.)

The US was not at war with Japan at the time, and today neither party has anything to gain by admitting any knowledge of the fate of the two aviators. The mystery remains unsolved. Amelia Earhart dared to reach new heights but, like Icarus, fell into the sea; she will always remain a legend in the annals of flight.

THE TRAGEDY OF GUERNICA

GUERNICA, SPAIN 1937

The Nazi general Hermann Goering used the Spanish Civil War as an arena for trying out the airmen and planes of his new Luftwaffe, the German Air Force. The Condor Legion was headed by Wolfram Von Richthofen, the cousin of the near-mythical Red Baron of World War I. Von Richthofen was eager to create his own myth as a combat pilot, likewise the crews of fighters and bombers of the Condor Legion were anxious to experience what they had been trained for: sudden coordinated air and ground assault – or, as it was soon to be known, 'blitzkrieg'.

Guernica, in Spain, is the cultural capital of the Basque people, seat of their centuries-old independence and democratic ideals. It had no strategic value as a military target in the Spanish Civil War. The apparent goal of the assault on Guernica was hitting a bridge over the Mundaca River on the edge of town, near an important road junction that possibly could be used in the future by Republican forces. But if the intent was only to hit the bridge, Von Richthofen would have used his Stuka dive bombers, capable of carrying a single bomb weighing 1,000 pounds. Equipped with the latest technology, a Stuka had a high chance of taking out the bridge with one direct hit. Even a near miss would have made a powerful shock wave that, if it did not cause the bridge to collapse, would doubtless have made it unsafe for traffic.

It was market day in Guernica when the church bells of Santa Maria sounded the alarm on 27 April 1937. People from

107

the surrounding hillsides crowded the town square. 'Every Monday there was a fair in Guernica,' says José Monasterio, eye-witness to the bombing. 'They attacked when there were a lot of people there. They knew when their bombing would kill the most. When there are more people, more people will die.'

For over three hours, 25 or more of Germany's best-equipped bombers, accompanied by at least twenty more Messerschmitt and Fiat Fighters, dropped 100,000 pounds of high-explosive and incendiary bombs on the town, slowly and systematically pounding it to rubble.

Eyewitness Luis Aurtenetxea told reporters, 'We were hiding in the shelters and praying. I only thought of running away, I was so scared. I didn't think about my parents, mother, house, nothing. Just escape. Because during those three and one half hours, I thought I was going to die.'

Another eyewitness, Juan Guezureya said, 'Those trying to escape were cut down by the strafing machine guns of fighter planes. They kept just going back and forth, sometimes in a long line, sometimes in close formation. It was as if they were practising new moves. They must have fired thousands of bullets.'

The fires that engulfed the city burned for three days. Seventy per cent of the town was destroyed. Sixteen hundred civilians – one third of the population – were killed or wounded.

But although the Condor Legion was made up of the best airmen and planes of Hitler's developing war machine, not a single hit was scored on the presumed target, the bridge – nor on the railway station, nor on the small-arms factory nearby.

Five days after the bombing, Pablo Picasso began expressing his outrage on a huge canvas, later titled after the town. In the painting, however, the enemy is nowhere to be seen. 'The omission conveys a chilling message,' Picasso revealed: 'to the victims of modern warfare, the enemy remains impersonal and unknown.'

HINDENBURG ABLAZE

NEW YORK, USA 1937

The terms 'zeppelin', 'dirigible' and 'airship' are used interchangeably for any type of rigid airship – a buoyant aircraft that can be steered and propelled through the air. Although neither Hitler nor Hermann Goering, the head of the Luftwaffe, believed that dirigibles had any value either as military or commercial aircraft, they allowed propaganda minister Josef Goebbels to take charge of the two mammoth zeppelins then in service under German control: the *Graf Zeppelin* and the newly launched *Hindenburg*, the ultimate luxury airship, which was put in service in March 1936.

The Germans used both ships both as instruments of propaganda and espionage as they crisscrossed the globe during 1936, flying north of the equator from May to September, and in the Southern Hemisphere the rest of the year. Huge swastikas were painted on the tail fins and loudspeakers made Nazi propaganda announcements when the giant ship toured cities that it passed. Thousands of small Nazi flags were dropped to float down like tiny parachutes to thrill schoolchildren and others that watched the giant zeppelin pass.

During the 1936 Olympics, which were held in Germany, the *Hindenburg* was everywhere, providing a sinister psychological edge for German athletes as it hovered over the games. In May 1937, after a late-summer run to Rio de Janeiro, the *Hindenburg* began its service to the United States with a flight from Berlin to New York under the control of Captains Truss and Lehman.

In the early days of airships, the primary lifting gas was hydrogen. And until the 1940s, most French, German and British airships continued to use hydrogen because it offered greater lift and was cheaper. However, hydrogen is also flammable when mixed with air. So the issue became one of safety versus cost. American airships had been filled with helium since the 1920s. Crucially, both the German ships were designed to be run with helium, but the United States had placed a ban on exporting any of its helium supply, so hydrogen had to be used instead.

On 6 May, the *Hindenburg* arrived in America and approached Lakehurst, New York, where it waited for a squall of wind to pass. At 7.20 in the evening, it headed for New Jersey and prepared to tie up at the mooring tower. Suddenly an explosion engulfed the rear of the dirigible and quickly spread to the entire ship, bringing it crashing to the ground in flames.

The flames – first visible towards the tail of the ship – swiftly caught on and the whole aft of the craft was engulfed in a fireball that towered hundreds of feet into the sky. As the ship burned, it lost its lift and fell to the ground, nose pointing upwards to the sky. Within just 37 seconds of the first flames being spotted, the *Hindenburg* lay on the ground, the skeleton of its framework the only thing visible through the fire. Passengers jumped from windows and ran for safety. One cabin boy had his life saved when a water tank burst above his head.

On the ground a radio reporter named Herbert Morrison was covering the airship's arrival and his horror-struck commentary was recorded for prosperity:

It burst into flames! . . . It's fire and it's crashing! It's crashing terrible! Oh, my! Get out of the way, please! It's burning, bursting into flames and is falling on the mooring mast, and all the folks agree that this is terrible. This is the worst of the worst catastrophes in the world! . . . There's smoke, and there's flames, now, and the frame is crashing to the ground, not quite to the mooring mast . . . Oh, the humanity, and all the passengers screaming around here!

Of the 97 people aboard, 36 died, including thirteen paying passengers – the first passengers of this kind killed in a dirigible accident. Captain Pruss was saved, but Captain Lehman died in hospital a few hours later. Before he died, however, he was interviewed by one of the investigators sent to determine what had happened. As Lehmann lay dying, he muttered that the explosion must have been caused by an incendiary bullet shot from the ground. His dying words, 'It must have been an infernal machine,' have often been quoted afterwards, though no one was quite sure what he meant.

In fact, it was determined that the accident had been caused by the new paint used on the *Hindenburg*, which contained an explosive mixture. Static electricity caused by the prevailing weather conditions would have been sufficient to have triggered the fire. But some of the surviving crew, including Commander Pruss, suspected the fire was due to sabotage.

Several people suggested that the saboteur might have been one Joseph Spah, a passenger who survived the disaster. On several occasions, Spah had gone into the bowels of the ship to visit his dog in the cargo area, which certainly gave him the opportunity to place a bomb. Others suspect that Erich Spehl, an introverted crewman thought to have had anti-Nazi leanings and who perished in the fire, might have been the saboteur.

The Germans conducted an elaborate Nazi funeral in New Jersey for the victims, milking the occasion for maximum propaganda and implying that the tragedy could have been averted if the United States had been willing to sell Germany some of its helium.

'WRONG WAY' CORRIGAN

ATLANTIC OCEAN 1938

When 31-year-old Douglas Groce Corrigan took off from Brooklyn's Floyd Bennett Field on 17 July 1938, in a modified Curtiss Robin aircraft he called *Sunshine*, he carried two chocolate bars, two boxes of fig biscuits, a quart of water and a US map with the route from New York to California marked out on it.

Corrigan had bought the aircraft from a scrapyard for $325, rebuilt it and modified it for long-distance flight. He had previously piloted the single-engine plane nonstop from California to New York and although the transcontinental flight was far from unprecedented, Corrigan received national attention simply because the press was amazed that his boneshaker aircraft had survived the journey.

Almost immediately after arriving in New York, he applied for permission to make a transatlantic flight from Newfoundland to Ireland, but aviation authorities turned him down, deeming it a suicide flight. His nine-year-old monoplane was too old and unsafe, they said, for such a long flight over water.

Instead, he was issued with a permit to fly back to the West Coast, and so he duly started out on 17 July ostensibly pointing his plane west. He took off but, much to the puzzlement of a few onlookers, he suddenly made a 180-degree turn and vanished into a cloudbank. Twenty-eight hours and thirteen minutes later, he landed in Dublin and instantly became a national hero, creating a household phrase still bestowed on those who do things the 'wrong way'.

Later, he recounted his hazardous trip. His 27-foot plane, which weighed 3,800 pounds, had fuel tanks mounted on the front. He had been flying east for ten hours when his feet suddenly felt cold. A leak had occurred in the main gas tank and gasoline was running all over his shoes and onto the floor of the cockpit. He was somewhere over the Atlantic Ocean at that point – and he was losing fuel at an alarming rate.

Corrigan flew on through the darkness. Time was not on his side, and the leak was getting worse. Before long, there was gasoline an inch deep on the cockpit floor. Just losing the gas was bad enough, but Corrigan was worried that it would leak out near the hot exhaust pipe – and he was well aware that he had no chance of surviving if that happened.

He knew he had to do something about the leak, but he did not have much to work with. He had only brought a screwdriver with him. With it, he punched a hole in the floor. The gasoline trickled out – on the side opposite the exhaust pipe. He was still losing fuel, but at least the plane was not likely to explode.

He had planned to conserve fuel by running the engine slowly, but now he realised that that would only give the fuel more time to leak out. He decided to run the engine fast instead, using the precious gasoline while he had it. He boosted his rpms from 1,600 to 1,900, then maintained that speed for the rest of the trip.

Corrigan flew straight ahead, hoping he would have enough fuel to reach land. When he saw a fishing boat, he went down close to the water and flew past it. Corrigan realised it was unlikely that such a small boat would be very far from shore. It looked like he was going to make it, and he opened a package of fig biscuits to celebrate.

He finished them and had started on a chocolate bar when land came into sight. Some time later, he recalled, 'I noticed some nice green hills.' It was not long before he reached Baldonnel Airport, in Dublin, where he landed. It was 18 July.

The first person Corrigan met was an army officer. The pilot introduced himself by saying, 'I left New York yesterday morning headed for California.' He added, 'I got mixed up in the clouds, and I must have flown the wrong way.' When officiallly asked for an explanation, he stated that, because of the fog on that fateful night, he had been told by airport authorities to take off toward the east and turn, above the Atlantic, turn and head west. However, he could only see out of the sides of the plane, he had no radio and his compass, which had been made during World War I, stuck.

As the ship bringing him home entered New York Harbour and past the Statue of Liberty, whistles started blowing and fireboats shot streams of water into the air. The Mayor's Reception Committee came on board and at noon the next day Corrigan was given a ticker-tape parade down Broadway in New York. RKO Studios made a movie about his feat entitled *The Flying Irishman* in 1939, though the true high point of his life came, he declared, when President Franklin Roosevelt assured him that he didn't doubt his story for a minute!

AMY JOHNSON

THAMES ESTUARY, ENGLAND 1941

Amy Johnson was British aviation's pin-up girl during the inter-war years after becoming the first woman to fly solo from England to Australia in May 1930. Her 8,600-mile flight took nineteen and a half days; the *Daily Mail* rewarded her with a £10,000 prize and she was awarded the CBE. The British press dubbed her 'Queen of the Air'.

When Germany invaded Poland in 1939, the Royal Air Force invited Johnson to join the newly established Air Transport Auxiliary, which ferried aircraft from factories to air bases. Ironically, though she was one of the most experienced aviators to join the ATA, Johnson would be the first to die. Her death was to be a controversial one, however.

On 5 January 1941, she took off, alone in an Airspeed Oxford Mk II, in thick, freezing fog from Blackpool Airport on a routine mission to Kidlington, a journey that should have taken an hour. Amy foresaw no difficulty. It was not until she actually began the flight and she had to land at a diversion airfield due to bad weather conditions that she fully realised just what she had taken on.

Once she arrived at Prestwick, near Manchester, Amy called the ferry pilots controller at Hatfield to report in and was told that she need not fly back as the weather was closing in rapidly and she may be too tired to concentrate fully on the remainder of her flight. She was offered the opportunity to return by train but chose to fly home instead. After spending the night in Blackpool with her sister's family she started out once again.

Weather conditions were still far from favourable when she left for the last leg of her journey, but she told onlookers that 'she would go over the top', meaning that she would fly over the cloud and miss all the bad weather. Unfortunately, the weather conditions worsened during her flight – only one of several factors that would lead to disaster.

One crucial element in the impending catastrophe was a new protective measure in operation along the coast of England of which Amy wasn't aware, whereby balloons were raised to prevent enemy aircraft from flying low to avoid interception by RAF fighters and so be able to strike their targets accurately. The idea was for the balloons to be flown from ground installations on the coast, and from ships just out to sea and in strategic harbour entrances, just below the cloud base. These were known as 'low zone' balloons. Amy Johnson, presumably lost above the clouds, would have seen one of these balloons through the cloud coverage and presumed that she was over land, possibly near the London balloon barrage, and that it was therefore safe to bail out.

On the afternoon of 5 January, a convoy of ships in the Thames Estuary spotted an aeroplane struggling through sleet. A parachute was seen coming down as the plane ditched into the river. HMS *Haslemere*, a cross-channel ferry, rushed to the rescue and Corporal Bill Hall of the RAF, who was aboard the ship, later submitted a report of what he had seen. According to Hall, the parachutist landed in the water and drifted close to the *Haslemere*. He heard someone call out that she was Amy Johnson, that the water was bitterly cold, and could they get her out as soon as possible. 'Hurry, please, hurry!' were the words he heard.

Seamen threw her a rope, but she couldn't get hold of it. Then someone dashed up to the bridge and reversed the ship's engines, as a result of which she was drawn into the propeller and, presumably, chopped to pieces. The *Haslemere*'s captain, Lieutenant Commander Fletcher, actually dived into the icy waters during the rescue. He was brought out of the water unconscious and died later of hypothermia – but without ever telling of what or whom he'd seen.

A week later, the drifter *Young Jacob* picked up several pieces of wreckage, including some yellow fabric from the undersurface of Amy's aircraft. It carried the black figures '35', which was part of Amy's identification number, V3540. Washed ashore on the Shoeburyness coastline the following week was a part of the tailfin from the Airspeed Oxford Mk II. The Queen of the Air was dead.

Newspaper headlines the next day, however, carried none of these details, simply claiming, 'Amy Johnson Bales Out, Missing!' and for a time confusion and fevered speculation reigned. Some of the crew of the HMS *Haslemere* claimed they had seen two bodies floating in the Thames estuary – even though Amy had set off alone.

An admiralty press release, which also stated that two bodies had been spotted in the water but which was quickly retracted, immediately led to rumours about Amy's death: that she had been on a secret mission, that she had a passenger on board (a 'Mr X') or that she was fleeing Britain to begin a new life abroad! Some said Amy was involved in the unofficial business of flying a spy out of the country who was actually her German lover! Others reckoned that she had been shot down by British anti-aircraft guns or that German planes could have taken her down.

The mystery passenger theory was at first put down to the fact that the observers, in fog and sleet, mistook her pigskin bag, which was fished out of the Thames after she crashed, for the head and shoulders of someone floating in the water. But a more likely explanation stems from the manoeuvre Amy had taken just prior to parachuting. Not wanting to leave the aircraft to crash on civilians, Amy would have carefully trimmed it for level flight before bailing out, the idea being that the aircraft would have continued on its way out to sea. To leave the Oxford in flight she would have to jettison the large cabin door, which could have been misinterpreted as the figure of a passenger.

However, without Lieutenant Commander Fletcher's account and a lack of further witnesses, it is likely that exact details of Amy Johnson's death will remain a mystery.

THE RUDOLF HESS MYSTERY

EAGLESHAM, SCOTLAND 1941

On 10 May 1941, Rudolf Hess, Hitler's deputy, made an infamous, almost incredible lone flight to Scotland under cover of darkness. And ever since he bailed out of his Messerschmitt 110 aircraft into a field near the Renfrewshire village of Eaglesham, some fourteen miles from his apparent target of the future Duke of Hamilton's home, speculation has raged over his motives and his state of mind.

Conspiracy theorists went into overdrive. Hess, some said, was lured here by British secret services . . . or the Duke of Hamilton was a Nazi sympathiser . . . or the man in the plane was not Hess but a doppelgänger . . . or Hess was trapped by a plan laid by intelligence officer Ian Fleming, the creator of James Bond . . . or the British royal family was 'in' on the scheme.

Hess's only injury from the ordeal was a broken leg. After surrendering to a farmer, David McLean, and being offered tea at McLean's cottage, he was taken into custody.

He then made a proposal – that Germany be given a free hand in Europe and handed back her African colonies (confiscated by Britain and France in the Versailles Treaty of 1919) in exchange for which Hitler would guarantee the security of the British Empire. Hess was analysed by a psychiatrist but, instead of being driven to London to meet Churchill and the King, was made a prisoner of war.

He would remain so until the end of the war. Sentenced in 1946 to life in prison for war crimes, he was kept as a prisoner at Berlin's Spandau prison until he was found dead in his cell in 1987, the victim of an apparent suicide – although some believe he was murdered. It was the last of many unsolved questions that have bedevilled that lone flight.

With the outbreak of hostilities in September 1939, it's clear that Hess gradually lost his position as Hitler's 'number two' to Martin Bormann and, as the war accelerated, his power seemed to wither. It has always seemed incredible, however, that he could have taken it into his head to approach the British with a plan to end the war without Hitler's knowledge.

One thing is for certain: when Hitler found out what Hess had done, he flew into a rage and swiftly followed Hess's suggestion – made in a letter to Hitler written before he left – that if his mission failed he could be disowned as being insane. It has subsequently been established, however, that Hitler not only knew of Hess's plan, but compelling evidence suggests the whole affair had Hitler's blessing.

Hess had clearly been planning to fly to England for some time. He was a skilled aviator and, in 1934, had won a hazardous air race around the Zugspitze, Germany's highest peak. Indeed, it has since been established that Hess took as many as twenty practice flights to familiarise himself with the plane and that Hitler's personal pilot, Hans Bauer, accompanied Hess on some of the flights.

On at least two occasions, 11 January 1941 and 18 March 1941, Hess actually flew toward the North Sea only to turn back because of engine trouble. Before the last two 'practice' flights, he gave his adjutant, Karl-Heinz Pintsch, the 'secret' letter for Hitler.

What's more, Reinhard Heydrich, head of SS Intelligence, flew as escort to Hess's flight to Britain. After refuelling in Cologne, Hess linked up with four fighter planes led by Heydrich, who followed him halfway across the North Sea. Heydrich could not have flown all the way to Scotland and then back to Norway, however, because his plane did not have the necessary navigation equipment or fuel capacity for such a flight.

He accompanied Hess for as far as he dared because Hitler did not want to take any chances. If Hess had been forced to ditch, or bail out, Heydrich would have been there to plot his position and arrange a seaplane rescue. Once over halfway, however, it was calculated that he would have little trouble from then on.

It has now been suggested that Hess was to meet with a faction of British royalty who wanted to arrange peace between Britain and Nazi Germany. However, Prime Minister Winston Churchill – who was against any such negotiations – got to Hess first when his plane landed and had him locked up, even though Hess, according to evidence, had been guaranteed safe passage by King George VI.

Here the story takes another odd twist. By 1942, two 'Rudolf Hesses' were imprisoned in Britain, one of them being the real Hess and the other being a Hess double, a subterfuge meant to impede any rescue attempts. Later that year, the real Hess was secretly moved from Wales to Scotland.

The Duke of Kent, part of the British royal faction trying to negotiate peace with Hitler, soon thereafter went on a supposed 'morale-boosting' flight to Iceland. The Duke's plane, unfortunately, exploded over Scotland. It has been suggested that, in fact, the Duke of Kent stopped on his way to pick up Hess so that they both could fly on to Sweden to continue secret peace negotiations, and that both Hess and the Duke perished in the plane mishap (which may not have been accidental!).

Thus, when World War II ended, the 'Rudolf Hess' tried at Nuremberg was not Hess, but the Hess 'double'. As evidence for this, Hermann Goering, Hitler's Luftwaffe commander, also tried at Nuremberg, had this to say about the supposed Hess on trial there: 'Hess? Which Hess? The Hess you have here? Our Hess? Your Hess?'

UFO

LOS ANGELES, USA 1942

On Wednesday, 25 February 1942, as war raged in Europe and Asia, at least a million Southern Californians awoke to the scream of air-raid sirens as Los Angeles County cities blacked out at 2.25 a.m. Twelve thousand air-raid wardens reported faithfully to their posts, most of them expecting nothing more than a dress rehearsal for a possible future event – an invasion of the United States by Japan.

The situation calmed down until 3.30 a.m., when the city was rudely awakened again, this time by sounds unfamiliar to most Americans outside the military services. The roar of the Coast Artillery Brigade's anti-aircraft batteries jolted them out of bed and before they could get to the windows the flashing 12.8-pound shells were being detonated in such quick succession that they were already raining back down as shrapnel. But what exactly had the guns had been shooting at?

Some days later, it was acknowledged that army listening posts had detected what they thought were five light planes approaching the coast on the night of the air raid. No interceptors had been sent out to engage them because there had been no mass attack. Various numbers of planes were later seen over various parts of the city and the anti-aircraft guns continued to pound the heavens. Later, however, eyewitness reports from thousands searching the skies with binoculars under the bright lights of the coast artillery verified the presence of just one enormous, unidentifiable, indestructible object that moved very slowly across the skies. Later, the 'object' proceeded at a leisurely pace over the coastal cities between Santa Monica and Long Beach before disappearing from view. No bombs had been dropped and no aeroplanes shot down and, miraculously, in spite of the tons of missiles hurled aloft, only two persons were reported wounded by falling shell fragments.

The blackout was not without its casualties, however. A state guardsman died of a heart attack while driving an ammunition truck, while heart failure also accounted for the death of an air-raid warden on duty. One woman was killed in a car-truck collision in Arcadia, and a Long Beach policeman was killed in a traffic crash en route to duty.

A Japanese vegetable man, John Y Harada, 25, was one of three persons arrested on charges of violating a county black out ordinance. Sheriff's Captain Ernest Sichler said Harada, driving to the market with a load of cauliflower, refused to extinguish his truck lights. Others held on similar charges were Walter E Van Der Linden, a Norwalk dairy man, accused of failing to darken his milking barns, and Giovouni Ghigo, 57, nabbed while driving to market with a truckload of flowers.

When daylight and the all-clear signal came, Long Beach took on the appearance of a huge Easter egg hunt. Whatever had been up there, had triggered an air-raid alarm that saw 1,430 rounds of ammunition released by the coast artillery. Children and even grown-ups scrambled through the streets and vacant lots, picking up and proudly comparing chunks of shrapnel fragments – personal trophies, mementoes of a very weird experience shared by all.

THE PLANE FROM NOWHERE

CALIFORNIA, USA 1942

On 8 December 1942, off the California coastline, United States Air Force radar picked up an unusual reading. What appeared to be an aeroplane was headed directly for the mainland – from the direction of Japan. This was highly unusual. Thus far, although only a year since the devastating aerial attack on America's fleet at Pearl Harbor, the Japanese had mounted no further attacks on American installations, certainly none on the American mainland. What's more, being just a single aircraft, the incident bore none of the usual markings of an aerial attack.

Two American war planes were sent to intercept the mysterious intruder but as they approached it, they were surprised to find that it was a P-40 – one of America's foremost fighters. What was odd about it, however, was that it bore military markings that had not been used since that attack on Pearl Harbor. When they managed to pull up alongside the craft they were further shocked to find the plane was riddled with bullets and that its landing gear had been blown away!

Puzzled as to how a plane in this condition could even fly, they then noticed that the pilot was slumped in the cockpit, his flight suit stained with blood. He wasn't dead, however. As they peered into the window, the injured pilot raised himself slightly, turned in their direction, and smiled. He then offered a tired-looking wave towards his two allies. Moments later the baffling craft plunged from the sky and smashed into the ground.

American troops hurried to crash site – but found no trace of the pilot or evidence of who he may have been. Neither did they find identifiable markings from the plane. What they did find was a document that investigators assumed to be the remains of some sort of diary. From this, they were able to deduce that the plane must have originated from the island of Mindanao, some 1,300 miles away!

So bizarre was this whole incident that various outlandish explanations were proffered. It was speculated that the fighter may have been shot down over a year earlier and the pilot had managed to survive on his own in the wild, scavenging parts from other downed aircraft, repairing his aeroplane, and somehow managing to navigate his way back to his homeland – over 1,000 miles of hostile territory! Such a theory was attractive – but couldn't explain how a heavy P-40 aircraft could ever have taken off without the aid of any sort of landing gear.

AIR RAID ON AMERICA

OREGON, USA 1942

Brookings, Oregon; a peaceful day in September 1942. Fishermen were slowly sailing out of port and the citizens were sitting down for breakfast. The sound of a small plane flying overhead alarmed no one. Little did anyone realise that they were in the midst of an air attack – the first and only manned aerial bombing of the American mainland.

Following the American Air Force's daring World War II air raid of Tokyo, the Japanese, still enraged at the invasion of their homeland, devised a secret plan to ignite the forests of the American mainland with incendiary bombs.

Chief Warrant Officer and pilot Nobuo Fujita was selected to lead the attack. The Japanese military believed an offensive could burn up a large part of the Northwest and destroy American morale. The bombs would explode and ignite the forest, the fire would spread to the cities burning homes and factories, spreading panic and fear.

On 15 August 1942, Fujita boarded a Japanese submarine for the trip to the American shore. Stored onboard the small sub was a single-engine aeroplane that would transport him and his navigator, Yukio Okuda, on their daring raid.

By early September, the ship had reached its planned position off the Oregon coast. Finally, on the morning of 9 September, the weather cleared and the sea was calm. Fujita was told to get ready. Along with his regular kit, he packed a family treasure – a Samurai sword that had been in his family for 400 years. If he was forced down, he could use

126

it to end his life rather than be captured by the enemy.

His GETA float plane was prepared and he and Okuda boarded. Moments later, the tiny aircraft and its two-man crew were catapulted into the skies and headed toward the Cape Blanco lighthouse on a southeasterly course into enemy territory. The secret mission to bomb Oregon was under way.

Fujita and Okuda proceeded east past Brookings and prepared to drop their load – two 160-pound incendiary bombs. An hour after leaving the sub, they were nearly in position, 8,200 feet over a heavily wooded forest. Fujita ordered Okuda to drop the bombs. Immediately afterwards, they set a course to the ocean and the sanctuary and safety of their submarine.

Although it was spotted by American planes, which dropped a number of depth charges, the Japanese sub slipped below the ocean surface and successfully hid on the bottom before eventually escaping.

About the same time, a little past noon, two lookouts radioed in a fire report. At 4.20 p.m., they located the blaze – a few small and easily extinguished fires that involved only seven trees. But, more importantly, they realised that the fires were not caused by lightning as they had originally suspected, but by bombs from an enemy aircraft. Excited, they radioed in their finding.

Within hours, the US military, the FBI, and other government agencies were on the scene – trying to piece together clues to how an enemy plane could have invaded and then escaped American airspace without a trace. Luckily, weather conditions were not favourable for a forest fire on 9 September.

Back on ship, Fujita, Okuda and the rest of the sub crew waited patiently off shore, preparing for another attack, which came twenty days later. This time, a grassy area east of Port Orford was targeted. Unlike the previous attack, neither bomb ignited and, to this day, neither has been located.

Their mission accomplished, Fujita and company sailed back to Japan. Okuda was later killed in action, but Fujita survived the war to become a successful businessman. In 1962, twenty years after the attack, he returned to Brookings as a guest of its citizens. To make amends for his attack, he

AMAZING MAGEE BRINGS THE ROOF DOWN!

ST NAZAIRE, FRANCE 1943

Sergeant Magee, 24, was one of the oldest of the ten-man crew who flew out of Molesworth, England, on a B-17 bomber nicknamed *Snap! Crackle! Pop!* The pilot was only nineteen. His seventh mission was a daylight bombing run on St Nazaire, in Occupied France, called 'Flack City' because of the anti-aircraft guns defending their submarine port. *Snap! Crackle! Pop!* was one of a group of 85 B-17s and went with a fighter escort.

Magee was a 5-foot-7-inch gunner, barely small enough to fit in the B-17's ball turret – a cramped, doughnut-shaped, plastic-glass-and-metal turret on the bomber's underside. It was such a tight fit – a gunner's knees were practically against his chest – that Magee had to leave his parachute on the deck of the four-engine Flying Fortress. The ball turret offered a panoramic view but was also a precarious target for German fighter planes. B-17 gunners had a high casualty rate.

Over the target area, flack damaged Magee's plane, and then German fighters shot off a section of the right wing. Magee, who was wounded, scrambled back into the cabin, only to find his parachute was ruined. The plane was seriously disabled and spinning out of control. He had no choice but to jump out at 22,000 feet – a drop of more than 4 miles – without a parachute.

As he fell from the plane, Magee asked God to save his life. 'I don't wish to die because I know nothing of life' was his appeal to the Almighty. Then he lost consciousness and crashed through the glass roof of the St Nazaire railroad station.

It's said that at that exact moment, a bomb exploded inside the station, the two forces cancelling each other out and breaking his fall.

When he regained consciousness, Magee said to his captors: 'Thank God I'm alive.' His injuries were numerous, however: 28 shrapnel wounds, including broken limbs; his right arm was nearly severed. The Germans decided that anyone who could miraculously survive deserved special attention. With the German medical assistance, Magee made a full recovery.

Two of his crewmen also survived. In all, 75 airmen died, seven US planes were destroyed and 47 were damaged that day. Magee remained a prisoner of war until May 1945. He was decorated for meritorious conduct and awarded the Purple Heart.

On 3 January 1993, Magee and the other two crewmen were guests of the St Nazaire townspeople. They hosted a banquet and erected a six-foot-tall memorial to salute the *Snap! Crackle! Pop!* crew.

'THE CURSE OF THE LADY BE GOOD'

SOLUCH, LIBYA 1943

The *Lady Be Good* was an American B-24D Liberator based at Benina Airfield in Soluch, Libya and commanded by First Lieutenant William J Hatton. Following a 4 April 1943 bombing raid on Naples conducted by the 376th Bomb Group, the plane failed to return to base. After attempts to locate the plane in Libya, its nine crewmen were classified as missing in action, and presumed dead, believed to have perished after crashing into the Mediterranean.

On 9 November 1958, British oil surveyors located the wreckage of the Lady Be Good 440 miles southeast of Soluch in the desert. Although the plane was broken into two pieces, it was immaculately preserved, with functioning machine guns, and a working radio. Evidence aboard the plane indicated that the men had bailed out. Records in the log of the navigator ended at Naples for reasons unknown. The United States Army conducted a search for the remains of the airmen. Finding no evidence of the men's progress, the exploration concluded that their bodies were buried beneath sand dunes.

In 1960, however, the bodies of eight airmen were found by a British oil exploration team. Five were found nearly 80 miles from the crash site, while another two were found another 20 miles and 27 miles farther north respectively. A journal found in the pocket of the co-pilot indicated that eight of the men had bailed out and had managed to make contact with one another by firing their revolvers and signal flares into the air. They had survived for eight days without water before perishing, but not before managing to trek over a hundred miles in searing heat. Three of the eight had eventually set off to try and find help while the other five waited behind.

The body of one of the three, the radio operator, was never found. The ninth man was found not far from the crash site. The other crew members had been unable to establish contact with him and presumed him lost. In fact, his parachute had failed, causing him to die during the evacuation.

Tragically, it appears that the crew could have survived had their escape maps covered the area in which they had bailed out, for they never suspected that they were more than a hundred miles inland! Had they travelled south instead of north, they would have come upon the oasis of El Zighen. On their way, they would also have found the wreckage of the *Lady Be Good* and have been able to retrieve the water stored aboard.

Their tragic misfortune appears to have been transferred to the remains of the plane itself. Numerous parts from the *Lady Be Good* were subsequently returned to the US for technical study. Some of these parts were then installed in other aircraft – which all then experienced unexpected difficulties. A C-54 in which several of the ill-fated plane's autosyn transmitters were installed had propeller trouble and the crew only managed to make a safe landing by throwing cargo overboard. A C-47 in which a radio receiver was installed had to ditch in the Mediterranean. Finally, a US Army 'Otter' plane in which seats from the *Lady Be Good* had been fitted crashed in the Gulf of Sidra with ten men aboard. No trace was ever found of any of them, but one of the few pieces washed ashore was a seat armrest from the *Lady Be Good*.

'APRÈS MOI LE DÉLUGE'

RUHR RIVER, GERMANY 1943

During World War II, a British plan was hatched to disable a series of German dams that provided hydroelectric power and water supplies over a large area. Aerial bombardment could create a devastating hit against the Germans. The plan was, however, fraught with problems.

The dams were already protected against the use of torpedoes. A normal bomb blast would simply be cushioned by the impact in the water. The only alternative was eventually invented by a British scientist, Barnes Wallis. He developed the spinning cylindrical bomb – a bomb in a barrel – which could skip and bounce along the surface of the water right up to the dam, where it would explode.

And so the famous Dambusters came into being under the command of Wing Commander Guy Gibson. The 617 Squadron was made up of British and Allied bombers, all coordinated under the umbrella of 'Operation Chastise'.

Their training itself was, of necessity, fairly bizarre. Normally, pilots were reprimanded for flying too low; the Lancasters were designed to bomb from 20,000 feet and up. Five hundred feet was considered low-level flying. Barnes Wallis's bouncing bomb would have to be dropped at a speed of 230 miles per hour and from a height of just 60 feet – dangerously low for a pilot.

Squadron 617 started at 250 feet and as Ken Brown, one of the pilots chosen commented, 'When we got used to it, we went down to 150 feet. This was really low. But then they asked us to start flying at 60 feet, at night – this was a whole new experience. It was frightening. You had trees; you had high-tension wires; many different obstacles. At that altitude, you can't be sloppy. If you dropped a wing at 60 feet, it'd scrape on the ground.'

A few days before the raids, they got their planes and for the first time saw Barnes Wallis's top-secret bomb. After two and a half months of training, Brown and the other air crew finally found out what they were supposed to destroy with the new bomb. 'Most of us thought it would be ships. Believe me, we were all really shocked when our commander told us we were going to do the dams, "the great dams of Germany",' he remembered. Indeed, it was to be a huge and highly dangerous attack – targeting the Mohre, Eder and Sorpe dams on the river Ruhr.

Everything went according to plan during the mission itself, which took place on 15 May 1943, and although the dams were not completely destroyed, they were irrevocably damaged. Millions of gallons of water gushed through the gashes and swept down the Ruhr Valley. Mines, houses, factories, roads and railways – all were destroyed in the path of the flood water for about 50 miles from the source.

The death toll was enormous: 1,294 civilians, 749 of them Ukrainian women and children trapped in a German prisoner-of-war camp below the Mohre dam. The Dambusters themselves also suffered very great losses: 53 men died, thirteen of them Canadians, and of the seventeen aircraft which took off on the first raid, only eight resumed the second. According to Brown, Barnes Wallis, the eccentric scientist who devised the bouncing bomb in his back garden, wept: '"All those boys. All those boys," he said.' However, pictures of the broken dams proved to be an immense morale booster to the Allies, particularly to the British, who were suffering continual German bombardment.

In fact, 'Operation Chastise' did not have the military effect that was at the time believed. Estimates show that before 15 May 1943, water production on the Ruhr was 1 million tonnes, which dropped to a quarter of that level after the raid. By 27

June, full water output was restored, thanks to an emergency pumping scheme inaugurated only the previous year, and the electricity grid was again producing power at full capacity. The raid proved to be costly in lives but, in fact, no more than a minor inconvenience to the Ruhr's industrial output.

Thirty-three of the surviving aircrew were decorated at Buckingham Palace on 22 June 1943. Guy Gibson was awarded the Victoria Cross. The squadron badge was chosen at around the same time, along with a suitable, if tongue-in-cheek, motto: 'Après moi le déluge'.

DEATH ON THE ROCK

GIBRALTAR 1943

When the Liberator aircraft carrying Polish general Wladyslaw Sikorski, the prime minister of the Polish government-in-exile during World War II, crashed soon after take-off from Gibraltar en route to London on 4 July 1943, there was immediate suspicion of sabotage. The bodies of all five passengers and crew, including Sikorski's daughter, were never found, although the Czech-born pilot, Max Prchal, was rescued by an RAF launch.

When Ludwik Lubienski, head of the Polish military mission in Gibraltar at the time of the crash, visited Prchal in hospital the next day, the mystery deepened. Lubienski had personally unfastened the inflated Mae West lifejacket worn by the pilot as he came ashore unconscious in the launch. However, the injured airman strongly denied that he had been wearing the jacket, which he insisted he always kept hanging on the back of his flying seat.

At the RAF court of inquiry into the crash days later Prchal stoutly maintained that he had not departed from his usual practice, and that when he started his take-off run, he was not wearing it. It was established, however, that when he was picked up out of the water he was found to be not only wearing his Mae West, but that every tape and fastening had been properly put on and done up.

The inquiry concluded that the crash was caused by the aircraft's controls jamming after take-off, for some unexplained reason. A report concluded that there was 'no question of sabotage' and that Prchal was in no way to blame, although his protestations concerning his lifejacket suggested to some that he knew the aircraft was going to crash.

Suspicions that Sikorski had been assassinated remained, however, including allegations that Winston Churchill, British prime minister at the time, had been part of the plot.

In 1969, Sir Robin Cooper, a former pilot, reviewed the wartime inquiry's findings. He wrote a memo to Harold Wilson's Cabinet, stating that security at Gibraltar had been casual, and that a number of opportunities for sabotage had arisen while the aircraft was there. Although he doubted sabotage had taken place, or that the pilot had crashed the aircraft deliberately, he added that, although involvement of the British could be excluded, the possibility of Sikorski's murder by 'persons unknown' remained a possibility. Who, Cooper wrote, could have jammed the aircraft's controls? No one had ever provided a satisfactory answer.

There were plenty of likely candidates in the area at the time. The head of the British Secret Intelligence Service's counter-intelligence department for the Iberian Peninsula from 1941 to 1944 was Kim Philby, the Soviet double-agent who defected in 1963, and later claimed to have been a double-agent since the forties. Before 1941, Philby served as an instructor with the Special Operations Executive – which specialised in sabotage behind enemy lines.

Then there was Lieutenant Commander Lionel 'Buster' Crabb, one of the first Royal Navy divers to examine the wreckage. Crabb later disappeared in mysterious circumstances in 1956 while on a secret underwater mission beneath a Soviet cruiser in Portsmouth Harbour. A headless body in a diving suit was found weeks later, amid unconfirmed speculation that Crabb had defected.

The Russians regarded Sikorski as a serious troublemaker and had the strongest motives for doing away with him. By the spring of 1943, he had been raising the issue of post-war borders with the Soviet Union and had travelled to the USA to lobby support from President Roosevelt. In 'April, he had lunched with Churchill in Downing Street, where he brought up the alleged massacre by the Russians of 10,000 Polish officers in the forests of Katyn, near Smolensk in the USSR.

Although Churchill, concerned that the alliance between Stalin and the West was fragile, urged caution, Sikorski called publicly for the International Red Cross to investigate the massacres. A furious Stalin promptly broke off diplomatic relations with the Polish government-in-exile. His anger was conveyed to Churchill at Chartwell by Ivan Maisky, the Soviet ambassador in England.

By a remarkable coincidence, Maisky had also arrived in Gibraltar on the morning of 4 July 1943, on his way to Moscow. His Liberator landed just after 7 a.m. – the time at which, evidence has subsequently confirmed, Sikorski's aircraft was left unguarded.

MUSSOLINI RESCUED

GRAN SASSO, ITALY 1943

In 1943, the formally pro-Nazi Italian government decided to change sides and align themselves with the Allies. On 25 July 1943, the Fascist dictator Mussolini was removed from his post, placed under arrest and imprisoned. In Germany, Hitler was devastated – his partner in crime and friend had been betrayed, possibly to be turned over to the Allies as a prisoner. He must be rescued! The task fell to Otto Skorzeny, commander of Germany's Special Forces.

The first step was to find Mussolini. After a long search, he was finally located at the Hotel Campo Imperatore, a winter sports centre on the Gran Sasso, the highest peak in the Apennine mountain range. The hotel was located on a crag 6,000 feet up the mountain, its only link with the outside world being a funicular railway running up the side of the mountain. He was guarded by a battalion of Italian policemen.

It was a difficult situation to assess. Various options had to be cancelled out – a ground assault would be too complicated and there was nowhere for paratroops to land safely. Eventually it was decided to use twelve gliders. Two would lead and secure the landing site followed by four more carrying Skorzeny and troops, who would storm the hotel. The remainder were to land at the bottom of the mountain, move rapidly overland and seize the bottom end of the railway to prevent reinforcements arriving.

However, things went badly from the start. The two lead gliders ran into bomb craters on take-off and never left the ground, leaving the glider carrying Skorzeny as the lead. They discovered the landing site was studded with boulders, a fact not revealed by aerial photos of the ground. Skorzeny and his men crash-landed, and immediately invaded the hotel and located Mussolini. The guards, dazed and bewildered by the speed of the assault, offered no resistance.

The original plan had been for the force to capture the nearby airfield and hold it while Mussolini was being taken away. This was done, but the rescue aircraft could not be contacted. A back-up plane was hastily arranged but damaged its landing gear on arrival. The only hope lay with a very small Fieseler Storch aircraft, and the man flying it: one Captain Gerlach. The landing space in front of the hotel was cleared of boulders and he managed to land. Very quickly, Mussolini was squeezed in behind Gerlach, with Skorzeny behind him.

The overloaded Storch just managed to gather speed as it bucked and bounced over the rocky surface. It then plunged over the edge of the plateau into the deep ravine below.

Gerlach, an accomplished airman, who had a reputation for performing miracles in the air, at last managed to lift the plunging aircraft from its nose dive just a few hundred feet above the valley floor. The three flew to Rome and from there Mussolini and Skorzeny were bundled on a transport plane out of Italy to Vienna and safety.

Upon receiving the news of the successful operation, an emotional Hitler told Skorzeny, 'You have performed a military feat which will become part of history. You have given me back my friend Mussolini.'

THE MYSTERY OF THE
UNEXPLAINED FALL

PENNSYLVANIA, USA 1943

One afternoon in late September 1943, the Brouse family were picking tomatoes in a field of their farm a mile west of Kratzerville, Pennsylvania, when their attention was drawn to the sound of an object hurtling towards the earth at a terrific speed. It hit the ground with such tremendous force that, 100 yards away, they felt the ground shake.

They'd just heard a plane pass overhead and, thinking that it might have been a mailbag dropped in error, they ran over to get a better look. They were horrified to discover the crushed form of a human being.

The next day, naval intelligence officers arrived and found two military service identification tags on the body. The dead man was identified as Carroll Rex Byrd, 26, a coast guard aviation pilot and radioman, and a resident of Tecate, California. He had served in the US Navy as a radioman for four years until his honourable discharge in 1938. In 1939, he joined the coast guard, serving two and a half years as an aviation radioman before heading off for flight training at NAS Pensacola, where he earned his 'wings' in April 1943.

As a formal investigation opened, people speculated as to how and why Byrd had fallen. Many in the local farming community were puzzled by the fact that the plane had continued its westward flight without slowing or showing any sign of distress. Had Byrd been murdered by another member of the air crew – by pushing his victim out of the plane?

Or was it simply a clear case of suicide? Then again, how could this experienced aviator have fallen through an open bomb bay? Maybe he'd just opened the safety hatch and been sucked out into the slipstream. There was even a theory that he could have been working on the plane when it took off and was kept hanging suspended in the air until he could no longer support himself!

The crew of the Coast Guard Goose (Grumman JRF-2/3/5G) quickly solved the mystery. They revealed to investigators that Byrd had, incredibly, crawled out of the plane in mid-flight simply to repair a radio antenna – and that they had not become aware of his disappearance until some twenty minutes later. This explained the strange, apparently unconcerned continuance of the plane on its course.

Carroll's wife later wrote a letter to Mr and Mrs Brouse, the farmers who had found his body, in which she revealed, 'My husband had always been daring to the point of disregarding rules and his own personal safety.' It was only after reading the letter and learning of the radio antenna, that Mr Brouse recalled that he'd found a piece of thin metal about half an inch wide and a yard long, resembling a whalebone, while working in his field. He'd joked with his wife about 'losing part of her corset' and thrown the piece of metal away. He promptly went out and found it again. Navy personnel later identified it as the part that Carroll had probably been working on when his tragic fall had occurred.

DIVINE WIND OF THE KAMIKAZE

LEYTE ISLAND, PHILIPPINES 1944

Kamikaze is a Japanese word – usually translated as divine wind – that came into being as the name of a legendary typhoon said to have saved Japan from an invasion fleet in 1281. In the English language, however, the word 'kamikaze' usually refers to suicide attacks carried out by Japanese aircrews against Allied shipping, towards the end of the Pacific campaign of World War II.

In February 1944, the Japanese military, though outnumbered by the Allies in terms of men and machines, were superior in terms of the numbers of soldiers willing to risk their lives rather than to be defeated. Whoever first suggested the kamikaze attacks is unknown, but most people believe it was Admiral Takijiro Onishi.

In October 1944, the Japanese were facing overwhelming Allied assaults on the Philippines. The Japanese 201st Navy Flying Corps – consisting of just forty planes – was given the hopeless task of assisting the Japanese Navy and in a meeting of air crew at Magracut Airfield near Manila, Onishi suggested: 'I don't think there would be any other certain way to carry out the operation than to put a 250-kilogram bomb on a Zero [a Japanese fighter plane] and let it crash into a US carrier, in order to disable her for a week.'

Commander Asaiki Tamai then asked a group of 23 talented student pilots, whom he had personally trained, to join the 'special attack force' (usually abbreviated to Tokkotai). Every pilot volunteered. Later, Tamai asked Lieutenant Seki Yukio to take command, which he was more than eager to do.

However, according to eyewitnesses, the first kamikaze attack was not carried out by Tamai's unit, but by an unidentified Japanese pilot. On 21 October 1944, the flagship of the Royal Australian Navy, the heavy cruiser HMAS *Australia*, was hit by a Japanese plane carrying a 200-kg (441-pound) bomb, off Leyte Island. The plane struck the superstructure of the *Australia* above the bridge, spewing burning fuel and debris over a large area. However, the bomb failed to explode; if it had, the ship might have been effectively destroyed. At least thirty crew members died as a result of the attack, though.

On 25 October, the *Australia* was hit again and was forced to retire to the New Hebrides for repairs. That same day, five Zeros, led by Seki, attacked a US escort carrier, the USS *St Lo*, although only one kamikaze actually hit the ship. Its bomb caused fires that resulted in the bomb magazine exploding, sinking the carrier. Others hit and damaged several other Allied ships.

The peak of the attacks came on 6 April 1945 during the Battle of Okinawa, when waves of planes made hundreds of attacks, in Operation Kikusai ('floating chrysanthemums'). These attacks, which expended 1,465 planes, created havoc: accounts of losses vary, but by the end of the battle, at least 21 US ships had been sunk by kamikazes, along with some from other Allied navies, and dozens more had been damaged.

Estimates of the overall damage caused to Allied shipping and the numbers of Japanese pilots who died vary widely. The Japanese claimed almost 4,000 men sacrificed themselves, sinking over 80 ships. American estimates are much lower, suggesting 34 naval losses and 2,800 kamikaze pilots dead. They also estimate that almost 5,000 sailors died in such attacks.

The Japanese military never had a problem in recruiting volunteers for kamikaze missions; indeed, there were three times as many volunteers as there were aircraft. As a result, experienced pilots were turned away, as they were considered too valuable in defensive and training roles. The average kamikaze pilot was a twentysomething studying science at university. Their motivations in volunteering varied from patriotism, to a desire to bring honour to their families, or to prove themselves personally – in an extreme fashion. It's been suggested, however, that many of the pilots who completed the attacks were second or third sons in the family, because the first-born son got to inherit the family business and therefore needed to be spared.

In public schools throughout Japan, students were effectively taught that dying for the Emperor was the right thing to do and that those who did would be worshipped when they died at the yakusuni shrine. By late 1944, a motto of *jusshi reisho*, which means, 'sacrifice life', was being promulgated throughout Japan.

Special ceremonies were often held, immediately prior to kamikaze missions, in which pilots, carrying prayers from their families, were given military decorations.

According to legend, young pilots on kamikaze missions often flew southwest from Japan over Mount Kaimon in the Satsuma Province. They looked over their shoulders to see this, the most southern mountain on the Japanese mainland and said 'goodbye' to their country, and saluted the mountain.

FRIDAY THE 13TH

CAMBRAI, FRANCE 1944

Warrant officer Andrew 'Andy' Mynarsky was a Canadian serving with the RAF during World War II. On 12 June 1944, he and the crew boarded a Lancaster bomber bound for an attack on the rail marshalling yards at Cambrai, France. Not only would it be the crew's thirteenth sortie; they would be over the target on Friday the thirteenth. Not normally superstitious, the crew could not avoid the omens in this case. Before take-off, Andy found a four-leaf clover in the grass by the planes. He insisted that his closest friend in the crew, tail gunner Pat Brophy, should take it.

They set off and during the raid the aircraft came under heavy attack and both engines failed. Hydraulic lines to the rear turret were severed and the fluid ignited, turning the rear of the fuselage into an inferno.

As the plane lost altitude, the crew bailed out. Andy left his post at the mid-upper turret and began to make his way to the rear escape door. Through the fierce flames, however, he could see his friend Pat, desperately trying to escape from the immobilised rear turret. He was trapped! The turret had jammed in such a position that the exit doors didn't line up and, in his frantic attempts to free himself, Pat had broken the manual escape back-up system as well. By now, all of the other crew members had made their escapes from the stricken aircraft.

With complete disregard for his own safety, Andy crawled through the flames to assist his fellow gunner. Not noticing that

146

his own flight suit and parachute had caught fire, he fought heroically to free the turret, but all his efforts were in vain.

'Completely ignoring his own condition in the flames, he grabbed a fire axe and tried to smash the turret free,' Brophy told *Reader's Digest* in 1965. 'It gave slightly, but not enough. Wild with desperation and pain, he tore at the doors with his bare hands – to no avail. By now he was a mass of flames below the waist. Over the roar of the wind and the whine of our two remaining engines, I screamed, "Go back, Andy! Get out!"'

Reluctantly, he had to comply.

'When Andy reached the escape hatch, he stood up. Slowly, as he'd often done before in happier times together, he came to attention. Standing there in his flaming clothes, a grimly magnificent figure, he saluted me! At the same time, just before he jumped, he said something. And even though I couldn't hear, I knew it was "Good night, Sir."'

Andy's parachute was severely damaged by the fire that had raged around him as he struggled to release his friend; he did not survive the jump. French witnesses saw him plunge earthward in flames but when they found him, he was so severely burned that he died within hours.

Ironically, Pat Brophy survived, unhurt. When the Lancaster crash-landed, two of its twenty bombs immediately exploded, throwing the tail gunner clear. His watch stopped at 2.13 a.m., on Friday, 13 June 1944.

THE DESERT FOX – OUTFOXED!

NORMANDY, FRANCE 1944

Late in the day on 17 July 1944, slightly more than a month after the Allied landings on the Normandy beaches on D-Day, German Field Marshal Erwin Rommel was returning to his headquarters at La Roche-Guyon. In spite of the best efforts of the forces under him, the Allies were breaking out everywhere. They enjoyed total air superiority and their ground-attack aircraft were roaming at will over the countryside, targeting anything that moved. The ditches were filled with the smoking hulks of destroyed German vehicles.

The Field Marshal was travelling hundreds of kilometres each day, meeting with his battle commanders, doing what he could, in a war that he knew was lost. On this particular day, as he was leaving the Command Post of the 1st SS Panzer Corps led by Sepp Dietrich, Dietrich suggested that he did not take the main road and that he should ride a German Jeep in order to be less conspicuous. The Field Marshal waved off such a suggestion.

He departed, as usual, in his personal car, a large open Horch. Rommel sat in the front, as was his habit. He liked to keep a map on his knee, so he could do the navigating. At the wheel was his regular driver, Daniel. In the back were three staff members.

In the late afternoon the same day, a Canadian Spitfire Squadron took off on an armed reconnaissance mission. Sometime into the sortie, one of the pilots, Charlie Fox, spotted a large black car travelling at high speed. With his number two following to watch his tail, Fox began a curving, diving attack to his left and started firing at approximately 300 yards. He hit the staff car, causing it to crash. At the time, he had no idea whose the car was, only that it was large black and open, gleaming in the sun without any camouflage, which was unusual.

Driver Daniel, seriously wounded, lost control and it hurtled on for several hundred yards before finally crashing into the ditch. The passengers in the back remained unhurt, though Daniel was to die shortly afterwards. Field Marshal Rommel was thrown against the windshield post. He lived but suffered a fractured skull, a broken cheekbone, an eye injury, and a concussion of the brain. His career was over. He was taken to a hospital and then to his home in Germany to convalesce.

Three days later, an assassin's bomb nearly killed Hitler during a strategy meeting at his headquarters in East Prussia. In the gory reprisals that followed, some suspects implicated Rommel in the plot. Although he may not have been aware of the attempt on Hitler's life, his 'defeatist' attitude was enough in itself to warrant Hitler's wrath.

Soon afterwards, Rommel was officially implicated in the assassination plot against Adolf Hitler. On 14 October 1944, General Wilhelm Burgdorf and General Ernst Maisel arrived at the Field Marshal's home. Rommel was given a choice – immediate death by poison or a public trial. If Rommel chose a court hearing, reprisals would be taken against his family. However, if he elected suicide his family would receive all pensions due and he would get a full military funeral. (Hitler obviously did not want to admit that Germany's most famous general had plotted against him.)

He was driven from his home towards Ulm, but, on the way, Burgdorf ordered the car to stop and told Maisel and the SS driver to leave for just a moment. When the two men returned, Rommel was dead, probably from a cyanide pill, which would have killed him almost instantly. At his state funeral three days later, the largest wreath came from Hitler. His death was officially said to have been a result of injuries from the air attack.

It would be another six years, however, before Fox was officially credited with bringing Rommel down. At first, the Americans claimed that one of their P-47s had shot up Rommel's car, though the Germans were adamant that it was a Spitfire.

Fox was subsequently named an honorary colonel of 412 Squadron in Ottawa.

JOE KENNEDY JUNIOR DIES

BLYTHBURGH, ENGLAND 1944

During World War II, Joseph Patrick Kennedy, the elder brother of future President John F Kennedy, was a volunteer US Navy pilot flying in B24 Liberators. He was stationed in England at Dunkeswell, Devon.

In July 1944, after completing his normal combat tour of thirty missions, he was ordered home. He had already had his personal belongings loaded on a transport plane bound for the USA when he got wind of 'Project Aphrodite'. This was a top-secret mission – to target the German V3 Supergun site at Mimoyecques, France. It involved low-level flying and a parachute jump. Kennedy volunteered and was accepted.

On 12 August 1944, a Consolidated Liberator bomber of the United States Navy Squadron VB-110 took off from an airfield near Diss in Norfolk. The crew consisted of only two men. Its captain was Lieutenant J P Kennedy and co-pilot was Lieutenant W J Willy.

The aircraft had been stripped of all armament to save weight, but broom handles were put into the turrets to fool the enemy. Twelve tons of Torpex explosive plus six demolition charges each containing 100 pounds of TNT had been packed into the aircraft. After setting a heading for the target, the crew were to bail out and the pilotless aircraft would then be radio-controlled to its final destination, which it would crash into.

The escorting aircraft were officially listed as two Lockheed Venturas, one of which was the radio-control aircraft, a De-Havilland Mosquito photographic aircraft (flown by Colonel

Roosevelt, the son of the US president at that time), two Lockheed P-38 Lightnings and two Boeing B-17 Flying Fortresses. Sixteen North American P-51 Mustangs were also detailed as top cover for the North Sea crossing to France.

Once the formation had cleared Halesworth, the Liberator switched over from manual flight to radio control. Lieutenant Kennedy, now flying as a passenger, radioed the codename 'Zoot Suit' to tell the other crews that everything was fine. Lieutenant Willy then switched on 'Block', which was the codename for the TV camera in the nose used to guide the drone onto the target.

While over Blythburgh, just before heading out to sea, the radio-controller in the mother-ship Ventura decided to feed a test course alteration to the bomber to check that the system worked. As soon as this signal was executed, at exactly 6.20 p.m., the Liberator was torn apart by an enormous explosion.

The most likely explanation for the catastrophic blast was the inadequacy of the electrical shielding on 'Block'. Such shielding is used as a screen to suppress or isolate an electromagnetic field that might otherwise cause interference with other circuits. In this case it seems that the interference triggered the detonator mechanism, which in turn set off the load of Torpex.

The wreckage was scattered over an area three miles long and about two miles wide. Three square miles of heath land was set on fire, 147 properties – some up to 16 miles away – were damaged, and hundreds of trees were felled as a result of the blast. Despite all this, no civilians were killed. However, no remains of Lieutenants Willy or Kennedy were ever found.

The string of tragedies that were to befall the unfortunate Kennedy dynasty had begun.

THE COLDITZ 'COCK' GLIDER

COLDITZ, GERMANY 1944

Colditz Castle had the distinction of being the only German POW camp that had more guards than prisoners. Nevertheless, Allied prisoners continued to tunnel, jump and sneak their way out of 'The Colditz Escape Academy' in surprising numbers. More ambitiously still, a certain group of recaptured RAF prisoners in Colditz planned to escape by air – in their own hand-built glider.

It was constructed inside a loft above the chapel; access was gained through a trapdoor in the floor. The necessary materials were, for the most part, scavenged. The prisoners obtained a few items through bribery: cases of glue and a metal drill, for example. They salvaged metal from cupboards and used it for the main wing supports. Floorboards and bed-slats provided most of the wood for the hundreds of ribs required to construct the body. Six thousand hand-fashioned pieces were needed for the wings alone. They made all their own tools with which to work – a plane from a table knife, drills from nails, saw handles from bed boards, and saw blades from both a wind-up record player's spring and the frame around iron window bars. For the glider's controls they expropriated electrical wiring taken from unused areas of the castle. Finally, to cover the whole wooden frame, they used bedsheets which were then sized with hot millet – taken from their rations – to make them stiff.

The finished machine was designed to take two prisoners out of Colditz, across the River Mulde and far enough to get a head start on the prison's guards.

On the day of the flight, a hole was to have been made in the west wall of the attic and the glider moved on to the roof of the chapel. The wings, measuring 16 feet each, would by then have been attached to the body and preparations made for the launch.

Bill Goldfinch, one of the men involved, admitted: 'Although we had made the glider, we had not worked out the best way to get it into the air.' One plan had been to fill a metal bathtub with concrete and attach that to the plane by a series of pulleys.

Dropping the tub 60 feet to the floor would have propelled the glider into the air, 300 feet above the surrounding countryside, allowing it to fly for about a mile.

In the last months of the war, a message was received from high command in Britain that there were to be no more escapes and when the conflict ended the glider was discovered still in its compartment. It was then shown to astonished guards, who had been totally unaware of what had been going on above the chapel.

The glider disappeared from its hiding place some time after the war ended, its ultimate fate unknown. During later visits to Colditz, survivors heard rumours that the aircraft had been burned. One story was that it was broken into firewood during the brutal winter of 1945–6, a time during which many Germans and Russians either froze or starved to death. Another story was that villagers felt 'disgraced' by its presence and publicly torched it. The truth will probably never be known, unless some of the Russians soldiers who occupied the town immediately after the war come forward.

One burning question remained, however: whether the plane would really have flown. That question was solved in March 2000. A glider made to the original plans drawn up on a single sheet of paper was towed on to a grassy area of RAF Odiham and John Lee, a lifelong glider pilot and manufacturer of several home-made planes, climbed into the tiny cockpit.

The signal was given to power up a 1,200-yard-long cable attached to the glider. It hurtled across the grass and then almost immediately into the air. The cable was released and it climbed to 500 feet, its wings perfectly level. The pilot showed the plane's manoeuvrability with a few deft turns before making a wide left arc and then coming in to land just a few feet from where he had taken off.

Bill Goldfinch, the only survivor from the team that built the original glider, watched with tears in his eyes. 'I always thought it would fly,' he said. 'There can't be any doubt now.'

CLARK GABLE'S WAR

THE RUHR, GERMANY 1944

Upon hearing of the attack on Pearl Harbor in 1941, both Clark Gable and Carole Lombard – Hollywood's Golden Couple – offered their services to the White House. Although told to continue making movies, Lombard was unhappy and suggested that Gable enlist in the army and earn a commission. While Gable dithered, and eventually started work on a previously scheduled film, Lombard set out in early January 1942 on a War Bond tour. She telegraphed Gable, 'Hey Pappy. You better get into this man's Army,' but, impatient to return home, she took a plane – instead of the train, as planned – which crashed into Table Mountain, near Las Vegas, on 16 January 1942. There were no survivors. President Franklin D Roosevelt decorated Lombard posthumously and offered a military funeral, but Gable had a private service, in accordance with her wishes.

Gable went hunting to escape his grief but by chance met an army air-force officer, Colonel Luke Smith, who told him he'd be doing the force a great service as a gunner – it would help to glorify the plane crews and the 'grease monkeys', he told the star.

And so Gable joined up – although MGM studios shrewdly arranged for his friend, cinematographer Andrew McIntyre, to accompany him. On 12 August, after being sworn in, Gable told the press, 'I have made application to be a gunner and I'm going to do my very best. There's nothing else to say.'

Soon after Gable's arrival on a posting to England with the 351st Bomber Group, Nazi radio propaganda broadcaster,

Lord Haw-Haw, while 'welcoming' the Group, added, 'among them is the famous American cinema star, Clark Gable. We'll be seeing you soon in Germany, Clark.' Hermann Goering even offered to handsomely reward any Luftwaffe pilot who downed Gable's B-17 bomber. Gable commented, 'How can I hide with this face? If I ever fall into Hitler's hands, the son of a bitch will put me in a cage like a big gorilla. He'd exhibit me all over Germany. If the plane goes down,' he concluded, 'I'll just go with the son of a bitch.'

Gable and McIntyre commenced work on what would become a fascinating documentary about the B-17s, called *Combat America*. Although it was suggested that Gable's flying missions were carefully selected so as to avoid any risks to the great man, Gable saw plenty of real action.

Flying in Major Theodore Milton's *Ain't It Gruesome*, Gable wedged himself in behind the top turret gunner for a better view and was amply rewarded: fighter planes made five passes, killing one man, wounding seven others, and damaging eleven of the 351st Bomber Group planes. At one point a 20-mm shell came through *Gruesome*'s floor, cut off the heel from Gable's boot, and exited a foot from his head, all without exploding. Gable commented, 'I didn't know anything about it until we had dropped eleven thousand feet. Only then did I see the hole in the turret.'

Gable's last mission was on 23 September, when 117 bombers, in a break from the Combined Bomber Offensive, attacked the French port of Nantes. Clouds forced all but 46 planes of the 351st and 91st Bomb Groups to abort. Gable's plane, Lieutenant Colonel Robert W Burns's *The Duchess*, got through, however. As they approached the target, fighters attacked head-on, closing to within yards. It was Gable's last chance for combat. Leaving his camera crew in the waist of the plane, he pounded away with a nose-mounted .50 calibre gun.

Later on, talking on the tarmac with Burns's crew and reporters, he said, 'It wasn't quite as tough as the Ruhr. But it was tough enough. I could see the German pilot's features. That guy won't be around very long if he keeps on doing that.

THE LITTLE PRINCE FALLS TO EARTH

LYON, FRANCE 1944

Antoine de Saint-Exupéry was famous on two counts. Firstly, as a daring French aviator in World War II and, secondly, as the author of *The Little Prince*, a tender fable about a prince from an asteroid who explores the planets – and then falls to Earth. The story was written in 1943 and soon became a twentieth-century children's classic. Saint-Exupéry also wrote about his aviation experiences in his works *Wind, Sand and Stars* and *Flight to Arras*, which dealt with a doomed reconnaissance mission.

In 1944, Saint-Exupéry served as a pilot for the Free French Air Force, based in Corsica. He was fifteen years older than his colleagues, and also overweight. He felt isolated and depressed and very pessimistic about his future. On 31 July, returning to Corsica from a photographic sortie to Lyon, he vanished.

Was he shot down over the Mediterranean? Was there an accident, or was it suicide?

Nothing further was discovered until, in 1998, 93 miles west of Marseilles, a fisherman retrieved a bracelet from the sea. This bore the names of both Saint-Exupéry and his wife, Conzuela Gomez Castillo, but it was widely thought to be a fake. The fisherman, Jean-Claude Bianco, later revealed, 'For years, people had their doubts, claiming I made it myself.'

But Bianco's discovery jogged the memory of a local scuba diver, Luc Vanrell. In the 1980s he had discovered what he thought might be the missing Lockheed Lightning plane nestled in the ocean bed not far from the rugged cliffs of Provence. He began to investigate records of downed war planes and, by 2000, he was convinced he had found the right one. He applied to the government for permission to have the pieces brought up for analysis.

A furious argument broke out. Many Saint-Exupéry fans resisted the efforts of those determined to retrieve the wreck. Perhaps they wanted to keep the mystery alive. Eventually, however, the wreckage was recovered. The plane's position on the seabed indicated that it entered the water at a near-vertical angle, suggesting an unconscious man at the controls. However, no body was found, and so the myth surrounding Saint-Exupéry's disappearance lives on.

After his death, a letter was found in Saint-Exupéry's room that bore witness to a man who felt deeply disillusioned with life, with very little will left to live. The last line bleakly stated: 'What can one say to mankind? What does one have to say to mankind?' Given such dark thoughts, it is certainly possible that the much-loved author's death was due to suicide.

FLOSSY'S FURY

TOULON, FRANCE 1944

The 17th Bomb Group was based 15 miles to the northwest of Decimomannu air base on the southern end of the island of Sardinia, near the town of Villacidro. Each group consisted of four squadrons with 25 operational B-26 Martin Marauder bombers in each squadron. Twenty-year-old Technical Sergeant George Moscovis was an engineer/gunner in the 95th Squadron of the group.

Sunday, 20 August was 'Organisation Day' – a very special day for the men of the 95th. On that date in 1917, during World War I, the 95th Squadron had been formed. To celebrate its proud heritage, a party was planned for that evening in the base theatre – good food, lots of beer and Sardinian girls to dance with. But first, there was a mission to fly, and today's targets were the heavy-gun emplacements that guarded Toulon harbour on France's south coast.

Sergeant George Moscovis and his friend Sergeant Bob McCluskey were together on *Flossy's Fury* – a plane with battle number five-zero on its tail – that would carry the one-ton demolition bombs. Moscovis, the flight engineer, would man the twin .50-calibre machine guns in the top turret, while McCluskey flew as radioman and handled a .50 calibre at one of the waist windows.

Like many of the other combat crew that day, McCluskey had experienced bad 'vibes' at the briefing, and when they drew their flight equipment, he had opted to take extra flak jackets; heavily leaded front and back, each weighed almost 20 pounds.

A jacket usually hung from the shoulders like an baseball umpire's chest protector, but the crew often took extras and strategically placed them under or over whichever other parts of their anatomy they most wanted to protect.

'There was heavy flak on the bomb run,' Moscovis recalled. 'You could feel the bombs go out, and I thought we were safe. But just as we started our break, we got two direct hits. The blast knocked me out of the turret, and when I found my chest pack, some of the silk was hanging out and the ripcord had been shot off, but I snapped it on.' By now, the plane was spinning down out of control and was completely engulfed by the billowing flames. The fuselage skin was too hot to touch.

'I started crawling back toward the tail to the waist window, when I saw McCluskey pinned under a bunch of flak suits. They were really heavy because of the G-forces, but I dragged the suits off him and got him to the waist window. There was no gun mounted in the left window, and I helped him go out, head first. We were really low by then, and I knew I had to get out. I squeezed out the waist window, and that's the last thing I remember.'

As he floated down, McCluskey watched the Marauder below him and saw it hit the ground and explode. He did not see another parachute, and he was sure his friend George had been killed along with the rest of the crew.

German soldiers still occupied Toulon, and when they found what appeared to be the lifeless body of Sergeant George Moscovis, they stripped him of his dog tags, his watch, an escape kit with $40-worth of francs and the bible he had carried on every mission. Then they ordered some French civilians to get rid of the body. The Frenchmen carried Moscovis to a small shed and laid him on a table, naked and covered only by a towel; they began to make a crude casket out of ammunition boxes and, by the time they had finished, it was almost dark. As they eased the body from the table into the coffin, George Moscovis regained consciousness.

'They all started to kiss me,' Moscovis said. 'Then they all began to cry. Then, damned, if I didn't cry, too.'

Germans were still everywhere in the city, and for several days the French 'underground' risked their lives to protect Moscovis and get him medical help. 'About four days later, these Free French had got me to a hospital, and they said they had a surprise for me,' Moscovis recalls. 'Into my room walked Bob McCluskey. I couldn't believe it and neither could he. We both cried like babies; each of us had thought the other was dead.'

Military records show that the day after Five-Zero's loss, the 17th Group Executive Officer Major Verl Oberlin submitted a confidential 'Disappearance of Missing Personnel' report on each crew member. The report on T/Sergeant Moscovis read in part, 'Only one parachute was seen to open as the plane went down – most likely, the waist gunner Sergeant Robert McCluskey. The crash was probably fatal to the other crew members.'

And the official 95th Squadron records for the 20 August mission read: 'One A/C was hit by flak immediately after bomb run. Flak hit between right engine and fuselage and A/C went into a sharp spin, fell on its back and exploded. One chute was observed to open.'

How did the miracle happen? If his parachute never opened, how did George Moscovis survive? 'I'll never know for sure,' Moscovis says. 'Maybe I hit on a sloped roof. Maybe a tree broke my fall.'

DID GLENN MILLER DIE IN A FRENCH BROTHEL?

ENGLISH CHANNEL 1944

On the afternoon of 15 December 1944, Major Glenn Miller boarded an RAF Norseman C-64 aircraft. The plane took off from an RAF base in England to take Miller to Paris, where he would join up with the rest of his band for a show.

Always nervous about flying, Miller expressed doubt about the single-engine plane. His fellow passenger, Colonel Norman Baesell, reminded him that Lindbergh made it across the Atlantic Ocean on one engine; they were flying only to Paris. 'Hey, where the hell are the parachutes?' Miller had asked. 'What's the matter, Miller, do you want to live forever?' the Colonel joked in reply. Shortly thereafter, the Norseman took off in the dense fog and disappeared.

Not until 24 December – after Miller's wife back home in New Jersey had been notified – was it announced that the famous bandleader was missing. Preoccupied with far larger problems in this decisive phase of the war in Europe, the American high command assumed that the Norseman had crashed into the Channel when its wings iced over or its engine failed. There was no search or inquiry into the tragedy.

Officially it was reported that foggy weather had led to the crash over the Channel – but no more details were given. Friends, fans and the troops themselves were not, however, satisfied with this story.

Miller was one of the premiere performers of the time, and

hugely popular. Wild rumours were rampant: he had been shot accidentally; his plane had been brought down by a German assassination squad; he had been taken for a spy and executed. Such stories continued for decades. In 1983, the bandleader's younger brother, breaking a forty years' silence, even claimed that he had died from lung cancer! In 1997, German journalist Udo Ulfkotte claimed he had evidence that Miller had actually arrived safely in Paris on the 14th, but had a heart attack on the 15th while consorting with a French prostitute, and that the American military had covered up the episode. Ulfkotte later claimed he'd been misquoted. It was the last of the fantasy tales.

A more likely explanation subsequently emerged soon after Miller's disappearance. Fred Shaw was a navigator with 149 Squadron, based in Norfolk. According to his logbook, on 15 December his squadron had been sent to make a bombing raid over Seigen, Germany. However, once the planes reached Brussels, they were told to abandon the raid because of bad weather. Returning home, they went instead to the southern jettisoning area fifty miles south of Beachy Head on the Channel to get rid of their bombs – a vital requirement for a safe landing.

Just after unloading the bombs, the bombardier in Shaw's plane called out that there was another plane below them. They looked out the window and saw a Norseman flying south at 1,500 feet. Bombs were exploding all around it and the pilot had completely lost control.

Just before it disappeared from Shaw's line of vision, it went into a tailspin. Seconds later the rear gunner called out that, 'There's a kite just gone in down under.' Shaw's aircraft then returned to base. Since they had never crossed into enemy territory, the crew never reported the plane they had seen go down over the Channel. It's possible, therefore, that Miller's plane had got lost in bad weather and strayed into the jettison area just as the squadron was dropping its bombs.

In 1985, British diver Clive Ward claimed to have found the remains of Miller's Norseman plane, undamaged, with no signs

'WHERE THERE'S FOO, THERE'S FIRE'

NORTHERN FRANCE 1945

On 10 March 1935, the *Chicago Tribune-New York Daily News* syndicate started distributing a comic strip called Smokey Stover, which continued successfully for decades. Smokey was a fireman who drove around in a two-wheeled fire-truck known as The Foomobile and was fond of saying, 'Where there's foo there's fire.' He also called himself a 'foo-fighter' rather than 'fire-fighter'.

So when American airmen, many of whom were fanatic comic readers, began seeing fiery, rounded unidentified shapes – glowing lights, eight or ten of them in a row, orange balls of fire, moving through the air at a terrific speed – it wasn't long before some wag suggested that they be called 'foo-fighters'. They weren't entirely a joke, however.

On a routine mission over Dijon, France, in late 1944, the 415th Night Fighter Squadron reported seeing mystery lights that disappeared before reappearing far off. No enemy plane showed up on radar, however. A few nights later another pilot and radar-observer, flying at an altitude of 1,000 feet, also saw a huge red light 1,000 feet above them, moving at 200 miles per hour. On 23 December, another 415th Night Fighter pilot, flying near Hagenau at an altitude of 10,000 feet, saw large orange glowing lights. After staying with the plane for two minutes, they peeled off and turned away, flying under perfect control, and then went out. This was the first and only suggestion of a controlled flying device. Although the men regarded these sightings with a certain amount of scepticism, official reports of the 'foo-fighters' had gone to group headquarters and had been noted. Various explanations were offered for the phenomena, none of them satisfactory and most of them irritating to the men of the 415th. There were suggestions that they might be a new kind of flare. That they were jet planes. That they could be flying bombs of some sort, either with or without a pilot. Or weather balloons. Perhaps even St Elmo's fire?

Throughout January 1945, the 415th continued to see the 'foo-fighters', and their conduct became increasingly mysterious. One aircrew observed lights, moving both singly and in pairs. On another occasion, three sets of lights, this time red and white in colour, followed a plane, and when the plane suddenly pulled up, the lights continued on in the same direction, before also suddenly pulling up to follow. The pilot checked with ground radar – he was alone in the sky, as was the case in every instance that foo-fighters were observed.

On the last appearance of the exasperating but potentially deadly lights, one pilot turned into them at the earliest possible moment and the lights disappeared. The pilot continued on his way, slightly perturbed, when he noticed lights far to the rear. The night was clear and the pilot was approaching a huge cloud. Once in the cloud, he dropped down 2,000 feet and made a 30-degree left turn. Just a few seconds later he emerged from the cloud – but with his eyes peeled to the rear. Sure enough, coming out of the cloud in the same relative position was the foo-fighter, as though to thumb its nose at the pilot. It then disappeared. This was the last time the foo-fighters were seen over Germany.

Intriguingly, the 'foo-fighters' phenomenon disappeared just at the point when Allied ground forces captured the area east of the Rhine. This was known to be the location of many German experimental stations. After V-E day, Intelligence officers put many such installations under guard, hoping to get valuable research information, including the solution to the foo-fighter mystery, but nothing substantial ever emerged.

However, during the last months of World War II, crews of

many B-29s over Japan saw what they also described as 'balls of fire' that followed them, occasionally came up and almost sat on their tails, changed colour from orange to red to white and back again, and yet never closed in to attack or crash, suicide-style.

One B-29 made evasive manoeuvres inside a cloud, but when it emerged, the ball of fire was following in the same relative position. The pilot reported it to be about 500 yards off, 3 feet in diameter, and to have a phosphorescent orange glow. No wing or fuselage – which might have suggested an aerial bomb or plane – was seen. The ball of fire followed the B-29 for several miles and then disappeared just as mysteriously as it had appeared in the dawn light over Fujiyama.

There may well have been plenty of foos, but in the end, thankfully, there was little fire.

THE LADY LYNN

NANCY, FRANCE 1945

With four injured crewmen and the right engine running rough and belching flame, *Lady Lynn*, a Martin B-26 Marauder bomber, was a heartbeat from disaster. And the nearest hope for salvation was an hour away.

Inside the cockpit, all was chaos. Bud Barrett's right hand was shattered, and he had a hole in his right thigh. Paul Ramsey's co-pilot controls had been shot out, and his face was peppered with Plexiglas fragments. Bombardier Russ Allen was on the floor in the nose with no parachute and both arms paralysed by his wounds. Hurricane winds of 185 miles per hour howled in through the nose and filled the cockpit with a bloody mist. *Lady Lynn* was a loose cannon – ready to blow and take everyone with it!

As he wormed into the pilot's seat, Ramsey glanced at Barrett's chute – pieces of torn silk gaped from flak holes. Bailing out had just ceased to be an option, at least for him and Barrett.

The crew stayed calm. Despite intense pain, Bud hobbled forward and had radioman Charlie Mellas buckle him into the co-pilot's seat. He wanted to give Ramsey moral support and any help he could. With his good left hand, Bud pulled his rosary beads from the pocket of his flight suit and hung them over the throttles. Without looking over, Ramsey gave a thumbs up. He pointed to the altimeter and Barrett nodded: 'We're not holding our altitude, Charlie,' he told Mellas. 'Toss everything you can overboard.' Mellas relayed the order, and the first thing to go was Sergeant Bob Blue's state-of-the-art

170

K-17 aerial camera. Waist guns, ammo, tools, flak suits and helmets followed. Only one more thing to go – the bomb load – and with the hydraulic system shot out, there was only one way to do it.

Mellas and engineer Dick Balinski balanced on the narrow catwalk in the bomb bay and began to unhook the clusters of fragmentation bombs from their shackles. Six 20-pound 'frags' were wired to a pipe on each of the twenty shackles. They uncoupled the 120-pound clusters one by one and passed them through the bulkhead to tail gunner Sergeant Rich Billington and Sergeant Blue. The clusters were bulky, and both teams handled them gingerly. If they accidentally pulled an arming wire loose the sensitive detonator might explode a cluster inside the plane. With strength born of fear, the four crewmen muscled all twenty bombs back to the waist windows and eased them overboard. With the plane stripped to its bare bones, the crew hunkered down in silence, trying not to think of the long haul ahead.

Bob Dietrich, the navigator, had been hit with dozens of shrapnel slivers, but he was on the radio with navigator, Ray Borden, asking for a heading to the nearest Allied field. 'We got three wounded [he ignored his own wounds] and the right engine's smoking. What's our best bet?' In seconds, he heard: 'The nearest field is at Luneville, about 160 miles on a heading of 285 degrees.'

By the time Luneville was in sight, the Marauder was down to 1,800 feet and straining to stay at that altitude. Charlie Mellas managed to rouse the tower operator: 'Luneville, we would like a straight-in approach. We have no hydraulics, an engine smoking and four injured crewmen on board.' Ramsey and Barrett were stunned when two red flares arched from the tower. 'Aircraft on fire, you cannot land here. Repeat, do not land. We have a squadron of our fighters due in; can't have a damaged aircraft closing our runway. Our pilots don't have enough fuel to divert.'

But the news got better. 'There's a "little friend" coming up behind you, and he'll escort you to a field at Nancy, only fifteen miles farther west. Good luck, guys.'

A Republic P-47 Thunderbolt fighter appeared just off *Lady Lynn*'s left wing, and Ramsey responded with a wave when the pilot waggled his wings. The fighter was flying tail low, hanging on the prop to fly slowly enough to match the B-26's speed – now down to 160 miles per hour. Barrett spotted the strip at Nancy and the tempo quickened.

Ramsey levelled the wings just as they skimmed over the runway threshold, and he chopped the throttles. The bomber hit hard and the gear collapsed. The plane skidded sideways in a nightmare roar of shattering glass and twisting metal. The right wing was ripped off, taking the fire with it and skewing the plane sideways with one last violent shudder. Then, all was still and very, very quiet.

They had crashed at an abandoned field, but the GI driver of a maintenance truck witnessed the landing and was there to help immediately. Being turned away at Luneville turned out to be a blessing because at Nancy there was a first-rate hospital. All the crew survived after treatment.

On the flight back the survivors played 'What if?' What if, on that mission, they had been carrying demolition bombs and flying in tight formation? What if *Lady Lynn*'s left engine had been hit? Almost surely, with either scenario, a multi-plane midair catastrophe would have been triggered.

But none of the 'what ifs' happened. A courageous crew stayed cool under fire. They put all their training into practice, worked together as a team and, with nothing to spare, their battered bomber held up just long enough to take them home. *Lady Lynn* had the dubious honour of being the last plane in the 320th Bomb Group to be shot down. In less than three weeks, the carnage ended. On 8 May 1945, after almost six years of fighting, the long, bitter struggle in Europe was over.

HANNA REITSCH'S DARING FLIGHT

BERLIN, GERMANY 1945

Hannah Reitsch, an enthusiastic admirer of Hitler, was also Germany's most accomplished female pilot. She could fly any type of aircraft, including helicopters, and she held more than forty altitude and endurance records. She was prepared to go to any length to help Germany win the war.

In 1943, concerned about the progress of the war, she offered to form a squadron of women pilots to fight for Germany, on the same terms as the men of the Luftwaffe. Although this plan was rejected, her idea for a suicide squadron that would strike at vital production centres in England was approved. The plan, however, was abandoned when the Allies landed in Normandy in June of 1944.

It was April 1945 when Hitler summoned Lieutenant General Ritter von Greim to his hideout bunker in Berlin for urgent talks. He knew that Germany was fast losing control of the war; Berlin itself was surrounded by Russians. It would be a very precarious operation to fly in to meet the Führer. Greim hatched a plan and enlisted the help of Hannah Reitsch.

On 26 April, they prepared to fly by night into Berlin from Gatow airfield, the only Berlin field still in German hands. They would then fly a single-engine Fiesler Storch (Stork) for the remaining distance and land within walking distance of Hitler's shelter. With Greim at the controls and Reitsch as passenger, the plane took off from Gatow under a whirling cover of German-Russian dogfights and continued at treetop level toward the Brandenburg Gate.

Street fighting was going on below them and countless Russian aircraft were in the air. After only a few minutes of flight, heavy fire tore out the bottom of the plane and severely injured Greim's right leg. By reaching over his shoulders, Reitsch took control of the craft and by dodging and squirming closely along the ground, brought the plane down on the main East-West axis road. Heavy Russian artillery and small-arms fire was spraying the area with shrapnel as they landed. A passing vehicle was commandeered to take them to Hitler's shelter, where Greim received first aid for his shattered foot.

There they were told of Nazi Reichsmarshall and Luftwaffe-Chief Hermann Goering's 'betrayal' in trying to broker a separate peace with the Allies. Greim and Reitsch begged Hitler to be allowed to remain in the bunker, and die with him if need be. Hitler consented. Later that first evening, Hitler called Reitsch to his room and handed her two vials of poison, one for herself and one for Greim.

However, Hitler still seemed to hold out hope of a German Army breakthrough from the south. He talked of little else, and on the 28th and 29th he was mentally planning the tactics that General Wenck, in charge of what was left of the army, might use in freeing Berlin.

At one-thirty on the morning of 30 April, Hitler came to Greim's room and said, 'Our only hope is Wenck and to make his entry possible we must call up every available aircraft to cover his approach.'

Hitler ordered Greim to return to Rechlin and muster as many planes as he could with the task of destroying the positions from which the Russians were preparing to launch their attack on the Chancellery.

Thirty minutes after Hitler had given the order, Reitsch and Greim left the shelter. Outside the city was aflame and heavy small-arms fire was already plainly audible a short distance away. SS troops brought up a small armoured vehicle, which took the two to where an Arado 96 plane was hidden near the Brandenburg Gate. The sky was filled with the thunder of shells, some of which landed so close that their vehicle was severely knocked about.

Reitsch later claimed that she was certain that it was the last plane available. The broad street leading from the Brandenburg Gate was to be used for take-off. Just over 1,300 feet of un-cratered pavement was available as runway. The take-off was made under a hail of Russian fire and as the plane rose to rooftop level it was picked up by countless searchlights and at once bracketed in a barrage of shelling.

Explosions tossed the craft like a feather, but only a few splinters hit the plane. Reitsch circled to about 20,000 feet, from where she could see a sea of flames beneath. The destruction of Berlin she later described as stark and fantastic.

Heading north, in 50 minutes they reached Rechlin Airport near Mecklenburg, where the landing was again made through a screen of Russian fighter craft.

But Hitler's last mad fling proved to be a delusion. General Wenck's army had long been destroyed or captured and capitulation was soon announced. Reitsch and Greim were soon in the custody of the American military authorities. Greim was taken to Salzburg, prior to being taken on to Germany as a prisoner of war, but committed suicide with Hitler's poison capsule on the night of 24 May.

Held for eighteen months by the American military after the war, Reitsch was interrogated and then released. She died in 1979 of a massive heart attack at the age of 67.

BRICKS AWAY!

BURMA, INDIA 1945

In April 1945, 436 (Tactical Airlift) Transport Squadron of the Canadian Air Force (Motto: 'We carry the load') was ordered to move operations from Akyab Island in the Bay of Bengal, down the Burmese (now Myanmar) coast to Ramree Island. The move was necessary to maintain supplies to the British 14th Army, which was advancing on the Japanese. Ramree had been shelled and extensively damaged and the instructions were to fly a load of bricks there so that the cooks could build ovens to serve the squadron's mess needs.

A C-47 'Gooney Bird', an aerial 'workhorse' of a plane, was transporting the bricks but, soon after take-off, the pilot found that he was having problems gaining altitude. Quite obviously it had been seriously overloaded. At this point, the co-pilot spotted a Japanese seaplane beached on a small island below. It was a perfect target!

They performed a few low passes over it, during which they pushed out as many bricks as they could. There was no sign of life around the enemy aircraft and it seems doubtful that any lasting damage was done – but it's certainly the only bombing raid ever carried out with bricks!

LITTLE BOY

HIROSHIMA, JAPAN 1945

In the summer of 1945, Colonel Paul Tibbets and his crew lifted off from Wendover, Nevada in a B-29 bomber named the *Enola Gay* (after Tibbets' mother) on their way to Tinian Island, in the Western Pacific Ocean. From there, they proceeded on to Hiroshima, Japan and at 8.15 a.m., 6 August, bombardier Thomas Ferebee released an atomic bomb, destroying the city and marking the beginning of the end of World War II.

For three years, hundreds of scientists and technicians had worked in the utmost secrecy at Los Alamos out in the desert of New Mexico to build the bomb. Originally the plan had been to drop it on Berlin, using Hitler's bunker as the target. But because the war in Europe had ended, it had been decided to drop it on Japan.

The crew for the mission was selected very carefully. Their training was so discreet and compartmentalised that they didn't even discuss it between themselves. They were ordered to ask no questions and they were sworn to secrecy. Their phones were tapped and their mail censored.

It wasn't until the flight was one hour away from Hiroshima on that fateful day that the crew were told that they were about to drop the world's first atomic bomb. Tibbets was carrying a sealed packet of suicide pills to be used by the crew in the event of capture if the plane was shot down. If anyone refused, he was to be shot. Co-pilot Robert Lewis, by contrast, carried a packet of condoms!

At 8.14 a.m. they all put on Polaroid goggles to protect their eyes from the ensuing glare. A minute later, the *Enola Gay*'s bomb doors snapped open and the world's first atomic bomb dropped clear of its restraining hook. Suddenly over 9,000 pounds lighter, the plane lurched upwards 100 feet.

Forty-three seconds later, having plunged nearly six miles, the atomic bomb (nicknamed 'Little Boy' – a reference to President Roosevelt) exploded over Hiroshima. On board, nobody spoke as a strange glow illuminated the instrument panel on the cockpit. Then came the shock wave, created by air so compressed that it seemed to 'take on a solid, physical shape' as it smashed against the plane. Slowly, a huge black mushroom over a mile wide developed beneath them – the base was shot through with flames: Hiroshima was perishing beneath it.

Eighty thousand of the estimated 320,000 civilians and soldiers in the city died. One hundred and eight of Hiroshima's doctors died along with 1,654 nurses. Only three of the city's 55 hospitals survived. Sixty-two thousand other buildings out of a total of 90,000 were destroyed.

During much of the flight, Lewis spent his time writing a diary on a notebook strapped to his knee. When Tibbets had asked him what he was doing, he replied, 'Writing my memoirs.' When told he wasn't allowed to do that, Lewis merely shrugged and went on writing. In 1971 he would sell his diary for $37,000. In the diary, Lewis had apparently written, 'My God, what have we done' at the moment of detonation. Years later, however, he confessed that he had actually written, 'Gee, look at the sonofabitch go!' Only when the *Enola Gay* had returned to base and Tibbets saw what Lewis had written, did he tell him to change it to something more appropriate.

When the *Enola Gay* landed back at Tinian Island, the crew were greeted by General Spaatz, who decorated Tibbets with the Distinguished Service Cross and the other crew members with Air Medals. Tibbets handed over his suicide pills to a doctor. Robert Lewis flushed his packet of condoms down a toilet.

Lewis later admitted that he'd envisaged he and the crew being feted as heroes. Instead they soon found themselves surrounded by controversy. When they returned to the United States, they found themselves bombarded with hate mail, and even death threats.

The money Lewis received from selling his diary paid for marble from which he began to sculpt religious motifs. His most famous was of a mushroom cloud. He called it 'The Divine Wind Over Hiroshima'.

Over the past half-century, some of the crew have returned to the city to take part in the annual commemoration celebrations, but Lewis never did. For him it was, 'just a job of work. I helped make the world a safer place. Nobody has dared launch an atomic bomb since then. That is how I want to be remembered. The man who helped to do that.'

FALLING DOWN THE EMPIRE STATE

NEW YORK, USA 1945

At 9.40 a.m., on Saturday, 28 July 1945, as workers went about their business in the Catholic War Relief Office on the 79th floor of the Empire State Building, a B-25 Mitchell bomber crashed right into them at 200 miles per hour. The impact reportedly tore off the bomber's wings while one engine was catapulted through the Empire State Building, emerging on the opposite side and crashing through the roof of a neighbouring building. The second engine and part of the bomber's landing gear fell through an elevator shaft. Its fuel tanks exploded, engulfing the 79th floor in flames. The fire was extinguished in forty minutes.

Lieutenant Colonel William F Smith Jr, a decorated veteran of World War II and experienced pilot, had been flying the twin-engine bomber from his home in Bedford, Massachusetts to Newark, New Jersey, but apparently lost his way in the dense fog that had enveloped Manhattan that Saturday morning in July. He had been scheduled to land at La Guardia Airport, and an air-traffic controller was guiding him towards his landing in New Jersey when Smith asked for and received permission to land in Newark instead. Flying past the Chrysler building he proceeded to bear right instead of left, and headed directly into the flight path of the Empire State Building.

A final last-minute attempt to rectify his mistake and climb the height of the building failed. The last words Smith spoke to the air-traffic controller were: 'At the present time, I can't see the top of the Empire State Building.'

Smith died in the crash, along with two other crew members. Eleven workers died in the Catholic War Relief Office, and at least two dozen people were injured.

Betty Lou Oliver was working as an elevator operator when the plane hit the building. She was badly burned, having been blown from her position on the 80th floor. Once she received first-aid treatment, she was put into another supposedly safe elevator in order to meet an ambulance waiting at the bottom. Unbeknown to rescue workers, however, the safety cables of this elevator had been cut when the plane penetrated the elevator shaft.

Witnesses heard what sounded like a gunshot as the cables snapped on the lift's descent. By freak coincidence, if the safety cables had worked as they should, the car would have automatically stopped at the 34th and 35th floors, which were known as blind hatches (meaning that there are no escape doors in the hatch), and would have forced rescue workers to spend considerable time breaking through layers of marble and concrete to get to her. Moreover, the car was on fire, which also could have meant Betty suffocating from smoke inhalation in the delay. However, once the cables snapped, the elevator car went into freefall and in a matter of seconds it had crashed to the basement.

Fortunately, the impact was cushioned by the broken cables, which had piled in a springlike spiral on the floor of the shaft. It is also thought that the narrow lift shaft served as a compressor for the air and therefore softened the blow.

Whatever the explanation when rescuers managed to cut through the mangled wreckage, they found Betty alive! The plunge of 75 storeys inside an elevator is currently the Guinness World Record for the longest elevator fall recorded!

MORSE CODE MYSTERY

SANTIAGO, CHILE 1947

On 2 August 1947, *Stardust*, a British civilian version of the wartime Lancaster bomber, took off from Buenos Aires Airport on a scheduled flight to Santiago. There were five crew members and six passengers on board, but *Stardust* never made it to Santiago. Instead it vanished without trace. One final strange Morse-code radio message – 'STENDEC' – was sent, after which, nothing more was heard from the plane.

Various questions were immediately posed: why did the plane crash without warning? Why was it so far from its planned route across the mountains? What was the meaning of the last mysterious message – 'STENDEC'? And, perhaps most mysteriously, why did the wreckage elude discovery for so long? For despite an immediate massive search of the Andes mountains, no trace of the plane was found for 53 years!

Early in 2000, however, the plane was discovered sitting on a glacier high up in the Andes, more than 31 miles from the area where it had last been reported. In February of that year, the Argentine army arranged a major expedition to visit the crash site beneath the massive Tupangato peak (22,310 feet). Their aim was to bring back the human remains found at the site so that an attempt could be made at identifying them. The expedition also offered crash investigators a unique opportunity to see if they could finally explain what had happened to the ill-fated plane.

The plane's main wheels were discovered, one still fully blown up alongside one of *Stardust*'s Rolls-Royce engines.

Damage to the nearby propeller indicated that the engine had been working normally at the time of the crash. The wreckage ultimately offered no real clues to explain why the crash had happened, though. A few human remains were discovered – a hand, parts of a torso half-buried in ice, fragments of hair – poignant reminders that this was, above all, a human tragedy.

The air-crash investigators therefore focused on the mystery of why the plane had not been found for so many years. Their analysis led them to suspect that the answer could lie with the glacier the wreckage was lying on. A glacial specialist in Mendoza suggested that if the plane had crashed on the upper part of the glacier it would have been gradually buried year by year by snowfall, until it became a part of the glacier itself. It would then have travelled downhill with the glacier under the influence of gravity. Eventually, it would have reached a warmer zone, and here the ice would start to melt. Gradually, out of the melting ice, came the remains of *Stardust*. She had been buried inside the glacier for more than fifty years!

The investigation then turned its attention to finding out why the plane been more than fifty miles off course when it crashed. How could a highly experienced crew make such a massive error? The team focused on a meteorological phenomenon that was virtually unknown in 1947 – the 'jet stream'. This high-altitude wind can blow at more than 100 miles an hour but, in 1947, very few planes flew high enough to encounter it. *Stardust* was one of the exceptions.

On the day of the flight, bad weather over the Andes could have persuaded the crew to fly close to the plane's maximum altitude, so they could fly above some of the weather conditions and above the mountains. *Stardust's* superior performance should have guaranteed its safety. But in fact, it could have been the decision to fly high that was at the root of the disaster.

Unknown to the crew, they were flying straight into the jet stream and, because of the bad weather, they couldn't see the ground, so they had no way of knowing that the jet stream was dramatically slowing them down. It meant that although the crew's calculations showed they had crossed the Andes, in fact the jet stream's powerful wind meant they were still on the wrong side of the mountains. So when Stardust began its descent, rather than being above Santiago Airport, it was on a collision course with Mount Tupangato!

The jet stream finally explained the reason for the massive navigational error and, therefore, the reason for the crash. But the investigators were still unable to explain one final mystery – the last radio message: STENDEC. It has been pointed out that STENDEC is an anagram of 'descent'. There have been suggestions that the crew might have been suffering from hypoxia (lack of oxygen), because the Lancaster was unpressurised and the plane was flying at 24,000 feet, which might have led the radio operator to scramble the message. Other explanations for the appearance of an anagram in an otherwise routine message included a dyslexic radio operator and/or receiver in Santiago, and playfulness on behalf of *Stardust*'s radio operator!

It seems clear, however, that STENDEC is not what the Morse-code message was meant to say. The word is meaning-less, and trying to use it as an acronym or an abbreviation yields little by way of explanation. It also seems clear that *Stardust*'s radio operator was not anticipating a crash, otherwise he would not have repeated the message three times. And why not use SOS, the internationally accepted distress signal?

Fiddling with Morse code seems to offer the best chance of getting close to an understanding of the message. But in the absence of a new clue, the truth as to what that final enigmatic radio message was intended to convey will probably never be known for sure.

THE GOOSE HAS LIFTED!

During World War II, shipyards across America were running at full production but enemy submarines were sinking Allied vessels nearly as fast as they could be built. Something had to be done.

The idea for an airship that could fly when necessary over danger might be the answer. Henry Kaiser, head of one of the largest shipbuilding firms of the time, enlisted the help of Howard Hughes, who was known as an innovator in aircraft construction and design. Between them they developed the idea of the HK-1 flying boat. This was its official name, bearing the initials of the principals in the project, but to most people it's always just been known as *Spruce Goose*. This was because Hughes, in order to meet wartime restrictions on steel, decided to build his aircraft out of wood mainly of birch, but also of spruce. It was laminated with plastic and covered with fabric.

The difficulties in constructing such a huge wooden frame (it had a wingspan of 320 feet and was powered by eight giant propeller engines), however, were considerable. What's more, Hughes would prove to be a demanding taskmaster during the period of development and construction. His attention to detail and insistence that everything on the new plane be nearly perfect, was largely responsible for both the beauty of the finished product and its not being ready to fly until after the war had ended! In the end, development of the *Spruce Goose* cost a phenomenal $23 million!

The timing of completion and final cost brought Hughes and the project under the critical eye of the post-war Congress. One senator grudgingly referring to the plane as 'The flying lumberyard' and Hughes was called to Washington DC in November 1947 to defend both the project and himself.

As if to demonstrate that he hadn't defrauded the government, Hughes, who always test-piloted his own planes, flew back to California during a break in the hearings to conduct a taxiing test for the HK-1 in Long Beach Harbour. During the test, the *Spruce Goose* actually took off and flew for about a mile in less than a minute!

Thousands of onlookers who had come to watch the aircraft simply taxi on the water were amazed when Hughes lifted his wooden behemoth 70 feet above the water and flew for several hundred feet before landing. It would be the only time the plane would ever be airborne.

This event, whether intended or not, put a halt to critics of the project and served as the finale for this gigantic aircraft – the project was dead. Although ruffled by the intense questioning he had endured, the 'flight' had vindicated Hughes and the project. The *Spruce Goose* was put into storage and remained hidden from public view, carefully preserved, until after Hughes's death in April 1976.

Why did Hughes never fly the plane again? Some said he was afraid to, but the more likely explanation is that there was no reason to continue. The war was long over. The need for big seaplanes had evaporated. Wood construction was obviously a dead end. Even before the flight Hughes admitted that the plane was too large to be economical. Claiming there were still research lessons to be learned, he stubbornly kept the work going until around 1952. But he became distracted by other ventures and his attention wandered from the *Goose*.

Nevertheless, Hughes, who became increasingly eccentric and withdrawn after 1950, refused to neglect what he saw as his greatest achievement in the aviation field. From 1947 until his death in 1976, he kept the *Spruce Goose* prototype ready for flight in an enormous, climate-controlled hangar at a cost of $1 million a year.

THE HOST WITH A GHOST

DALKEITH, SCOTLAND 1947

Ben Bell had been a fighter pilot during World War II and had seen a lot of action. After the war had ended, he retired from the services and lived comfortably as a civilian. In 1947, he was invited to stay with a friend who owned a large house in Dalkeith, near Edinburgh.

After dinner on the first evening the men retired to the drawing room with a box of cigars and a bottle of brandy. The conversation soon turned to the recent war in Europe. Ben was an excellent raconteur and his friend enjoyed his hair-raising account of life in combat. Hours later they eventually bade each other goodnight and went to bed.

After a time, Ben awoke. Needing to relieve himself he set off down the corridor and turned left into what he thought was the bathroom. Instead, he was surprised to find himself in a very comfortable, spacious lounge. Sitting in one of the armchairs was a rather distinguished-looking gentleman wearing a smoking jacket and slippers. He bade Ben sit down – 'Sorry I missed your stories earlier, old chap. I'd have loved to have heard them. Shot a few Germans down myself, you know!'

For twenty minutes or so the two men shared a whisky and exchanged stories, although whenever Ben tried to get the man to be specific about his wartime exploits the old pilot refused to be drawn. Tired, Ben eventually excused himself and, after finding the real bathroom, returned to bed.

The next morning, at breakfast, Ben inquired why the old pilot he'd spoken to in the early hours wasn't joining them. No one knew who he was talking about. Insistent, he took the curious entourage up the stairs and confidently opened the door he'd walked through the previous evening. He expected to see the lounge he'd sipped whisky in earlier but, instead, found himself staring into a broom cupboard.

Ben's host looked disturbed and took the guests back downstairs. He explained to Ben that formerly there had been an extra wing to the house, which had been pulled down. Where the broom cupboard now stood had once been the entrance to a lounge that was always used by his host's grandfather, who had been a World War I fighter pilot. Ben was then shown a group photograph of a few men. 'Is the man you chatted with in that photograph?' 'Yes, that's him there,' Ben answered, recognising immediately the man he had met the previous night. His host concluded, 'Well then, it looks like you've been talking to my grandfather. He died just two years ago.'

CROYDON GHOSTS

LONDON, ENGLAND 1947

A completely new St Paul's Church now stands proudly on the Roundshaw housing estate, on the edge of Wallington, Surrey. Rededicated on 25 January 2003, it replaced an earlier one built in 1980, which had been known as 'The Propeller Church' because of its striking cross, made from an aircraft propeller. The propeller cross has been re-erected on the new church – but why a propeller in the first place? Because the housing estate the church served was built on the old Croydon aerodrome, famous for its role in World War II and subsequently as the world's first international airport.

However, there are other remnants from the aerodrome's flying days that remain – though somewhat less acceptable from a Christian point of view. No less than three specific hauntings have been (and continue to be) experienced in various sectors of the estate – manifestations closely linked to its aviation past.

The most impressive is that of three ghostly nuns seen by various people in an area that was formerly a part of one of the runways of the original aerodrome. It has been established that three nuns, Mother Superior Eugen Jousselot and Sisters Helen Lester and Eugene Martin of the Congregation des Filles de la Sagasse, were three of twelve passengers killed when a Spencer Airways Dakota crashed during a snowstorm in January 1947. The plane was bound for Salisbury and collided on the runway with another aircraft returning to Czechoslovakia. One of the ghost's witnesses was so distressed at seeing the figure of a nun in her sitting room in 1976 that she

189

moved out of her house, though the phantoms are normally seen on the road.

The second ghostly visitation is the sound of community singing that can be heard occasionally from the main boiler house that serves the estate. It was here, during World War II, that a bomb destroyed the canteen while a number of pilots and their friends were having 'an enjoyable social'.

Thirdly, early morning travellers have seen a ghostly motorcyclist driving rapidly, but silently, along the main road and, on turning towards the boiler house, vanishing. It was at this spot that a fighter pilot was killed early in the 1940s.

FLYING SAUCERS ARRIVE

MOUNT RAINIER, USA 1947

The name 'flying saucer' was first coined in 1947 and arose from a misquote in an interview given by one Kenneth Arnold. He was describing something he had seen while flying his private plane near Mount Rainier in Washington on 24 June, at around 3.00 p.m.

At about 9,000 feet, a flash of light caught Arnold's eye. He turned and saw a procession of nine objects flying from north to south in front of his plane. They were flat and heel-shaped, very shiny, and they moved erratically. He later recalled in a TV interview: 'These objects more or less fluttered like they were, oh, I'd say boats on very rough water or very rough air of some type, and when I described how they flew, I said that they flew in the same way one takes a saucer and throws it across the water. Most of the newspapers misunderstood and misquoted that too. They said that I said that they were saucer-like; I said that they flew in a saucer-like fashion.' Whatever the exact term he used, he estimated their size at about two-thirds that of a DC-4, a large, four-engined passenger airliner, and he calculated their speed at over 1,500 miles per hour by timing their travel between two mountain peaks.

Arnold was the owner of the Great Western Fire Control Supply Company and flew his small plane from town to town to demonstrate his fire-control equipment. He was also a member of the sheriff's 'aerial posse' of Ada County, Idaho and a relief US marshal. He had been returning that day from a business trip in his plane when he heard that a C-46 marine

191

transport plane had gone missing in the Yakima, Washington area. He immediately flew to lend what assistance he could to the search for the downed plane.

When Arnold landed at Yakima, after telling some other pilots about what he had seen, he went to Pendleton, Oregon, to make a report to the FBI. The FBI office being closed, he told his story to the *East Oregonian* newspaper instead. Some months later, his story was sensationalised in the pulp magazine *Amazing Stories* in an article he wrote himself. And the rest is history.

Sightings like Arnold's – and even more fantastic stories, including actual contact with occupants of the saucers, as well as rumours that the US government had salvaged a crashed alien spaceship – flourished in the late 1940s. In response, the US government created a group to investigate these reports. Operating under several names, the best known being 'Project Blue Book', the air force continued to investigate UFO reports for some twenty years or more.

Arnold, a Republican, ran unsuccessfully for the post of Lieutenant Governor of Idaho in 1962.

THE DISAPPEARANCE OF FLIGHT 19

FORT LAUDERDALE, USA 1947

Flight 19 originated at the US Naval Air Station in Fort Lauderdale, Florida. On 5 December 1947, Five TBM Avenger torpedo bombers carrying fourteen men took off at roughly 2.10 p.m. on a routine navigational training mission. Led by instructor Lieutenant Charles Taylor, the assignment was to fly a three-legged triangular route with a few bombing practice runs over the sea.

At 3.45 p.m., Fort Lauderdale tower received a call from the flight but, instead of requesting landing instructions, the flight leader sounded confused and worried, saying that he couldn't see land and that they seemed to be off course. When the flight-control tower asked for his position, there was silence.

The tower personnel could see no sign of the planes in the clear Florida afternoon. Eventually, the flight leader announced, 'We cannot be sure where we are. Repeat: Cannot see land.'

The tower then lost contact with the flight for about ten minutes. But when contact was regained, it wasn't the voice of the flight leader that was heard but those of the crew – sounding confused and disoriented, and, according to one of the tower personnel, 'more like a bunch of boy scouts lost in the woods than experienced airmen flying in clear weather': 'We can't find west. Everything is wrong. We can't be sure of any direction. Everything looks strange, even the ocean.' After yet another delay, the tower operator learned, to his surprise, that the leader had handed over his command to another pilot for no apparent reason.

193

Twenty minutes later, the new leader called the tower, his voice trembling and bordering on hysteria. 'We can't tell where we are ... everything is ... can't make out anything. We think we may be about 225 miles northeast of base...'

For a few moments the pilot rambled incoherently before uttering the last words ever heard from Flight 19: 'It looks like we are entering white water ... We're completely lost.'

A thirteen-man Martin Mariner PBM flying boat was immediately dispatched from Miami to search for the missing airmen. It was a huge craft loaded with electronic tracking gear and carried enough fuel to remain airborne for 24 hours, but it had to turn back when its antenna iced over. A second flying boat took off from the Banana River Naval Air Station. By 7.47 p.m., after a few routine transmissions, it too fell silent. In a few short hours, the Bermuda Triangle (an area of sea between Bermuda, Puerto Rico and Florida) had apparently swallowed up six planes and 27 trained men.

Coast Guard and Navy ships and aircraft combed the area for the six aircraft. They found a calm sea, clear skies, middling winds of up to 40 miles per hour and nothing else. For five days almost 250,000 square miles of the Atlantic Ocean and Gulf were searched. Yet not a flare was seen; not an oil slick, life raft or telltale piece of wreckage was ever found.

Various rational explanations have been put forward for what had happened. In 1945, pilots flying over water had to rely on compasses and knowing how long they'd been flying in a particular direction, and at what speed, to judge their position. After the bombing run on this particular day, Taylor apparently got hopelessly lost. Both of the compasses on his plane were malfunctioning and transcripts of in-flight communications suggest he wasn't wearing a watch. The Navy's final report surmised that Taylor thought he was west of the Florida panhandle – a region which includes the sixteen westernmost counties in the State – when actually he was east of it when he got lost. Consequently, he refused to fly due west, which would have brought him to the shore from which they all had taken off. Radio communication with Florida coastal stations was being interrupted constantly by broadcast radio in

Cuba. Even after repeated urgings from flight controllers in Florida, Taylor refused to change to the emergency radio frequency for fear of losing contact with the other four planes, even though they had been lost so long they were running out of fuel. Taylor eventually formulated a plan; as soon as the first plane's fuel level dipped below ten gallons, all five planes were to ditch at sea.

The Avenger or 'Iron Bird' as it was sometimes known, was an extremely rugged plane. Pilots sometimes called them Grumman ironworks as they weighed more than 10,000 pounds empty. When ditched, the Avenger would go down hard and fast. The possibility of anyone surviving a landing in high seas was slim, the chance of surviving the night in the cold waters in heavy seas was nil; the likelihood of the wreckage making a quick descent to the bottom was high.

Ultimately, the official report on the disappearance of Flight 19 blamed pilot error. Taylor's family protested and, after several reviews, the verdict was changed to 'causes or reasons unknown'.

Perhaps this ambiguous conclusion is the reason why the disappearances have subsequently been attributed to the machinations of enormous sea monsters, giant squid, or even extraterrestrials. Alien abductions, the existence of a mysterious third dimension created by unknown beings, and ocean flatulence – the ocean suddenly spewing great quantities of trapped methane – have also been suggested as culprits.

Only by discovering the downed planes might the truth be discovered, but searching for wreckage in such a vast area would be like trying to find a needle in a haystack. What's more, US Navy officials have estimated that more than 130 aircraft litter the sea bottom in the area of the Bermuda Triangle – the area was a virtual graveyard for TBM Avenger torpedo bombers.

Then the unexpected happened. The worst national air tragedy in United States history occurred in 1986. On 19 January, Space Shuttle *Challenger* exploded moments after lift-off from Cape Canaveral. The debris fell into the ocean at about the same area many people believed the lost Avengers to be. Quite by accident, the underwater search for the *Challenger* wreckage uncovered a plane submerged at a depth of 400 feet of water. Believing the wreckage was that of a twin engine DC-3, the *Challenger* searchers ignored it.

But one salvage expert didn't, and in July 1990, using a submersible, he dived on the wreckage. The Avenger has several distinctive features to it, and he hoped to be able to spot any or all of them. One was the bomb bay located under the fuselage, another was the wheel well under the wing, and the most unusual feature was a balled turret behind the pilot, which protected the gunner. Even though the plane found was upside down and partially buried in the sand, all three distinctive features were plainly visible. The submerged plane was an Avenger.

After recovering various parts of the plane it was discovered that several serial numbers partially matched those of one of Flight 19's planes, though the salt corrosion was too severe for positive identification.

The weirder possibilities remain, therefore. Why did both of Lieutenant Taylor's compasses fail so shortly after pre-flight checkout? And how did the airmen become convinced that the first leg of their flight had taken them so far south rather than east? Even with the most modern technology and suppositions, the evidence does not explain how a planned two-hour training flight became a wandering, five-hour flight to nowhere.

THE CANDY BOMBER

BERLIN, GERMANY 1948

Following World War II, the Allies – the US, the UK, France and Russia – agreed to split occupied Germany and its capital city, Berlin, into four sectors. The Russians had decimated the heavily defended Berlin in a series of street battles that cost an estimated 200,000 Russian casualties. Intent on exacting revenge on the Germans, they then blocked off outside access to Berlin and, by 1947, the German inhabitants were starving.

The only access to the city open to US forces was through a narrow air corridor into Berlin's Templehof Airport. The Russians had threatened to shoot down any planes that strayed from that corridor. The Cold War had begun. A constant stream of C47 and C54 cargo planes flew in and out of the narrow Templehof corridor transporting water, coal, food, tools and medicine to supply the inhabitants.

A US pilot, Gail Halvorsen, watched the children of Berlin scrambling about in the rubble, some barefoot; it made him think of his own family at home. So Halvorsen came up with an idea to make their lives a little more bearable. He and his crew collected their candy rations and those of their friends and began fashioning tiny parachutes out of handkerchiefs with which to drop the candy to the children as the planes flew in on their approach.

When his superiors found out about what he was doing, he was at first reprimanded. But on reflection, they relented – after all, the exercise was clearly beneficial to the children. Halvorsen was encouraged to continue.

There was an extraordinary response to the candy bombing. A little boy, whom Halvorsen later met as a 60-year-old man in Berlin, explained its role in raising morale. He said he was ten years old during the blockade and, one cloudy day on his way to school, suddenly down came a parachute and landed at his feet – with a fresh Hershey chocolate bar from America attached! Needless to say, he was astonished at the sight – but it was not the chocolate itself that was important. The act signified that someone outside the blockaded city knew he was there. It wasn't chocolate, it was hope. He said that applied to everyone in the city.

The operation was dubbed 'Little Vittles' (victuals) and Halvorsen became known as the 'Candy Bomber' to the GIs and as 'Uncle Wiggly Wings' to the German children, because he'd wiggle his plane's wings as he came in, to alert the kids about an imminent sweet drop.

The story was soon picked up by the press in the USA. Once the American people became aware of the extent of the suffering of the Berliners, a heartfelt pouring of aid began to flow. Along with the necessities for survival, now clothes, shoes and toys were being flown in. Some of the parachutes were even constructed with donated silk scarves.

By January of 1949 Lieutenant Halvorsen had air-dropped more than 250,000 parachutes loaded with candy on Berlin, bringing a little joy to the 100,000 children of the city during the Russian blockade.

On the fiftieth anniversary of the Berlin Airlift in May 1998, 77-year-old retired Colonel Halvorsen took to his controls once again and dropped 10,000 tiny parachutes over the now-united city.

CHASING BALLOONS?

KENTUCKY, USA 1948

On 7 January 1948, Thomas Mantell, the pilot of a P-51 Mustang fighter, was killed while pursuing an unidentified flying object near Godman Air Force Base, Kentucky. His is considered by some researchers to be the first human death that can be attributed to a UFO.

The incident began at 1.20 p.m., when the tower at Godman Army Air Force Base at Fort Knox, Kentucky, received a call from the Kentucky State Highway Patrol, who said they were taking calls about a UFO. The object in question was described as huge metallic sphere with a red-and-white light on the bottom, which was drifting across a large area of Kentucky.

It was then reported visually from the control tower of Godman Air Force Base.

For about an hour and 25 minutes, dozens of people, including base commander Colonel Hix, watched as the UFO seemed to hang motionless in the southwestern sky.

Three planes from the Kentucky National Guard were asked to investigate, Captain Mantell, piloting a P-51, among them. Around 2.40 p.m. they began climbing in the direction of the UFO in an attempt to intercept it.

At 15,000 feet, Mantell radioed the control tower that the UFO was 'metallic and tremendous in size' and 'appears to be moving about half my speed'. With the UFO still above him, he reported he would continue to climb.

All three aircraft reached 22,000 feet, at which point Lieutenant A W Clements and Lieutenant B A Hammond turned back. The oxygen equipment of one of the fighters had failed and military regulations required that oxygen be used above 14,000 feet.

Mantell, however, who had no oxygen equipment on his aircraft, continued upwards. The last that anyone saw of him, he was still heading toward the 'UFO', but he made no more radio calls to either his wingmen or the control tower at Godman. By 3.15 p.m. everyone had lost both radio and visual contact with him.

Some time later, William C Mayes, a resident of rural Franklin, 'heard a funny noise as if [an aircraft pilot] were diving down and pulling up, but [the plane that he saw] wasn't, it was just circling. After about three circles the aeroplane started into a power dive slowly rotating. It started to make a terrific noise, ever increasing, as it descended. It exploded halfway between where it started to dive and the ground. No fire was seen.'

When firemen dragged the body of the partially decapitated Mantell from the wreckage, they noticed that his shattered wristwatch had stopped at 3.18 p.m.

An accident investigation began immediately. Crash investigators thought it most likely that Mantell had blacked out at about 25,000 feet, while his P-51 continued up to 30,000 feet, lost power, levelled off, and then circled before going into a power dive.

While it appears Captain Mantell passed out and crashed due to a lack of oxygen, the question as to what he was chasing and the circumstances surrounding his crash remain confused. There were said to be mystery wounds on Mantell's body, that the aircraft was riddled with nearly microscopic holes; outside forces were rumoured to have knocked the plane from the sky.

Eventually, the established official line was that Mantell, a World War II combat pilot veteran, and recipient of the Distinguished Flying Cross for valour, had been climbing past safe limits – and unwittingly chasing the planet Venus! However, this theory failed to account for many other aspects of the case, including Mantell's reference to a very large, metallic object. After researchers demonstrated that the planet Venus was only 33 degrees above the horizon at the time, and at only half its maximum brightness, the air force retracted its original statement and claimed that Captain Mantell had been chasing a US Navy Skyhook balloon, although they were unable to locate any records of a balloon being launched at that time.

That might have been because it was then part of a secret Navy project about which none of the witnesses would have known. At least two separate observers in Kentucky and Tennessee on the afternoon in question had seen what they first took to be a UFO; on closer telescopic observation, they saw it was a balloon.

Captain Mantell's remains were brought back to Louisville and buried at Zachary Taylor National Cemetery. On 19 September 2001, the Simpson County Historical Society unveiled a historical marker in honour of Thomas F Mantell, Jr.

GLASS COFFIN

COLLINSVILLE, USA 1948

On 18 October 1948, First Lieutenant Eugene 'Gene' Erickson of Collinsville, Illinois, and two other airmen died when their C-54 Skymaster crashed trying to land at Rhein-Main Air Base in Germany. The three were among the 31 Americans killed between 24 June 1948 and 30 September 1949, during the Berlin Airlift.

After Erickson's wife had been informed, the local newspaper made the announcement of his death. She heard nothing further for quite some time. For reasons that still aren't clear, Erickson's body was not sent home right away. In fact, it wasn't until New Year's Eve that his wife received word that the body was on its way to Collinsville.

Mrs Erickson told the funeral home that she didn't want anything done to her husband's body until she had seen it, although the funeral home and her family tried to talk her out of her decision. Erickson's father also insisted on there being a closed casket as, with a heart condition, he felt he could not stand seeing his son. But Mrs Erickson was adamant – her husband would not be buried until she had seen his body.

When she finally met the casket with its military escort at the Collinsville train station, she was told by the escort that they were to deliver the casket to the funeral director, who would then call for her. When at last she got inside the funeral home, the lid was up – and she couldn't believe her eyes. 'It was just as if he had laid down and died,' she commented later. 'They had sealed him in glass! The upper half of the coffin was all sealed in glass and he had been embalmed!'

Over the succeeding years, she managed to piece parts of the story together from records and by talking to others involved in the airlift. Her husband had received some kind of injection to preserve his body and been embalmed and prepared to conceal any damage from the crash. The East German authorities had then held a funeral ceremony for him.

'I don't know why just him,' Mrs Erickson said. 'But when we went [to Germany] for the tenth anniversary, no one would believe me, that they held a funeral for my husband and then shipped him home in a glass coffin.'

THE MURDER OF STANLEY SETTY

ESSEX MARSHES, ENGLAND 1949

Sulman Seti was born in Baghdad of Jewish parents. After World War II, having changed his name to Stanley Setty, he became involved in various illegal activities, such as acquiring and selling stolen cars, and forging petrol coupons. His partner in crime was one Brian Donald Hume who, in 1941, had been invalided out of the RAF, suffering from meningitis. Ultimately, a quarrel broke out between the two of them, ostensibly because Setty had kicked Hume's dog. Setty was last seen on 4 October 1949, when he was known to have £1,000 in £5 notes in his possession.

Some weeks later, a farm labourer named Stanley Tiffin was shooting ducks at Tillingham, on the Essex marshes, when he found a large parcel floating in the water. Opening it, he found it to be the torso of a man. An examination revealed that the man had been killed by stab wounds and that it was Stanley Setty. His car was later found abandoned at St Pancras.

Newspaper reports of the crime soon covered all the front pages. As a result of the publicity, the police were contacted by the United Services Flying Club at Elstree, who said that a club member called Brian Douglas Hume had hired a plane to fly to Southend and been seen loading a large parcel into it. On arrival at Southend, however, there was no longer a parcel in the plane, although there was some damage to one of its windows. Further enquiries revealed that after the flight Hume had paid for a taxi from a roll of notes. Hume was arrested, but all the police could prove was that he had dumped the body –

they couldn't prove he had committed the murder.

Hume asserted that the parcels were being carried on behalf of smugglers, who had told him they contained a printing press for forged petrol coupons. He claimed that he had been asked to throw them out over the sea; the money was to pay for completing the task.

Police searched Hume's apartment (above a greengrocers' shop in the Finchley Road, just opposite Golders Green Station) and found blood under the floorboards of the hall and living room. Further investigation revealed a left-luggage ticket for Golders Green Station, which turned out to be for a blood-stained suitcase.

Hume then claimed that he'd found the blood in his flat and cleaned it up, assuming that Setty had been murdered by the smugglers, whom he named as three men called Greeny, Mac and The Boy.

At his subsequent trial for murder, the jury were unable to reach a verdict. Hume pleaded guilty to being an accessory to murder and was given a life sentence, for which he served twelve years' imprisonment.

On his release in 1958, Hume confessed to the murder, admitting that he had killed Setty during an argument at his apartment and describing the crime in a popular newspaper. He had murdered Setty, he said, with a Nazi SS dagger and, the same day, had dropped the head and legs into the English Channel from the aeroplane. The next day, managing to avoid both his wife and the cleaning lady, he asked a decorator to paint over the bloodstains on the wall and even asked the man to help him carry the parcel, which contained the torso, downstairs and into his car. This time, however, he misjudged the route of his flight and mistook the watery marshes for the Channel. The law of double jeopardy meant that he could not be tried again for the same crime, however.

Hume went on to commit bank robberies in England and Switzerland and was soon back in prison after he shot and killed a taxi driver in Switzerland in January 1959. This time, he received a life sentence with hard labour. In 1976, he was judged to be insane and was returned to Broadmoor Hospital in Berkshire, England.

A MURDER IN THE FAMILY

QUEBEC, CANADA 1949

As a young man, Albert Guay sold watches and jewellery on commission. When World War II broke out, he got a job at Canadian Arsenals Limited at St Malo. There he met his wife, Rita Morel. The arsenal closed in 1945 and Guay opened a jewellery and watch repair shop. By the late summer of 1949, however, he was facing severe personal and financial problems – his business wasn't going well, and the debts were piling up.

Guay was a jealous and possessive man, who nonetheless had a taste for extramarital affairs. He met seventeen-year-old Marie-Ange Robitaille, they began dating, and Guay, using the assumed name of Roger Angers, bought her an engagement ring.

When Rita found out, she confronted the pair in the Robitaille's living room. Guay then took Marie-Ange to Port Sept-Iles, where they lived together for a time, but eventually the young girl left him, citing his marriage as the reason.

Guay moved back with his wife and appeared to be attempting a reconciliation. In fact, he was putting together a plan he hoped would take care of his situation – to kill his wife and collect the insurance. He enlisted one-time girlfriend Marguerite Pitre and her brother, Genereux Ruest, who worked from his wheelchair as a clock maker in Guay's shop. Guay made a dynamite bomb and Ruest built a timer for it.

In September 1949, Guay asked Rita to travel to Baie-Comeau to pick up some jewels. Guay had to insist, because Rita balked at making the trip. Ultimately, she agreed to do her husband the favour.

On 9 September, Guay drove his wife to Quebec Airport, where he bought a $10,000 flight-insurance policy on her life as she boarded a CP Airlines flight for Baie-Comeau. Shortly before take-off, Marguerite Pitre arrived at the airport by taxi and air-freighted the package bomb to Baie-Comeau. Ruest had timed the device to explode over the St Lawrence River, from which evidence might never be recovered, but it detonated above deep woods, plunging the twin-engined DC-3 to earth and killing all 23 people aboard.

The insurance policy led police to Guay. As investigators closed in he became worried about leaving witnesses and persuaded Pitre to down a concoction of pills he had brewed. She survived the attempted poisoning, however, and when questioned by police in hospital admitted delivering a package to the airport for Guay, though she claimed she did not know what its contents were.

Guay went on trial in 1950. A jury quickly convicted him and he received the mandatory sentence of death by hanging. In the death cells, and hoping to save himself, he implicated Pitre and her brother as co-conspirators. His statement particularly damaged the defence of Pitre. Guay was hanged in 1951, Genereux Ruest in 1952. Marguerite Pitre, the last woman to be hanged in Canada, never wavered from her claim of innocence right up to her execution in 1953.

Author Roger Lemelin, a friend and neighbour of Guay, based his novel, *Le Crime d'Ovide Plouffe/A Murder in the Family* on the story. Denys Arcand turned the novel into a movie in 1984.

UNLUCKY 13TH AGAIN!

NORTHOLT, ENGLAND 1950

Twenty-six-year-old Susan Cramsie was the stewardess on a British European Airways Viking flight bound for Paris on the evening of 13 April 1950. As the plane crossed the French coast near Dieppe, she thought she smelled something acidic towards the rear of the plane. Before she had time to investigate, an explosion tore though the fuselage of the aircraft, leaving two large holes.

She later recorded the midair bomb in her diary as follows: 'Took off at 8pm for Paris – never got there!! Explosion in loo mid-Channel!'

Cramsie was badly injured in the explosion, and spent seven months in and out of hospital with shoulder, back and arm injuries. Such was the force of the explosion that the lining in her handbag was torn out, and the tobacco was separated from her cigarette papers. Passengers were unable to give her a relieving shot of morphine because the first-aid box was attached to the rear door, which was hanging off its hinges in midair!

The captain, Ian Harvey, 29 at the time, immediately suspected his plane had been struck by lightning and, with great skill, he regained control of the Viking, gradually turned it and landed back at Northolt Airport, with no loss of life. Already a decorated RAF war hero, he was later awarded a George Cross for his courage and skill.

Two days after the explosion, detectives from Scotland Yard were instructed to begin inquiries into an act of sabotage.

MI5 and MI6 were also involved. Police and aviation experts quickly eliminated lightning as the cause, concluding that a bomb – an 'infernal machine', as it was officially named – had been planted in the lavatory compartment, although they found no evidence of a detonator, or timing device, or even burns on the interior of the plane. Neither were they able to establish with any authority who might have planted it, or why.

The Scotland Yard investigation remained classified for more than half a century. Released by the National Archives in August 2005, the secret papers accuse a French passenger of making a suicide attempt – a theory made 'in the absence of any direct evidence'.

At the time, speculation as to the bomb's intended target was rife. One newspaper report suggested someone had a grudge against Cramsie, although attempted suicide on her part was ruled out when police concluded that she could not have concealed a bomb in her tight-fitting uniform.

The passenger list revealed a number of other intriguing potential targets: a member of Lord Montgomery's staff, a US special representative, a French engineer working in Indo-China. Interestingly, among the crew was the radio officer, Thomas Holmes, 33, who had been working with British South American Airways when two planes disappeared in the Bermuda Triangle.

However, suspicion finally lighted on the man in seat 30: Alfred Calmet, aged 52. He was the last person to visit the lavatory before the bomb went off and apparently spent several minutes there. Calmet was a petty con man with six convictions and had been involved in a deal to sell alcohol from Britain to the United States at the end of Prohibition.

Calmet claimed he had been on a day trip, visiting banks to arrange a deal selling barrels made on his French estate. Mysteriously, he had made an appointment to return to a bank the next morning, knowing he was already booked on a return flight that evening. The French police revealed that Calmet's wife had been having an affair with the son of the local mayor. And Mr Robine, his fellow passenger, confided that Calmet told him at Northolt after the explosion that he had recently insured his life for 10 million francs.

A police investigation concluded: 'The motive was suicide, contemplated because of impending financial troubles coupled with domestic unhappiness. There is his statement of new insurance policies to the value of 10 million francs, which would not be payable if suicide was proved. Opportunity exists in France to obtain explosives. By flying over the route in the morning Calmet would know the best time to carry out his plan.'

With no forensic evidence, nor eyewitnesses, Calmet was never charged. He made a fleeting return to London in August 1950 for single day. Police had him under surveillance but lost him in the early evening and he slipped out of the country before they could question him further.

Miss Cramsie, meanwhile, went on to become Chief Air Stewardess for BEA, and received £2,500 compensation for her injuries. She vowed, however, never to fly on the 13th of the month again.

ONE LUCKY MAN

KOREA 1952

On a bone-chilling, miserably windy day in 1952, in the middle of the Korean War, 400 feet above the snow-covered ground, Captain Fred C Seals, Jr, fell out of his aeroplane, a C-46 Commando. Improbably, he lived to tell the tale and, to this day, old men stop him and ask if it is true. In fact, he lived because he fell right back into the plane!

A 1944 graduate of Texas A&M University, Seals saw three wars from the 'front row' as a B-17 pilot over Germany during World War II, as a recalled pilot for the Korean War and as a cargo pilot flying out of Da Nang during the Vietnam War. But he will always be known for a mission he carried out in March 1952 in South Korea while trying to re-supply troops.

Seals was at the controls of the C-46 Commando. The wind, howling at fifty miles per hour and dropping the temperature below zero, pitched the twin-engine aeroplane up and down, back and forth, and kept blowing the supply pallets way off course as the crew threw them out of the side of the plane.

The crew got so sick they couldn't keep working. So Seals unstrapped his seatbelt, told the co-pilot to take over and went back to do it himself.

'The plane was bouncing fifteen, twenty feet at a time and fishtailing,' Seals remembered. 'I'm trying to hang on. Before the co-pilot could give the green light to drop the cargo, the plane dropped and fishtailed, and it went right out from under me.'

Seals remembers two thoughts he had very clearly as he looked below and saw only the ground – to watch out for the plane's horizontal stabiliser and to figure out which way North Korea was!

'Then I'm back in the plane on my hands and knees,' he continued. 'Now I'm disoriented.'

To this day, Seals is unsure how long he hung in the air, though it was obviously just a few seconds but 'long enough for me to orient myself'. He also isn't sure exactly how he ended up back in the plane, except to guess that it dropped and fishtailed again and 'scooped me up'.

The amazed crew told their commanders, who told air-force information officers, who in turn told reporters.

Seals is now 83, a retired colonel and wing commander who makes his home in Norman, Oklahoma. 'After the news got out, I got cards and letters from people all over the world, men I'd served with who wondered if I was the same Fred C Seals. There's many a time I've thought, "Why in the Sam Hill am I here?"' he reflected, only to answer: 'By the grace of God.'

NEVIL SHUTE AND THE PROPHECY OF THE COMETS

1953

Nevil Norway was one of the leading aeronautical engineers in Britain during the twenties and thirties, and a fellow of the Royal Aeronautical Society. When he began writing, in the twenties, he feared that a reputation as a writer of fiction might harm his engineering career. For this reason, he published his books under his two Christian names – Nevil Shute – and engineered under his 'real' name – Nevil Norway.

Shute produced a number of bestsellers, including *On the Beach* and *A Town Like Alice* and, in 1948, *No Highway* – which was about a new aeroplane called the Reindeer that mysteriously crashes in Canada. In the novel, a structural engineer, named Theodore Honey, is sent to investigate the crash. Honey has his own theory that Reindeers suffer a metal fatigue failure after about 1,400 hours in the air, but no one takes him seriously. Halfway across the Atlantic, Honey, who's pretty oblivious to his surroundings, discovers he's travelling in a Reindeer. A few questions reveal that this particular plane has been in service for just about 1,400 hours. Honey suddenly has to assume responsibility for saving 200 people who feel no need of being saved from anything. The book was later made into a film called *No Highway in the Sky*, starring Jimmy Stewart as Honey, and Marlene Dietrich.

The book was written while the de Havilland Comet was in its final stages of design. (It will be remembered that Comet was, along with Dasher and Prancer, one of Santa Claus's famous reindeer!). The Comet jet was put into service in 1952 but disaster struck three times after just one year of service.

Leaving Calcutta, one Comet disintegrated in a thunderstorm. When investigators couldn't find any other cause, they blamed the storm. Eight months later, a second Comet blew up in clear sky, 27,000 feet over the Island of Elba, off the coast of Italy. It was hard to recover much from the ocean, so that crash also went undiagnosed. Then a third Comet exploded over the Mediterranean, three months later. This time, the whole fleet was grounded.

A more intense search of the latest crash site finally yielded some wreckage, which showed the failure had occurred in the cabin area. The engineers then carried out a huge fatigue test on an actual Comet. They varied the cabin pressure hydraulically while they flexed the wings. After 3,000 pulsations, a crack appeared near a cabin window and quickly spread. The Comet's designers had overlooked stress concentrations at rivet holes near the windows.

The windows were redesigned, and a new safe Comet went into service in 1958.

How had Nevil Shute anticipated the Reindeer disaster? Perhaps he had simply followed his keen engineering instincts, which took him where real life eventually took the Comet.

THE MAD MAJOR FLIES UNDER A BRIDGE TOO FAR

LONDON, ENGLAND 1953

Christopher Draper was a gifted and courageous World War I fighter pilot. After obtaining an Aviator's Certificate in October 1913, he entered the Royal Naval Air Service in January 1914 and on 7 July 1917 he became the first person ever to engage an enemy aircraft over London when he entered what became an enormous 100-aircraft dogfight.

His nickname of 'The Mad Major' (in its early days the RAF used Army ranks) came about when, flying towards the front lines in France, Draper accidentally flew under a bridge while in full view of a large body of troops. The troops cheered so heartily that Draper repeated the stunt wherever possible.

After the war, Draper continued to fly as a stunt pilot at air shows and in motion pictures. In April 1919 he piloted the first flight of the British Aerial Transport Company's FK26s, the first plane specifically designed to carry passengers.

In 1930, however, as part of a protest over the way the government had treated war veterans, he set out on the first of a number of attempts to fly under all of London's bridges over the River Thames. Due to bad weather, he only managed to fly under two, but the following year, promoting a budding acting career as 'George Mannering', Draper succeeded in flying under them all.

In 1932, invited to participate in an 'Aces of the Air Tour' of Germany along with air aces from many nations, Draper was introduced to Chancellor Adolf Hitler and, as a result of his long-standing criticism of the British government's treatment of veterans, was listed by the Nazi Party as a potential sympathiser. After his return to England he was contacted and asked to spy for the Germans. He agreed but immediately informed MI6, who decided to use him as a double agent to feed false information to the Nazis, a situation that continued for four years until the Germans realised they were being duped.

In World War II Draper rejoined the RAF, commanding squadrons in West Africa and the Far East but saw relatively little action. After the war, however, he once again became upset at the government's treatment of veterans. In 1953 and now aged 61, he once again protested by flying under the Thames bridges from Waterloo to Kew – this time with a passenger in a plane with a 36-foot wingspan! He was arrested and charged with flying too low in an urban area.

Although he pleaded guilty to dangerous and low flying in contravention of the Air Navigation Order, 1949, Draper argued that there was 'more clearance under the bridges than in close-formation flying'. What's more, he asserted that if there had been engine failure he would have landed 'in the only safe landing place in London'. He also declared that it was a tragedy that, at the age of 61, and in full possession of his faculties, he was unable to find any sort of steady job.

He was given a conditional discharge and fined ten guineas but his protest worked. Soon afterwards, he was offered a contract with a motor firm!

BOMB KILLS MOTHER

DENVER, USA 1955

On 1 November 1955, a United Airlines Douglas DC-6B flight from Denver to Seattle crashed eleven minutes after take-off from Denver Colorado's Stapleton Airport bound for Portland, killing all 39 passengers and five crew members.

The plane had been travelling at several hundred miles per hour, when there was a loud bang followed by a gigantic blast that ripped the fuselage into a thousand pieces, sending debris, luggage and passengers tumbling into space. Since the fuel tanks were almost filled to capacity, an immense fireball was detonated, which enveloped the entire aircraft.

Just outside Denver city limits, local farmer Conrad Hopp was in his fields when he heard the loud noise and looked up. 'It sounded like a bomb went off,' he later told the press, 'I ran out and saw a big fire right over the cattle corral. I hollered back to my wife that she'd better call the fire department . . . then I turned around and it blew up in the air!' Other witnesses watched in horror as aircraft pieces fell from the sky, twisting and turning until they crashed into the distant plains.

Evidence eventually cast suspicion on a relative of one of the passengers. Jack Gilbert Graham was a petty criminal – a married father of two who managed a drive-in restaurant in Denver. Forensic experts determined that the explosion had been centred in a gift-wrapped parcel in luggage checked onto the jet by Daisie King, Graham's mother, who had died in the crash. She had been staying with the family in Denver, apparently unaware of the consuming hatred her son felt for her.

The principal motive for the bombing turned out, in fact, to be a claim for $37,500 worth of life-insurance money, from policies bought in vending machines by Graham in the airport just before take-off. (Flight insurance could be bought at airports back in the 1950s.)

According to the FBI, Graham said that he put together a bomb consisting of 25 sticks of commercial dynamite, two blaster caps, a timer with a maximum capability of 90 minutes and a small battery. He said that he wrapped up the device like a Christmas present and placed it in his mother's luggage just before she left the house for Stapleton. Having set the timer for the full ninety minutes, Graham said that he knew he had to hurry in order to get his mother onto the plane and in flight before the time would expire.

After the plane took off, he went to the airport coffee shop, where he had coffee and munched on doughnuts. When he heard the news that a plane had gone down outside the City of Longmont, he knew that his plan had worked.

Graham displayed no sorrow or remorse for his crime and refused to file any appeals. Shortly before his execution by gassing in the Colorado State Penitentiary on 12 January 1957, Graham told a warder, 'As far as feeling remorse for those people [who died], I don't. I can't help it. Everybody pays their way and takes their chances. That's just the way it goes.'

NEWLYWED TAKES A FATAL STEP

NORTH CAROLINA, USA 1956

Piedmont Airlines Flight 5, carrying 24 passengers, departed Charlotte at 5.44 p.m., six minutes late, heading for North Carolina and Tri-Cities, Tennessee. At around six o'clock it was travelling at an altitude of 6,500 feet, near Shelby, North Carolina.

The seatbelt sign had been left on since take-off because Captain Baxter B Slaughter, Jr, anticipated turbulence, which had not developed. However, while the purser was on the flight deck obtaining information for a passenger, the aircraft suddenly yawed to the left as the cockpit door-warning light came on.

The first officer and purser immediately went to the rear of the cabin, where they found the main cabin door fully open. A woman passenger, who was in the lavatory when the door opened, was assisted past the open door by two crew members. A quick check revealed that a passenger named Oren A Pruitt was missing.

The Pruitts had been the original cause of the flight's delay, having arrived at the airport too late to claim their reservations on an earlier flight. They had been transferred to Flight 5 and had been seated in the rearmost aisle on the left side of the plane.

The couple were on their honeymoon, and had been drinking. It seemed that Oren Pruitt had been waiting for the lavatory to become available and, growing impatient, had apparently attempted to use what he thought was an alternative lavatory.

Passenger witnesses stated they heard a sudden rush of wind – Pruitt had, in fact, opened the main cabin door! They watched horrified as he fought frantically to hold on to the door frame – but he was sucked out and fell to his death.

After the air crew had managed to close the door, the plane proceeded to Asheville, where it made a routine landing and the flight was cancelled.

THE DAY THE MUSIC DIED

CLEAR LAKE, USA 1959

The 1959 'Winter Dance Party Tour' was planned to cover 24 American cities in a short three-week time frame (23 January–15 February) and Buddy Holly would be the biggest headliner with his band, the Crickets. Waylon Jennings, a friend from Lubbock, Texas, and Tommy Allsup would go as backup musicians. Ritchie Valens, one of the hottest artists at the time, J P Richardson (aka The Big Bopper), and Dion and the Belmonts would round out the list of performers.

Halfway into the tour, and tired of travelling on buses prone to mechanical breakdowns and faulty heating, Holly chartered a private plane to fly himself and two band members to Fargo, North Dakota, immediately after their 2 February performance in Clear Lake, Iowa.

Tommy Allsup and Waylon Jennings agreed to fly with them but both were persuaded to give up their seats. J P Richardson, who was coming down with the flu, managed to talk Jennings into giving up his seat so that he could arrive at the next tour stop early and have a little extra time to visit a doctor.

When Holly learned that Jennings wasn't going to fly, he said, 'Well, I hope your old bus freezes up.' Jennings responded, 'Well, I hope your plane crashes.' This friendly banter between friends would haunt Jennings for years.

Ritchie Valens spent the evening prior to the flight trying to convince Allsup to give up his seat on the plane, but Allsup, who needed to pick up a registered letter waiting for him in Fargo, demurred. Finally, just as Allsup was about to leave the

Surf City ballroom for the airport, he gave in and agreed to flip a coin with Valens for a spot on the aeroplane. Valens won the coin toss, and Allsup stayed behind to ride the bus to the next destination.

The plane, a red-and-white single-engine Beechcraft Bonanza, took off in the cold, windy, early morning hours of 3 February amid light snow flurries. It never reached Fargo. Shortly after take-off, one wing hit the ground and the small plane corkscrewed over and over, skidding some 500 feet across a snow-covered field, before coming to rest against a wire fence. The three young stars were thrown clear of the plane, leaving only the pilot inside. All died instantly. Due to the bad weather, they were only discovered by searchers the next morning.

Irving Feld of General Artists Corporation, who had booked the tour, promised the remaining members that they would be flown back to Lubbock for the funeral if they agreed to keep a performance date in Moorehead the next night. But the promise was never kept. The performers were forced to finish the tour, and never made it to the funeral.

Over the years there has been much speculation as to the cause of the crash – even sabotage was considered. The most obvious cause, however, was the bad weather. Because of the snow, visibility would have been almost nil; the flight should never have taken off.

After the death of Buddy Holly, the Crickets used various lead singers on their records. One was David Box – together they recorded 'Peggy Sue Got Married'. In the early 1960s, Box was working with local Houston band Buddy and the Kings, with Buddy Groves on vocal/guitar, Carl Banks on bass and Bill Daniels on drums. Daniels was a qualified pilot and the quartet hired a Cessna Skyhawk 172 to take them to a gig in Harris County on 23 October 1964. On the return flight the plane crashed nose first and overturned. There were no survivors.

The urban legend that 'American Pie' was the name of Buddy Holly's plane the night it crashed is untrue, however. The aeroplane, chartered through Dwyer's Flying Service in

Clear Lake, Iowa, had no name. Its only designation was its wing registration number, N3794N. Don McLean used the name 'American Pie' for his famous song about the day the music died.

THE SPY FROM THE SKY

SVERDLOVSK, USSR 1960

The Cold War between the USA and the Soviet Union had been raging for some years when, on 1 May 1960, Francis Gary Powers took off from Peshawar, Pakistan, at the controls of a new Lockheed U-2 high-altitude reconnaissance aircraft.

The plane was the brainchild of the CIA. It was capable of travelling at altitudes of up to 70,000 feet and was carrying state-of-the-art photography equipment. The CIA boasted it could take high-resolution pictures of headlines in Russian newspapers as it flew overhead! The CIA also assured President Eisenhower that the Soviets did not possess anti-aircraft weapons sophisticated enough to shoot down the high-altitude planes. In the unlikely event that it was brought down, it was equipped with self-destruct mechanisms that would render any wreckage unrecognisable and the pilot was instructed to kill himself in such a situation.

Powers, a CIA-employed pilot, was to fly over some 2,000 miles of Soviet territory to Bodo military airfield in Norway, collecting intelligence information en route. Roughly halfway through his journey, the 'impossible' happened. He was shot down over Sverdlovsk in the Ural Mountains. Forced to bail out at 15,000 feet, he survived the parachute jump but was promptly arrested by Soviet authorities.

Assuming that the aircraft would have automatically destroyed itself, the US government issued a cover statement indicating that a 'weather plane' had veered off course and supposedly crashed somewhere in the Soviet Union. This enabled Soviet Premier Khrushchev to pull off one of the most dramatic moments of the Cold War by producing not only the mostly intact wreckage of the U-2, but also the captured pilot – very much alive! Eisenhower had to publicly admit that it was indeed a US spy plane, but he refused to apologise. An imminent international summit was subsequently cancelled and relations between East and West fell to an all-time low.

In August, Powers pleaded guilty to espionage charges in Moscow and was sentenced to ten years' imprisonment – three in prison and seven in a prison colony. Fortunately for him, two years later, in February 1962, he was exchanged for Soviet Colonel Rudolf Abel in the most dramatic East–West spy swap ever to occur in Cold War Berlin.

Powers stepped onto the eastern end of Berlin's Glienicke Bridge spanning the River Havel. At the other end of the bridge stood Colonel Rudolf Abel, seized earlier by US security agents after setting up a Soviet spy network in New York in the late 1950s. At a precisely arranged signal, the two men strode on to the bridge, Powers heading westward, Abel eastward. In the middle of the bridge they passed each other silently, with barely a nod of their heads.

Upon returning to the United States, Powers was cleared by the CIA and the Senate of any personal blame for the U-2 incident. Privately, however, he was shunned by his former colleagues for failing to destroy the plane and kill himself.

In 1970, he published a book, *Operation Overflight*, about the incident and eventually died in 1977 at the age of 47 when a television news helicopter he was piloting crashed in Los Angeles.

On the fortieth anniversary of the famous incident, on 1 May 2000, US Officials presented Powers's family with the Prisoner-of-War Medal, the Distinguished Flying Cross and the National Defense Service Medal during a thirty-minute ceremony held at the Beale Air Force Base, north of Sacramento and home to the modern US U-2 force.

The ceremony ended with a fly-by of a lone U-2 plane.

THE RIGHT STUFF

EDWARDS AIR FORCE BASE, USA 1963

Chuck Yeager is the world's most famous test pilot – not only because of the records he set, but also because of his determination, his ability to remain calm in difficult situations, and his ability to quickly analyse problems and find a solution. He needed all those qualities when flying the experimental Lockheed Starfighter NF-104 in 1963 at over twice the speed of sound.

This revolutionary aeroplane could theoretically climb to over 120,000 feet. On the fourth flight, Yeager planned to exceed the magic 100,000-foot level. He set off the rocket boosters at 60,000 feet and the plane roared upwards. When he reached 104,000 feet, however, trouble set in. The NF-104's nose wouldn't go down. It went into a flat spin and tumbled down uncontrollably.

At 21,000 feet, Yeager desperately employed the tail parachute, which briefly righted the plane, but the nose promptly rose back up and the NF-104 began spinning again. He rode it down to about 6,000 feet, and ejected.

Normally, the rocket seat in which the pilot sits should blow the pilot out and away from the aeroplane at a velocity of about one hundred miles per hour. In this case, however, the plane was also falling at about 100 miles an hour, so the two were falling simultaneously and dangerously close to one another.

Immediately after this, the belt holding the pilot into his seat also blows open, thus propelling him into freefall, and ready to open his parachute. The belt 'blew' successfully but, though now freefalling, Yeager found that his parachute – which should have been slowing him down – for some reason hadn't opened and was, to use his words, 'flopping about in the breeze'. At the same time, the seat from which he'd been ejected and which was falling alongside him had become entangled in the shroud lines of his parachute!

After some desperate manipulation, involving the opening of a smaller canopy on top of his main parachute, the major canopy opened. Unfortunately, this only succeeded in causing the rogue seat – in particular, that part of the seat containing the rocket motor, which still had burning propellant spewing out of it – to hit Yeager full in the face-piece of his pressure suit. The visor was torn open and the burning propellant sprayed into his suit, which, containing 100 per cent oxygen, ignited like a blow torch.

Fortunately, the broken visor cut into his eyebrows so that his eye sockets filled with blood, which protected Yeager's eyeballs from the flames. However, his neck and shoulders were now being badly burned and it was very difficult to breathe. He was stunned from the blow, but knew that, in order to stop the fire, he had to raise the broken face-visor in order to shut off the oxygen flow from the kit in the back of his pressure suit. Fortunately, the relevant button on his pressure suit helmet worked, the visor rose and the fire inside the suit abated.

He just had time to swing his parachute a couple of times before painfully hitting the ground. It had taken just four minutes from the first spin to this final impact. Since he had been talking to flight control all the way down, help arrived within five minutes of the time he landed. Yeager's face was blackened and burned, but he was standing upright with his chute rolled up and his helmet in his arm when the rescue helicopter landed!

A flight surgeon gave him a shot of morphine and took him back to the hospital where they had to cut the pressure suit off him. He required extensive skin grafts for his burns. But he had clearly proved himself to be made of the right stuff.

ALFALFA LANDING

NORFOLK, USA 1966

May 1966. It was midday on the Dicke farm, and the family had just sat down to lunch when they heard a heavy, low, rumbling sound immediately above them. They rushed to the window – and could hardly believe their eyes. A DC-3 airliner was sliding across their alfalfa field!

Earlier, Flight 787 commanded by Al Bergum, with assistant Tom Truax, had left Omaha, Nebraska on its scheduled route to Norfolk, Sioux City, Yankton, Sioux Falls, Brookings, Watertown, Fargo and – ultimately, much later that night – its destination of Grand Forks.

However, a short way into the 92-mile flight, the plane suddenly backfired and a fire broke out. Black smoke and flames belched from the left-side engine, which the crew were unable to control.

With approximately fifteen miles remaining to their next stop, Norfolk airport, Bergum faced a difficult decision. Below him, eastern Nebraska's terrain consisted mostly of farm land. Very likely the aeroplane would be able to continue on to reach the airport, but this hope had to be balanced against the safety of 26 passengers and a crew of three. Reluctantly, he made his decision. Bergum quickly briefed the crew and radioed Norfolk to inform them of the impending off-airport landing.

He indicated an emergency descent, actuated the alarm button to warn the passengers to 'Brace for Impact' and selected an appropriate field for the rapidly approaching landing. Although no obstructions threatened the flight path, the field's short length presented a challenge of a different kind. The braking system usually imposed by the landing gear couldn't be used, therefore, lower than normal power had to be sustained to provide the necessary airspeed to be able to stop within the field.

Approaching touchdown, the DC-3 skimmed the tops of the trees and finally began to glide through the alfalfa crop. Both propellers dug into the ground as the aircraft slid precariously straight ahead to an eventual stop. There was a silence. They had made it safely to ground! The fire was swiftly brought under control and the passengers began to leave the plane – disoriented, but very relieved.

Meanwhile, farmer David Dicke had run from the kitchen to the machine shed. Fortunately, a hay wagon was already hitched to his tractor and he drove straight towards the aircraft disregarding the farm lane's conventional path through a gate! The end result was a new pathway. As it was customary for 'company' who dropped in for a visit to be offered coffee and refreshments, he promptly invited the startled passengers to climb onto the wagon's flatbed so he could take them all back to the farmhouse, where they and the crew enjoyed coffee and cookies.

Using the farm's party-line phone, Bergum got through to North Central's chief pilot in Minneapolis–St Paul and described the aeroplane's condition and location 'in an alfalfa field on the Dicke farm, ten miles south and three miles east of Norfolk'.

The passengers and crew were later transported to the Norfolk airport terminal, where a replacement DC-3 was awaiting them. No one was sure how many people wished to resume their trip! In the event, every passenger elected to re-board the flight with Bergum and – shortly thereafter – Captain Bergum taxied out and departed to a huge round of applause.

AIR CON

MIAMI, USA 1966

Back in the 1960s, a young American by the name of Frank Abagnale was earning himself a reputation as the country's most talented and notorious con man. In a five-year spree of forgery and fraud, he impersonated his way around the United States, assuming and divesting himself of identities as he went: doctor, lawyer – and, eventually, airline pilot.

Pilots, particularly those who worked for Pan American Airlines, were highly respected back in the 1950s and 1960s. If Abagnale were able to get a hold of a pilot's uniform, he would have greater success with cashing bad cheques. He thus contacted a purchasing agent at Pan American Airlines' corporate headquarters and told them he was a pilot for the company and that the hotel he was staying at in New York had lost his uniform.

He was instructed by the agent to visit a company specialising in Pan Am uniforms on 5th Avenue, and that very day was fitted with a Pan Am co-pilot's uniform, charged to a false employee number he invented while filling out the paperwork.

To make his new persona more believable, he obtained a Pan Am pass card by simply contacting the company responsible for making both the passes and IDs for Pan Am and pretending to be a purchasing officer interested in buying new ID cards for his own company. During an interview with the sales representative, Abagnale noticed in a catalogue a sample ID similar to that used by Pan Am. He had the salesman make him a sample pass with his name and picture on it that was almost an exact replica of the Pan Am pass, but without the logo. Frank then bought a model Pan Am plane, removed the famous airline symbol and carefully placed it on the ID pass card. The finished product looked almost flawless.

He then familiarised himself with the airline business, mainly by posing as a student doing a research project at Pan Am's headquarters. Most importantly, he discovered the practice known as 'dead-heading'. This was the privilege accorded to airline employees that allowed them to fly for free to far-off destinations on other airlines to fulfil specific job requirements. The employer would almost always cover the expenses of the trip. If he were able to pose as a pilot, he might be able to hitch some of these free rides on aeroplanes around the world!

The last hurdle Abagnale had to overcome was to obtain an FAA licence, without which he would not be able to impersonate a pilot. He solved the problem by obtaining a plaque from a firm specialising in mounting licences in silver. The FAA had a mail-order branch within the company. Abagnale falsified his name as Frank Williams and sent away for the plaque. Upon receiving it, he took the plaque to a printer and had it downsized, mounted on special paper and laminated.

Abagnale now had in his possession a replica FAA licence, a Pan Am pass card, a working knowledge of the aviation industry, a company uniform and the audacity to pull off a remarkable con. Using his new alias, he went to various banks and opened accounts, wearing his pilot's uniform.

Eventually, Abagnale felt confident enough to attempt 'dead-heading' on a flight to Miami. He boarded an Eastern Airline 727 plane in his uniform after filling out a form stating his name, employee number and other pertinent information. When on the plane, he made his way to the cockpit, eventually discovering the 'jump seat', which is where airline personnel can sit when 'dead-heading'.

To Frank's surprise and relief, the pilots took little interest in him and the flight was uneventful. He landed a short while later in Miami. For the next couple of years, 'dead-heading' would be Frank's preferred method of travel. It was free and he had access to anywhere in the world to cash his dud cheques. Moreover, Pan Am unwittingly picked up the tab for his accommodation while abroad, which served as an additional benefit throughout his criminal career.

Over a period of five years, Abagnale would use eight different identities and pass bad cheques worth over $2.5 million in 26 countries – providing money for a lifestyle during which he dated flight attendants, ate at expensive places, bought expensive clothing and travelled for free.

Eventually he was arrested in France in 1969, after an Air France attendant recognised his face from a 'wanted' poster. When the French police apprehended him, 26 countries wanted him to be extradited! After serving jail sentences in France and Sweden, he was deported to the United States. He was sentenced to twelve years in a federal prison for multiple counts of forgery.

Abagnale is now a multi-millionaire through his legal fraud detection and avoidance consultancy!

COOPER – OR THE REAL McCOY?

SEATTLE, USA 1971

On 24 November 1971, an American travelling under the name of Dan Cooper hijacked a passenger plane flying from Portland, Oregon, to Seattle, Washington. He was dressed entirely in black and wearing sunglasses, and threatened the crew with a bomb that he said was in his suitcase. He instructed them to complete the flight, then released all the passengers at Seattle-Tacoma International Airport in exchange for $200,000 and four parachutes.

He then ordered the crew to fly towards Mexico at low speed and altitude, with the landing gear down. At some point during the journey he jumped out of the rear stairway of the aeroplane with the money and parachutes.

His descent, however, went unnoticed by the United States Air Force F-106 jet fighers tracking the airliner. Despite an exhaustive eighteen-day search of the projected landing zone, no trace of the man or his parachute was found.

On 7 April 1972, four months after the Cooper hijacking, Richard McCoy, Jr, boarded United Flight 855, a Boeing 727, during a stopover in Denver. The plane was en route from Newark, New Jersey, to Los Angeles, California, with 85 passengers and a crew of six.

McCoy was a 29-year-old Vietnam veteran, helicopter pilot and skydiver – and at the time he was having serious financial problems. Approximately twenty minutes after take-off, he was seen to be holding a hand grenade. When an off-duty pilot attempted to tackle him, he pulled out a handgun and handed the pilot an envelope with instructions. Like Cooper before him, he demanded $500,000 in cash and four parachutes. The crew complied and the passengers were released in San Francisco. He then instructed the crew to fly to Utah, and he bailed out over the city of Provo.

This time, however, McCoy was arrested two days after the hijacking following a fingerprint and handwriting match-up. Inside his house, FBI agents found a jumpsuit and a duffle bag filled with cash totalling $499,970. McCoy protested his innocence, but was convicted and received a 45-year sentence.

Once incarcerated, using his access to the prison's dental office, McCoy made a fake handgun out of dental paste. He and a crew of convicts then escaped in August 1974 by stealing a garbage truck and crashing it though the prison's main gate. It took three months for the FBI to locate McCoy, in Virginia where, after a gunfight, he was killed.

The tantalising question remained, however: was McCoy actually Cooper, repeating his crime, or was he a copycat?

The question became academic when, in August 2000, a widow in Pace, Florida named Jo Weber claimed that her late husband, Duane Weber, had told her just before his death in 1995 that he was Cooper. She checked into her late husband's background and found that he'd served in the Army during World War II and later had spent time in a prison near Portland Airport. There were other clues too. Mrs Weber recalled that her husband had once had a nightmare during which he had talked in his sleep about jumping from a plane. She had also found an old plane ticket for Northwest Airlines that referred to the Seattle-Tacoma Airport in his papers. However, one of the most convincing pieces of evidence Mrs Weber discovered was a book on the Cooper case that she found in the local library containing notations that matched her husband's handwriting.

Recently, facial recognition software has been used on 3,000 photographs (including that of Weber and two other suspects) that identified him as 'the best match'.

Following three similar (but less successful) hijackings in 1972, the Federal Aviation Administration required that all

Boeing 727 aircraft be fitted with a device known as the 'Cooper Vane', a mechanical aerodynamic wedge that prevents the rear stairway from being lowered in flight.

WINGS OF HOPE

AMAZON RIVER 1971

On Christmas Eve 1971, seventeen-year-old Juliane Koepcke was on a flight with her mother from Lima, Peru, to Pucallpa, where they would rendezvous with her father, biologist Hans Koepcke. She had just graduated from the German high school in Lima and was preparing herself for a career in zoology. Her holidays had started and the family were looking forward to spending a happy Christmas together.

All was well until the Lockheed Electra, known as *Mateo Pumacahua*, suddenly hit a freak storm. Juliane looked out the window to see the right wing aflame. The crew fought to regain control but the stricken aircraft plunged from the sky. The wings were torn off and it came crashing down into a remote mountainous region of the Amazon. Juliane remembered falling and tumbling through the air – and then nothing.

She awoke three hours later, still strapped into her seat. There was a strange, eerie silence everywhere. She began looking for her mother, but all she found were empty seats and a row of three dead young women, covered in flies. Miraculously, she had only fractured her collarbone, gashed her right arm, and lost her vision in one eye. Of the 92 people on board, Koepcke appeared to be the lone survivor.

Although in a state of profound shock, she remembered her father's advice: heading downhill in the jungle leads to water, and water leads to civilisation. She had to try and save herself. Eventually, she found a stream and began nine days of wading through knee-high water and fighting off swarms of insects and leeches. On the ninth day, she found a canoe and shelter. Then she waited.

Hours later, local lumbermen returned and found her. They tried to get her to eat but she was sick and refused food. Insects had buried eggs in her skin and they were beginning to hatch. One of the men poured gasoline on her and, she revealed to the London *Daily Mail*, 'I counted thirty-five worms that came out of my arms alone.'

The next day, a group of Peruvian hunters arrived and took her to the town of Tournavista, where a local pilot flew her to her father in Pucallpa. When rescue crews finally located the aircraft with Koepcke's help, they discovered that as many as fourteen others had survived the initial crash but were unable to seek help as the teenager had, and died awaiting rescue.

How had the miracle happened? It has been suggested that rising winds slowed her fall and caused her to spiral rather than plummet straight down. She had then landed on a bed of branches and vines.

Koepcke is now a biologist in Germany and her ordeal was the subject of the 1999 Werner Herzog documentary *Wings of Hope*.

VESNA VULOVIC

CESKA, CZECHOSLOVAKIA 1972

As a teenager, Vesna Vulovic, a Serb from Belgrade, liked the Beatles and sang their songs with friends. After her first year in university, she went to England to improve her command of English. Later, Vesna met a friend in JAT (Yugoslav Airlines) uniform, decided that she looked nice and calculated that, as an air hostess, she would be able to visit her favourite city of London once every month.

She had only been flying eight months and didn't even have a permanent contract when, on 26 January 1972, the DC-9 aeroplane she was travelling in, along with 28 passengers and crew, blew up over Czechoslovakia (now the Czech Republic). A bomb in the cargo section planted by the Ustashe Croatian separatist group had exploded at an altitude of approximately 33,000 feet.

The plane disintegrated and fell into the mountains below. But incredibly, Vesna survived the fall. She sustained a fractured skull, two broken legs, and three broken vertebrae – one of which was crushed, leaving her paralysed from the waist down. No other passengers survived.

The 22-year-old wasn't even supposed to have been on the plane. As she later stated in an interview, it was another Vesna who should have been on the flight but she'd been happy with the mix-up as it allowed her to make her first trip to Denmark.

As she suffered amnesia from one hour before the accident until one month afterwards, she recalls nothing of the event itself, but later learned that a former German nurse, Bruno

Henke, saw her legs sticking out of the fuselage. She was in the middle part of the plane with her head down and a colleague lying on top of her. A catering trolley was pinned against her spine and had kept her in the plane. Henke had been with Hitler's troops as a medic during the Second World War and knew how best to treat her at the site of the accident.

Henke cleared Vesna's airways before rushing her to hospital. Three days later she awoke from a coma in a hospital in Ceska, Karmenice. Seeing her parents, she asked them why they were in Slovenia, which is where she thought she still was, having just visited Ljubljana before going to Copenhagen.

Nobody is quite sure how she survived. Physicists say that in any fall above 2,000 feet the body will reach a terminal velocity of 120 miles per hour (a speed at which you cannot go any faster because of air resistance). Vesna had two factors on her side. First, the drag on the tail section of the plane was sufficient to apparently cause it to spiral down at less than terminal velocity. Second, the part of the plane she was in hit the side of the mountain at an angle and continued to travel on – and thus not all of the forward momentum was stopped at once.

Vulovic spent several months in and out of hospitals and operations eventually allowed her to walk once again. At first, however, the police were concerned enough for her safety to place a guard at her door. It was thought she had seen the man who may have put the bomb on the plane in Copenhagen. So, nobody was allowed into her room except her parents and doctors in case the Ustashe tried to kill her as the only surviving eyewitness.

After the accident, Vesna was keen to continue flying. She explained in one interview, 'You must remember that I had no memories of the accident. To this day I enjoy travelling and have no fear of flying.'

She wanted to go back to her old job but JAT officials, not wanting the public to associate the tragedy with their airline, refused to allow her to fly with them. Instead, they gave her a desk job negotiating freight contracts. After eighteen years, however, she was forced to retire, primarily because of her views about Slobodan Milosovic. She was trying to persuade her colleagues not to vote for him and eventually found that her pay was being secretly reduced.

In retirement, Vesna continued her campaign against Milosovic and was regularly seen demonstrating in the streets of Belgrade. While the police made arrests, Vesna remained untouchable as she was – and remains – a national hero.

When the Milosovic regime finally tumbled, Vesna was on the balcony at the city hall as one of the celebrities making victory addresses that were the entrée to a night of partying for the Serbian people.

Vesna's remarkable escape from death gave her an entry in *Guinness World Records*. She received her medal at a ceremony in London, where she met Paul McCartney. Vesna told him he was 'the most fabulous man in England' and that it was because of him that she had started flying!

She returned to the accident scene on 27 January 1997 where she met her rescuers and placed memorial flowers at the monument for the others that had died in that terrible explosion.

FLIGHT 401

MIAMI, USA 1972

On the night of Friday, 29 December 1972, Eastern Airlines Flight 401 was carrying 176 people and nearing its destination at Miami Airport. Flying the L-1011 jumbo jet were Captain Bob Loft and Second Officer Don Repo, who were engaged in carrying out routine landing procedures when a warning light flashed on the control panel indicating a problem with the landing gear.

This distraction may have been the reason why neither of them noticed that the plane was actually descending around 200 feet per minute faster than they had thought. Seconds later the airliner crashed into the Florida Everglades, killing 101 people immediately. Both Captain Loft and Officer Repo survived the initial impact, but Loft died before he could be pulled from the burning, twisted wreck and Repo died a day later.

The cause of the crash was traced to a couple of design faults on the control panel, which Lockheed rapidly corrected. Eastern Airlines salvaged undamaged parts of the stricken aeroplane and redistributed them among similar aircraft in their fleet. But afterwards, a series of very strange incidents were reported on various flights. It appeared as though the ghosts of the two pilots were taking to the air again.

Repo's apparition appeared frequently on one particular plane, both in the cockpit and in the galley, the area where flight attendants prepared passengers' meals. He seemed to be especially concerned with flight safety, and was reportedly once seen fixing a faulty oven circuit.

241

On another occasion, a flight attendant saw Repo's face looking at her from an oven in the galley of a Tri-Star 310. Understandably alarmed, she fetched two colleagues, one of whom was a flight engineer who had been a friend of Repo's, and who recognised him instantly. All three heard him warn them to, 'Watch out for fire on this aeroplane.' The plane later encountered serious engine trouble and the last leg of its flight was cancelled. The galley of the Tri-Star 310 had been salvaged from the wreckage of Flight 401.

On another occasion, a female passenger made a concerned enquiry to a flight attendant regarding the quiet, unresponsive man in an Eastern Airlines uniform sitting in the seat next to her. He subsequently disappeared in full view of both of them, and of several other passengers, leaving the woman hysterical. When later shown a sheet of photos depicting Eastern flight engineers, she identified Repo as the officer she had seen.

Loft's ghost was also seen on various flights, usually sitting in first class or in the crew's cabin. A stewardess once confronted him, asking what he was doing on the plane as she had not seen him board and could not identify him on the passenger list. Receiving no reply, she reported it to her flight captain who walked back with her. He recognised Loft, who disappeared immediately, in front of a dozen people.

Later that year, one of the vice-presidents of Eastern Airlines boarded a Miami-bound Tri-Star plane at JFK Airport and spoke to the uniformed captain sitting next to him in first class. Suddenly, he recognised him as Loft, but once again the apparition disappeared.

The airline suggested that those who reported such incidents seek psychiatric counselling at the company's expense. Nevertheless, all of the salvaged parts of the ill-fated Flight 401 were eventually removed from the aircraft they had been put into, whereupon the paranormal sightings ended.

CROATIAN HIJACK

LA GUARDIA, USA 1976

One of the strangest air-piracy incidents occurred in 1976, when a group of political activists decided to hold a political seminar in the sky .

TWA Flight 355 was bound for Chicago when it took off from La Guardia on 10 September 1976. The plane, with 86 passengers and a full crew aboard, was taken over by five hijackers a short time later. They claimed to have bombs. The leader of the group, Zvonko Busic, was fighting for independence for Croatia from the then Yugoslavia. With him were his American wife, Julienne Busic, and three sympathisers.

Their plane 'bombs' were determined later to be fakes. But Busic had a plan to convince authorities in New York that he meant what he said. He planted a bomb in a coin-operated locker at Grand Central Station in New York and told police where to find it.

The captain immediately radioed the contents of the note to authorities and dialled the skyjack code for the air-traffic control radar location centre. Meanwhile, Zvonko Busic entered the cockpit wearing what appeared to be three sticks of dynamite connected to a battery. Busic ordered Captain Carey to fly the aeroplane to Europe. En route to Montreal for a refuelling stop, Busic explained that the purpose of the hijacking would become clear when the authorities read the note accompanying the bomb in the subway locker and that, upon receipt of a prearranged codeword indicating that their demands – the release of Croatian prisoners and the distribution of Croatian-independence propaganda in both France and the United States – had been met, the hijackers would surrender in Europe. At the same time, Julienne Busic was handing out copies of leaflets to the passengers, seeking their support for a free Croatia, independent of Yugoslavia. Zvonko Busic also wanted the leaflets dropped over London and Paris from the plane.

Throughout the ordeal, Julienne Busic conversed freely with the passengers and encouraged them to ask questions about the propaganda. Petar Matanic's assignment was to stand up at the front of the passenger section with a tear-gas gun, apparently to keep order. Like Julienne Busic, Matanic talked with the passengers throughout their ordeal, further explaining the purpose of the hijacking.

Meanwhile, responding to the hijack note that Captain Carey had transmitted, members of the New York City Police Department Bomb Squad located subway locker 5713 and found that it contained what appeared to be a bomb and additional propaganda. While attempting to deactivate the bomb, one officer was killed and one was seriously injured.

The hijackers demanded that their materials be published in the following day's editions of the *New York Times* (all three editions), *Los Angeles Times*, *Chicago Tribune*, *International Herald Tribune* and *Washington Post*.

After the aircraft landed in Paris, Zvonko Busic told Captain Carey that now they need only await reception of the prearranged codeword. Twelve nerve-racking hours followed for Carey and his passengers, and as time passed, still no code word was received. The passengers were twice herded together in the centre of the cabin while Zvonko Busic and Vlasic threatened to kill them. Eventually, Julienne Busic left the aircraft to contact information sources in the United States to confirm that the two propaganda texts had been published as demanded. Two hours later, she telephoned Zvonko Busic on the aircraft and told him that the demands had been met.

At various stops, approximately forty passengers were released – those who had medical problems, pressing engagements, weddings, graduations and the like. And some of the passengers who could have left actually said they wanted to stay on the plane until the end, that they considered it an 'adventure'. After their arrest, many of them wrote letters to the trial judge asking for leniency, and for years afterwards, several corresponded with Julienne directly and even visited her in prison.

The hijackers finally surrendered in Paris, after French police shot out the tyres of the plane and talked them into giving up. The hijackers were taken back to New York on another flight.

At the subsequent trial, Zvonko Busic freely admitted his role as the mastermind and attempted to take full blame for the hijacking. He also admitted having placed the bomb in the subway locker. Julienne Busic testified that she never intended to participate in the hijacking, but only went along with her husband because she thought she was pregnant and feared she would never see him again if she refused.

The others claimed that they had only joined Busic to travel to Chicago for a secret political meeting where they were to deliver the leaflets. Once on the plane, they insisted, Busic forced them to cooperate in the hijacking with the threat of death.

The Busics received life sentences and the three accomplices received thirty-year sentences. While in prison, Julienne Busic began to feel remorseful and even considered becoming a nun. She then struck up an acquaintance with Kathleen Murray, the wife of the New York City police officer killed while trying to deactivate the bomb.

In April 1987, Zvonko Busic briefly escaped from his upstate New York prison. Guards found a dummy dressed in his clothing in his bed. He broke through a plasterboard ceiling in the prison gymnasium, then dug a hole under a fence in the recreation yard and worked his way through security wire before running into woods next to the prison. He was recaptured a month later as he sat on the porch outside a rural Pennsylvania store.

Busic is regarded as a national hero in Croatia, which finally won its independence after he had spent 21 years in prison.

PEDALLING ACROSS THE CHANNEL

ENGLISH CHANNEL 1979

In 1976, Paul MacCready found himself in deep financial trouble. He had guaranteed a loan for a relative's business that had failed and he was now $175,000 in debt. He had a wife and three young children and a small engineering business of his own. It was a source of severe concern – where was he to find the money?

MacCready had always been interested in flight of all kinds, and now he suddenly remembered the Kremer Prize for a successful human-powered flight. It came with $100,000 in prize money – which would go a long way to paying off his debt. Suddenly, human-powered flight seemed important. He had trained as a navy pilot and had a PhD in aeronautics and so he decided to try and invent something that would meet the requirements of the competition.

He began to study in greater detail how birds fly, particularly large hawks and vultures. Scale also began to interest him – the larger the wings, the less power was needed to fly. He eventually calculated that a very light 96-foot-long wingspan, built like a hang-glider, would only require about 4 horsepower to fly – the same as that generated by a bicyclist.

It took six months of nonstop work for MacCready and his team of friends and family to build the Gossamer Condor. They used simple light materials – piano wire, aluminium tubing, and lots of tape – and managed to keep the weight down to 70 pounds. Bryan Allen, the pilot/engine, said flying it was 'like pedalling a house'. Nevertheless, on 23 August 1977, with

247

Allen at the pedals, the Condor flew the Kremer course and won the prize!

Soon after this, Kremer offered a much bigger prize for crossing the 22-mile English Channel, again under human power. MacCready still needed money. He had sunk so much into building the Condor, that he'd wiped out only a third of his original debt. 'The prize money, equivalent to $214,000, was enough to pay all the expenses on the project and pay off the rest of the loan,' he later explained. 'We realised if we just made a variation of the Gossamer Condor, with carbon spars and more ribs and so on, we could make the Gossamer Albatross and get it across the Channel.'

Two years later, on the morning of 12 June 1979, moving slowly through the air just a few feet above the choppy waters of the English Channel was one of the oddest-looking flying machines ever built. Almost 100 feet wide and sheathed in a shiny, semi-transparent skin, the Gossamer Albatross had a big propeller at its back but no engine to speak of. Instead, in an enclosed pod hanging beneath the huge wing, was Bryan Allen, once more furiously pedalling to make the craft go.

After almost three hours of physical effort, Allen gently landed the plane on the beaches of England. MacCready, who had been in a boat following the slow, tense journey from the shores of France, rushed to join the celebration.

Today, the Gossamer Condor hangs in the Smithsonian Institution's National Air and Space Museum, alongside the Wright brothers' plane, the *Spirit of St Louis*, and an Apollo Lander. The Albatross is on display at the Smithsonian Institution's Udvar-Hazy centre.

The Albatross went on to form part of an even more ambitious project – scaled down to three-quarters of its previous size and dubbed the Penguin, and with Paul MacCready's thirteen-year-old son Marshall aboard, it achieved the first-ever solar-powered flight with a human pilot on 18 May 1980.

DEATH IN THE DESERT

TEHRAN, IRAN 1979

On 4 November 1979, the US Embassy in Tehran, Iran was seized by anti-American student demonstrators in the wake of the Iranian revolution. The subsequent capture of many American hostages marked a climax in the history of US/Iran tensions and one of the lowest points in American foreign policy. The Iranian government condoned the actions in the aftermath, rendering all negotiation attempts impossible.

To mount a rescue of the hostages, the Americans faced a daunting task. The hostages were heavily guarded in a massive embassy compound that was surrounded by 700 miles of desert and mountains in every direction. There was no easy way to get a rescue team into the embassy. However, political negotiations to free the hostages continued to go nowhere and the tension was mounting.

Military experts were called upon to put together a team that would attempt a very daring rescue attempt. The players were all well-trained and ready to go. But something horrific happened in Iran's Great Salt Desert.

Because the Americans had no inside sources of information to supply details on the physical layout of the embassy, the numbers and locations of the Iranian guards, and, most important, the location of the hostages, Delta Force, as the team were called, had to plan to search up to six buildings in the embassy compound where the hostages might be held. That required its commander to increase the size of his assault force, which meant more helicopters were needed.

After testing and rejecting alternatives, it was decided to use Air Force C-130 Hercules transports rigged with temporary 18,000-gallon fuel bladders to refuel the helicopters on their way to Tehran.

However, that decision led to the requirement of finding a spot in the Iranian desert where the refuelling could take place on ground that would support the weight of the gas-bloated Hercules. US intelligence found and explored just such a location, about 200 miles southeast of Tehran. In planning and training, this site was known as Desert One.

On the first night, six Air Force C-130s carrying 132 Delta commandos, Army Rangers, and support personnel and the helicopter fuel would fly from the island of Masirah, off the coast of Oman, more than 1,000 miles to Desert One, being refuelled in flight from Air Force KC-135 tankers.

Nine Navy RH-53Ds would lift off from the aircraft carrier USS *Nimitz*, about 50 miles south of the Iranian coast, and fly more than 600 miles to Desert One. After refuelling, the helicopters would carry the rescue force to a hideout in hills about 50 miles southeast of Tehran, then fly to a separate hiding spot nearby. The C-130s would return to Masirah, refuelled again in flight.

The next night, Delta would be driven to the embassy in vehicles obtained by the agents. A team of Rangers would go to rescue the three Americans held in the Foreign Ministry. As the ground units were freeing the hostages, the helicopters would fly from their hiding spot to the embassy and the Foreign Ministry.

Three Air Force AC-130 gunships would arrive overhead to protect the rescue force from any Iranian counterattack and to destroy the jet fighters at Tehran Airport. The choppers would fly the rescue force and the freed hostages to an abandoned air base at Manzariyeh, about 50 miles southwest of Tehran, which was to be seized and protected by a Ranger company flown in on C-130s. The helicopters would then be destroyed and C-141s, flown in from Saudi Arabia, would then fly the entire group to a base in Egypt. From the beginning of this complex operation, problems occurred. When the helicopters eventually took off, they were told to fly below 200 feet in order to avoid radar signals, even though none had previously been picked up below 3,000 feet! This caused them to fly into a dust storm. The dust cloud became an extended torture for the helicopter pilots, who were trying to fly formation and visually navigate at 200 feet while wearing crude night vision goggles.

Two helicopters consequently lost sight of the main task force and had to land, out of action. A third had landed earlier when a warning light showed up on the control panel. Thinking the craft unsafe to fly, its crew abandoned it in the desert. All the men were subsequently picked up by the following choppers but the task force was now down to six helicopters, the bare minimum needed to pull off the rescue. The first group of three helicopters arrived at Desert One an hour late, with the rest appearing fifteen minutes later. Almost immediately, the rescue attempt was dealt its final blow. One of the remaining choppers had lost its primary hydraulic system and was judged unsafe to use fully loaded for the assault. Only five were now serviceable and six were needed. The doomed mission was aborted.

However, a bad situation became dramatically worse when, as it was being manoeuvred in bad visibility to another position, a helicopter drifted into a parked C-130 aircraft, slicing into it with its spinning rotors and igniting a raging fire. Red-hot chunks of metal flamed across the sky as both machines burst into flames and munitions were torched off. With the flaming wreckage hitting the three nearest helicopters, their crews quickly fled. Eight US soldiers were killed.

Mercifully, the order came to blow up the parked aircraft and exit the country. However, in the dust and horrendous confusion, this order did not get through; those who could escape, did. The aircraft were left intact and top-secret plans fell into the hands of the Iranians.

The next day, the soldiers waiting at Desert Two were almost captured. The mission's failure and its disastrous aftermath were a huge blow to American morale.

The hostages were eventually released after 444 days in captivity.

A HAUNTED HANGAR

COSFORD, ENGLAND 1980

In one of the hangars at RAF Cosford Air Museum in Shropshire stands an Avro Lincoln, a long-range bomber constructed in 1945, and the last of her kind. An historic plane, she is also something of a mystery.

One evening in 1980, a member of staff was locking up this particular hangar when he happened to glance over at the Lincoln, and was certain he saw someone moving inside. He turned on the lights and searched the aircraft, but there was no one there. As he turned off the lights, he saw a strange 'cloud' hovering overhead near the aircraft.

Several days later a mechanic was working inside the plane under poor lighting conditions. Dropping a spanner, he bent down to feel for it in the dark when, suddenly, an invisible hand thrust the spanner into his outstretched fingers as if trying to help him.

A number of other mechanics working in the hangar subsequently reported that tools, spare parts and other items required for restoration work suddenly appeared at their side without warning, as if someone was invisibly helping them in their work.

On one occasion, an electrician working on the Lincoln, fifteen feet above the hangar floor, accidentally fell – but instead of injuring himself, as had happened in a previous accident, he claimed he merely floated gently to the floor, where he landed without so much as a scratch.

Furthermore, numerous unexplained mechanical sounds were heard (and recorded) in the hangar. While sceptics attributed these to changes in temperature causing the hangar structure to 'settle', a number of researchers identified the sounds with specific noises one would expect to hear in a busy, working aircraft hangar. One investigator also recorded the sound of a Consul navigation beacon, even though that piece of equipment had last been used in 1956.

In spite of this catalogue of strange phenomena, however, few people have reported proper sightings of the ghost responsible. Several people have apparently seen a young man sitting in the rear gun turret. Others have seen him in the navigator's seat farther forward. But who was he?

It has been claimed that the plane is haunted by the spirit of one 'Master Pilot Hiller', who was the last pilot to fly her at the end of her commission in 1963. Tragically, Hiller died shortly after in an air crash at Cosford. Legend has it that, on at least one occasion, he said that after his death he would come back to 'haunt his baby' – i.e. the Lincoln bomber.

Unfortunately, 'Master Pilot Hiller' never existed. Records show that the bomber was last piloted not by Hiller, but by one John Langley in April 1963. Hiller's name appears in no official records. And no aircraft crashed in or near Cosford in 1963.

It seems that the ageing Lincoln bomber may be haunted, but by whom or what remains a mystery.

FLYING HIGH AGAIN

LEESBURG, USA 1982

In 1979, ex-Black Sabbath singer Ozzy Osbourne was looking to start a new band. Another rock star recommended Randy Rhoads and although Osbourne appeared initially uninterested in the youngster, after Randy walked in with a Les Paul and a Fender practice amp and started warming up, Osbourne immediately gave him the job. He later described Randy's playing as like 'God entering my life'.

Osbourne's band were touring America in March 1982 and, having played at the Civic Coliseum in Knoxville, Tennessee, they were headed in their tour bus to Orlando, Florida for the following Saturday's 'Rock Super Bowl XIV'.

On the way to Orlando they were to pass by the home of their bus driver Andrew C Aycock, who lived in Leesburg, Florida, at Flying Baron Estates. This consisted of three houses with an aircraft hangar and a landing strip owned by Jerry Calhoun who, as well as being a country and western musician in his earlier days, now leased tour buses, which he kept at the Estate.

The band needed some spare parts for their bus and Aycock, who had picked up his ex-wife at one of the band's shows, planned to drop her off in Florida. The bus arrived at Flying Baron Estates in Leesburg at about 8.00 a.m. on the 19th and parked approximately ninety yards away from the landing strip and close to the front of the house.

In spite of having driven all night, Aycock and his ex-wife, Wanda, went into Jerry Calhoun's house to make some coffee.

Some of Osbourne's band were asleep in the bus while others got out and stretched.

Stored inside the aircraft hangar at Flying Baron Estates was a red-and-white 1955 Beechcraft Bonanza F-35 aeroplane. Aycock possessed a pilot's licence but, unbeknown to anyone at the time, his medical certificate had expired, thus making the license invalid. Nevertheless, he took the plane up without permission and, with keyboardist Don Airey and the band's tour manager as passengers, began a brief daredevil flight, diving and flying low to the ground.

A little while afterwards Aycock took Rachel Youngblood, the group's hairdresser, and lead guitarist Randy Rhoads up for a few minutes, performing the same tricks, taking the plane low towards the ground, at times below tree level. Fatally, however, he then decided to 'buzz' the band's tour bus. He did this not once but four times – on the last, the plane's left wing struck the side of the bus. The plane spun off, hitting a nearby pine tree, before crashing into a garage and exploding into flames. There were no survivors.

The plush travelling bus, equipped with stereo, television and video games, received minor damage. Several broken side windows and a punctured side panel were the only evidence of the disaster. The two-storey house owned by Calhoun, however, was considered to be a total write-off. The roof, upper bedrooms and garage were completely gutted by fire while fire-fighters on the scene said there was probably structural damage to the concrete block walls of the home. The owner, who was inside the house during the impact, miraculously escaped without injury. Two cars, an Oldsmobile and a Ford Granada, were also destroyed when the plane hit the wall and splashed gasoline over the area.

Ozzy Osbourne and other band members, who had been sleeping, at first thought they had been involved in a traffic accident! Once they learned of the catastrophe, they refused to play at Orlando's 'Rock Super Bowl XIV' which, however, went ahead as planned. Osbourne fans might well have contemplated the irony of one of Rhoads's and Osbourne's last songs, 'Flying High Again', and its lyrics: 'Got a crazy feeling I don't understand – Gotta get away from here. Feeling like I shoulda kept my feet on the ground – Waiting for the sun to appear.'

COUCH POTATO TAKES OFF

LOS ANGELES, USA 1982

Larry Walters, a truck driver from southern California, had always dreamed of flying but had been unable to become a pilot in the United States Air Force due to bad eyesight.

However, on 2 July 1982, he made his dream come true. He fastened 42 surplus helium-filled balloons to an aluminium garden chair and launched himself into the stratosphere from his girlfriend's backyard in San Pedro!

Lawn-chair Larry, as he was instantly dubbed, carried various supplies with him. He took along a large bottle of soda, a parachute, a portable CB radio to alert air traffic to his presence and a gun to shoot the balloons one at a time to descend. He also took a camera, but later admitted, 'I was so amazed by the view I didn't even take one picture.'

However, Walters didn't realise how powerful the buoyancy of the balloons would be. When he cut a rope holding him to terra firma, he took off with such a jolt that another anchor rope broke under the stress and he shot upward so quickly that he lost his spectacles.

He floated around the LA basin for several hours and reached altitudes of up to 16,000 feet, where he was spotted by pilots from both TWA and Delta Airlines.

It was cold at 16,000 feet and he started shooting some of his balloons to descend, but when he accidentally dropped his BB gun he had to wait for his rig to come down on its own. He eventually landed in a residential neighbourhood in Long Beach where he got tangled in some power lines, causing a power blackout.

He later told *New York Times* reporters, 'It was something I had to do. If I hadn't done it, I would have ended up in the funny farm. I didn't think that by fulfilling my goal in life – my dream – that would create such a stir and make people laugh.'

The stunt earned Walters a $1,500 fine from the Federal Aviation Association, which cited him for four violations of the Federal Aviation Act, including 'operating a civil aircraft for which there is not currently in effect an airworthiness certificate' and 'operating an aircraft within an airport traffic area without establishing and maintaining two-way communications with the control tower'.

He also won the top prize from the Bonehead Club of Dallas for achieving the altitude record for gas-filled clustered balloons (which could not be officially recorded because he was unlicensed and unsanctioned). He also appeared on *The Tonight Show* and was flown to New York to be on *Late Night With David Letterman*, which he later described as 'the most fun I've ever had'. He was in brief demand as a motivational speaker after his flight and quit his job as a truck driver, though he was never able to make much money from his fame.

Walters gave his 'aircraft', which he'd dubbed 'Inspiration 1', to admiring neighbourhood children after he landed – which he later regretted, especially after the Smithsonian Institute requested to preserve it in their museum. He would, in fact, never see his chair again.

He died on 6 October 1993 after hiking to a remote spot in Angeles National Forest and shooting himself in the heart. He left no clues as to the motive for the suicide.

GIMLI GLIDER

GIMLI, CANADA 1983

In Western Canadian slang, 'to pull a Gimli Glider' is to make a spectacular foul-up. The legend originated in the following manner.

On 23 July 1983, a Boeing 767-200 jet, Air Canada Flight 143, ran out of fuel over northern Canada. Due to the failure of the automatic fuelling system and a series of computing errors by the flight and refuelling crews, the plane had taken off with under half the required amount to complete the journey.

At 41,000 feet, over Red Lake, Ontario, the cockpit warning system chimed four times, and indicated a fuel-pressure problem on the left side. The pilots, thinking a fuel pump had failed, turned it off. The computer then erroneously indicated that there was still plenty of fuel. A few moments later a second alarm sounded, and the pilots decided to divert to Winnipeg. Within seconds the left engine failed completely.

While they attempted to restart the engine and arranged for an emergency landing in Winnipeg, the warning system sounded again, this time with a long 'bong' that no one present could recall ever hearing before. The sound was in fact the 'all engines out' sound, something that had never been simulated in their training. Seconds later the right-side engine stopped and the 767 lost all power, including electrical power to the instrumentation screens.

One of the lost instruments was the vertical-rate indicator, which would have let the crew know how fast they were sinking and therefore how far they could glide. The engines also supplied power to the hydraulic systems, without which a plane the size of the 767 could not be controlled. Fortunately, Boeing had planned for this possible failure and included a device known as a ram air turbine that automatically popped open on the side of the plane, using some of the plane's residual velocity to spin a propeller-driven generator, which provided enough power to the hydraulics to make it controllable.

The pilots immediately opened the emergency guide, looking for the section on flying the aircraft with both engines out – only to find there was no such section!

Pilot Bob Pearson thus glided the plane at 220 knots, his best guess as to the optimum airspeed, while co-pilot Maurice Quintal began making calculations to see if they'd be able to reach Winnipeg. When they discovered this wasn't possible, it was decided to try for a landing at Quintal's former RCAF base at Gimli.

Unbeknown to Quintal, since his time in the service Gimli had been turned over to the use of the general public. Apart from serving as a club for flyers and skydivers, it was now a popular venue for drag racing! To make matters worse, on this particular day, the area was also covered with cars and campers for 'Family Day'.

As they approached Gimli, the main nose wheel of the landing gear, despite being built to open by swinging backwards with the force of the wind, wouldn't lock. The ever-reducing speed of the plane also made it increasingly hard to control. It also became apparent that they were too high, and so Pearson executed a manoeuvre known as a 'sideslip' to increase their drag and reduce their altitude.

As soon as the wheels touched the runway the pilots slammed on the brakes, blowing out several of the plane's tyres. The plane came to rest, nose down due to the unlocked nose gear, only a few hundred feet from Family Day at the end of the runway.

Miraculously, no one was hurt, although there some individuals sustained minor injuries when exiting via the rear slide which, due to the raised elevation of the tail, was hanging almost vertical.

A minor fire in the nose area was soon put out by drag-racers who rushed over with fire extinguishers. Mechanics quickly repaired the minor damage and flew the plane out two days later. Within weeks it was fully repaired and back in service.

As an ironic side note, the mechanics sent out from Winnipeg Airport in a van also ran out of fuel on their way to Gimli, and found themselves stranded in the backwoods of Manitoba! Another van had to be sent to pick them up.

As of March 2005, the 'Gimli Glider' was still in service with Air Canada.

SOUTH AFRICAN DEATH FLIGHTS

KWAZULU/NATAL, SOUTH AFRICA 1983

In May 2000, at the trial of South Africa's Wouter Basson for alleged human-rights abuses, a crowded courtroom of Pretoria's High Court heard the grizzly confession of Johan Theron, a former information officer of South Africa's apartheid government's Special Forces. According to Theron, the execution of hundreds of South West African People's Organisation (SWAPO) activist prisoners had been seen as a solution to the increasing prison inmate population of several defence force camps. Between 1979 and 1987 he was involved in the deaths of more than two hundred men using various methods, including burning, beating, poisoning and strangulation.

In 1983, for instance, in northern KwaZulu/Natal, Theron claimed to have been instructed by Basson to tie up three prisoners to a tree overnight and smear their bodies with jelly-like lethal toxins. The primary aim was to test the toxic agent to see if it was capable of causing death. The men did not die as easily as he expected, however, and the next day were still clinging to life. So he decided to get rid of them in another way.

He loaded them into a small plane and flew off towards the ocean. According to an article South Africa's *Sunday Times*, during the flight Theron injected the three men with lethal muscle relaxants before dumping their bodies into the sea some 100 miles off the coast.

After a couple of hair-raising incidents in which Theron had to kill awakening prisoners who were in the process of being transported with his bare hands, he asked Basson, then the leader of an elite Special Operations medical unit whose personnel accompanied SF operatives into the field, to provide him with drugs to ensure that the prisoners would not wake up and begin struggling for survival. According to Theron, Basson thereafter supplied him with a 'cocktail' consisting of the drugs Tubarine and Scoline, which were normally used to collapse the lungs during surgery but which would cause paralysis and death if administered in high doses to living prisoners. Because of the painful nature of such a death, Basson later allegedly provided Theron with the anaesthetic ketamine so that the victims could first be put to sleep.

Theron claimed that Basson, the former head of South Africa's chemical and biological warfare programme, readily supplied the lethal drugs, which he used on the majority of his victims.

Earlier, a retired French Foreign Legionnaire claimed he'd witnessed Basson injecting political prisoners from the Zimbabwe African National Liberation Army with poison in their stomach during a flight over Mozambique territory in 1979. The men were then thrown alive from an aeroplane. Before the poisoned, unconscious men were thrown from the plane, they were dressed in camouflage uniforms and supplied with guns and false papers. They were then sprinkled with an unknown powdery substance, which the witness believed was poison or some kind of lethal chemical agent meant to contaminate other rebel soldiers who may happen upon the bodies.

Basson was thought to have been involved in around 24 'death flights' between 1979 and 1987. Theron, however, explained to the court that he could never bring himself to throw a man out of a plane while he was still alive. 'He had to be killed first,' he said.

TIME SLIP

GRAND TURK, BAHAMAS 1983

The question of whether parallel dimensions exist is a complicated and, as yet, unanswered one. Occasionally, however, an incident occurs that tilts the argument towards the affirmative.

In 1983, Carolyn Cascio was ferrying a passenger to Grand Turk, Bahamas, in her Cessna 172 aircraft. The weather was clear and as the plane approached the airport runway, the tower tried to contact her, asking for her identification. However, there was no answer. The plane simply circled the airport in a holding pattern, watched in bewilderment and increasing consternation by the airport officials below. There seemed to be no obvious sign of distress, and the plane was operating normally. Cascio was a licensed and competent pilot, and knew everyone at the airport. What could be the problem? They tried again, asking her whether there was a problem and what her intentions were. It was then that something both bizarre and disturbing occurred. Because Cascio had apparently left her microphone keyed in the open position, those in the control tower were able to hear what appeared to be a conversation between herself and a passenger.

At first she seemed to be puzzled by what she was seeing below her, and suggested that she had made a wrong turn – there was, she said, nothing to be seen below her, no houses, no airport, no nothing! The passenger simply agreed with her. Neither of them could see the airport they were circling! They had continued circling because, according to Cascio's calculations, they ought to have been over Grand Turk by now – which, of course, they were.

Realising that something was seriously wrong, airport control desperately tried to contact her over the radio, but to no avail. After half an hour of circling, the airport picked up Cascio's last, chilling words. 'Is there no way out of this?' she said, before apparently making a decision to fly to another island. At that, she simply banked sharply to the left and flew out across the sea. The aircraft flew off into a low-lying cloud bank, but did not come out the other side. Neither Cascio, her passenger, nor the aircraft were ever seen again.

ROUND THE WORLD IN NINE DAYS

1986

The first nonstop un-refuelled flight around the world took place between 14 December and 23 December 1986, and was achieved by pilot Dick Rutan and co-pilot Jeanna Yeager – no relation to Chuck – in an aircraft (*The Voyager*) designed by Burt Rutan, Dick's brother.

Although the aircraft itself weighed only 939 pounds, at take-off from Edwards Air Force Base in California, fuel, pilots and supplies added up to a gross weight of 9,694.5 pounds! In fact, the large amount of fuel contained in *Voyager*'s wing tanks caused them to bob up and down while accelerating down the runway, and in the process, about a foot of each wing tip was chipped off. Rutan and Yeager circled the airfield and checked their plane's handling conditions; fortunately, the plane seemed sound enough to continue the journey.

The two pilots endured severe physical and mental demands during their record-breaking trip. To combat inevitable fatigue, they tried to rotate their duties, one crew member flying the aircraft, the other resting. Initially, they tried to work in two-to-three-hour shifts, but things did not always go according to plan. What's more, they found it extremely difficult to manoeuvre themselves into comfortable sleeping positions within the confines of *Voyager*'s small cockpit, which was only the size of a telephone booth.

At the time of the flight, there was no access to Libyan airspace – for political reasons – and they were forced to re-route their flight, costing them precious fuel. Later, they used up even more fuel to avoid storms that constantly threatened to rip the fragile plane apart. They even had to fly around the 600-mile-wide Typhoon Marge. While such manoeuvring helped them escape physical harm, it only added to their mental stress. Each time they had to adjust their flight plan by climbing above a storm, or going around one, they burned more fuel, and since *Voyager* had started the trip on a very tight fuel budget, they grew increasingly concerned that they might not have enough to complete their journey.

Finally, as the coast of California came into view, it seemed that they were home and dry; but then disaster struck! One of the two fuel pumps on board the *Voyager* malfunctioned and stopped pumping! The only working pump was hooked up to empty fuel tanks, due to eight days of flying, so Rutan began working frantically to swap the pumps while Yeager piloted the plane. But even when the pumps had been switched, the fuel still would not flow.

Finally, they realised that it was the altitude of the plane that was keeping the fuel away from the good pump. Yeager aimed the *Voyager* down toward the ocean. At the new altitude, the fuel rushed through the lines and found the good pump. The plane was flying again!

Rutan and Yeager completed their journey, touching down at Edwards Air Force Base at 8.06 a.m. on 23 December 1986. The entire 24,986-mile trip had taken 9 days, 3 minutes and 44 seconds, or a little more than 216 hours. During their trip, they had averaged around 116 miles per hour and when they landed, they had only a couple of gallons of fuel left.

HAVE A NICE DAY!

TEMPLETON, USA 1987

On 7 December 1987, USAir employee, David Burke, was dismissed from his job by his supervisor, Ronald Thompson, for stealing money from a beer fund kept by flight attendants. During the hearing he'd pleaded in vain for leniency. As he left his office, he was told to have a nice day, to which he replied, 'I intend on having a very good day.'

He later boarded the Pacific Southwest Airlines daily non-stop flight between Los Angeles and San Francisco, the flight also taken by Ron Thompson every day to commute home from the USAir Headquarters. Using his USAir credentials, Burke was able to bypass security carrying a loaded .44 Magnum pistol.

Once the plane was airborne, he wrote a note on an airsickness bag: 'It's kind of ironical, isn't it? I asked for leniency for my family, remember? Well, I got none, and now you'll get none.'

Upon reaching cruise altitude, Burke left his seat and headed to the lavatory, dropping the note into the Thompson's lap. On his return, a few moments later, Burke took out his handgun and shot Thompson. He then moved towards the cockpit door. With remarkable understatement, a flight attendant told the cockpit crew that, 'We have a problem.' The captain replied, 'What kind of problem?' Burke then appeared at the cockpit door and announced, 'I'm the problem,' simultaneously firing two more shots that killed the pilots.

Several seconds later, the flight recorder picked up increasing windscreen noise as the aeroplane pitched down and began to accelerate. A final gunshot was heard as Burke fatally shot himself.

The plane then descended to 13,000 feet, when, travelling at terrific speed, it broke apart and crashed in a farmer's field in the Santa Ana Hills near Templeton, California.

So completely did the plane disintegrate that those arriving on the scene found nothing that resembled a large airliner. In fact, there were no pieces bigger than a human hand, leading some to think that what had crashed was a small aeroplane full of newspapers.

After the discovery of the handgun, forensic experts found a small piece of skin wedged between the trigger and the barrel. By matching the skin prints to the passenger manifest, they were able to conclude that the gun had been in the hand of USAir employee David Burke at the time of impact.

The accident caused the end of Pacific Southwest Airlines, which in April 1988 was absorbed into USAir. Because his employer had not confiscated all of his work identification, Burke had been able to move unchallenged through the airport, according to Ronald Wecht, a San Francisco lawyer who represented family members who sued the airline and others. They received more than $20 million in out-of-court settlements.

Strict federal laws were passed after the crash, including a law that required 'immediate seizure of all airline employee credentials' upon termination from an airline position. Another policy was put into place whereby all members of any airline flight crew, including the captain, be subjected to the same security measures as the passengers.

MATTHIAS RUST LANDS HIS PLANE IN RED SQUARE

MOSCOW, USSR 1987

At around 7.30 p.m. on 28 May 1987, a white single-engine Cessna with West German markings flew over Lenin's mausoleum and landed near the Kremlin wall on the 750-yard-long Red Square in central Moscow. The small plane, piloted by a West German teenager named Matthias Rust, had flown 550 miles from Helsinki, Finland, to Moscow across one of the most closely guarded borders in the world.

Rust had started his flight in Hamburg, and refuelled at Helsinki, where he told air-traffic control that he was going to Stockholm. However, once he had taken off, he turned eastward and disappeared from Finnish airspace.

Heading towards the Baltic coastline, he turned towards Moscow when, by chance, the combination of a national border guard's holiday and lax security allowed him to fly into Soviet territory unnoticed. Although his plane was observed at various points along the way, it was flying so slowly that air reconnaissance was difficult!

When he came down in Red Square, curious onlookers and tourists believed that Rust was part of an air show, and immediately crowded round when he stepped from the plane. Very quickly, however, he was whisked away by the Russian authorities. The event proved to be an immense embarrassment to the Soviet government and military, and the repercussions in the Soviet Union were immediate: Soviet leader Mikhail Gorbachev sacked his minister of defence.

Rust, meanwhile, was put on trial in Moscow on 2 September 1987 for violating Soviet airspace. Described by his mother as a 'quiet young man . . . with a passion for flying', Rust argued that he had merely been trying to promote world peace. He carried with him copies of a plan he had developed for a worldwide democracy, which he referred to as 'Lagonia'. In the event, he was sentenced to four years in a labour camp for hooliganism, disregard of aviation laws and infringement of the Soviet border.

After serving some fifteen months, during which time he lost more than 10kg and suffered severe stomach problems, he was returned to West Germany on 3 August 1988. He worked for some time in a hospital in Rissen, Germany where he fell in love with a nurse. However, when his romantic advances were rejected he attempted to murder her by stabbing her with a knife. For this, he was sentenced to two and a half years in prison.

He was released after five months, however and, in April 1994, Rust announced that he would return to Russia, visiting an orphanage, for which he had become the patron. He then disappeared for two years, working as a shoe salesman in Moscow.

Two years later, at the age of 28, Rust returned to Germany and married an Indian girl named Geetha, the daughter of a wealthy Indian tea-salesman. He converted to Hinduism, but in 2001 appeared in court on a charge of stealing a cashmere pullover.

Rust now lives in Berlin with his second wife, Athena.

Today, a wealthy Japanese businessman owns Rust's aircraft, keeping it in a hangar until its value appreciates.

MODERN-DAY DAEDALUS

CRETE 1988

On the Greek Island of Crete lie the ancient ruins of Knossos, where a mythical inventor named Daedalus – considered to be the father of aviation – was said to have been imprisoned three thousand years ago, along with his son Icarus. Daedalus built wings of feathers and wax so that he and his son could fly to freedom across the sea. But Icarus was overwhelmed by the sense of power he experienced and flew too close to the sun, which melted his wings. Daedalus flew with more restraint and made it safely to the nearest island, Sontorini.

In 1985 a team of engineers from MIT set themselves the target of building a machine by means of which a man might fly the Daedalus route from Crete to the island of Santorini, 74 miles north – over three times the existing world record for human-powered flight.

They proceeded to build an aeroplane not of wax and feathers, but of carbon-fibre composites and plastics. It gave a whole new meaning to the word 'spindly'. Its wingspan outreached a Boeing 727's, but it weighed only 70 pounds. They named it, inevitably, *Daedalus*.

The most serious problem in achieving the feat, however, was going to be human endurance. The team carefully studied anatomy and metabolism. After extensive testing of 24 men and one woman, four world-class competitive cyclists were recruited to fill out a five-pilot team. Four of the five had no flying experience and so went into flight training in California while keeping up an intensive training regime, cycling at least 400 miles per week.

On Crete, the five pilots went on a rotating schedule, like baseball pitchers, so that one was always on a two-day taper of rest and ready to make the flight. Weather was a major factor. Finally, in the third week of April, the forecast improved. On Friday, 22 April, a flight was scheduled. Kanellos Kanellopoulos was up in the rotation and would be *Daedalus*'s pilot. He would be required to burn up his body energy at the rate of one kilowatt for four hours' running and, to sustain him on the trip, the team developed a special drink, one that would maintain balances of glucose, sodium, carbohydrates, electrolytes and water. Kanellopoulos would have to drink about a gallon of it during the flight.

The weather cooperated. He took off and was airborne over the sea at 14 miles per hour and a heart rate of 140 beats per minute. He flew on average a mere 5 metres above the water. Four hours later, *Daedalus* approached its final goal, the island of Santorini.

However, the head wind was strong now and as the plane approached the coast, Kanellopoulos had to attempt a landing parallel to the beach for an upwind touchdown. Then disaster hit. A gust of wind snapped the tailbone and then the wing and *Daedalus* settled into the sea just short of the beach. The pilot swam to shore, disappointed but at the same time exhilarated with the partial success of the flight.

The mythical flight of *Daedalus* was not completed. What went wrong? Were the gods unwilling to cooperate? Were they angry? It should be noted that the *Daedalus* pilot used a glucose drink throughout the flight and used leg power instead of arm power. So the gods had reason to be concerned, and perhaps, intervened?

PILOT SUCKED OUT

BIRMINGHAM, ENGLAND 1990

Nigel Ogden is a survivor. As an air steward, he had experienced an engine blow-out, a hold-door falling out and a near catastrophe in a thunderstorm a few thousand feet above the Alps. In 1990, however, in the skies above England, he survived probably one of the strangest of all near-disasters in the air.

Piloted by Tim Lancaster and co-piloted by newcomer Alistair Atchingson, Ogden's BAC111 took off from Birmingham, England on 10 June 1990 with 86 passengers on board. It was a holiday flight to Malaga and the passengers were relaxed.

Thirteen minutes after take-off, however, at about 17,000 feet, there was an enormous explosion. The cabin crew thought at first that a bomb had exploded. However, the truth was more prosaic, though equally shocking. While climbing past an altitude of 17,300 feet, the windshield on the pilot's side experienced a catastrophic failure. British accident investigators would later determine that 84 of the 90 retention bolts in the windshield were of a diameter smaller than specified. The extreme air-pressure difference between the outside and inside air had thus been able to blow the windshield out.

Worse was to follow. Explosive decompression made the whole cabin mist up like fog for a second – and the plane started to plummet. It was at that moment that Ogden suddenly realised that pilot Tim Lancaster had been sucked head first out of the cockpit! His shirt had been pulled off his back and his

274

body was bent upwards, doubled over round the top of the aircraft. The high speed of the aircraft was keeping him pinned in this position.

Incredibly, however, the back of his knees had caught onto the windshield frame and his upper body was hanging outside the aeroplane with his back against the upper fuselage. His ankles, meanwhile, were jammed against the pilot-side control stick, disconnecting the autopilot, while the flight door was resting on the controls. This crazy set of consequences was now sending the plane hurtling down at nearly 399 miles per hour through some of the most congested skies in the world.

Ogden jumped over the control column and grabbed Lancaster round his waist to avoid him going out completely. Everything was being sucked out of the aircraft: even an oxygen bottle that had been bolted down went flying. Ogden was holding on for grim death but could feel himself being sucked out too when a steward, John Heward, rushed in and grabbed Ogden's trouser belt to stop him slipping further. He then wrapped the captain's shoulder strap around him. Luckily, Alistair, the co-pilot, was still wearing his safety harness from take-off, otherwise he would have gone, too.

Lancaster's face was now banging against the windscreen with blood coming out of his nose and the side of his head, his arms flailing. Most terrifyingly, although his face was hitting the side screen, his eyes were wide open.

By now, Alistair was talking to air-traffic control, who were talking him through a landing at Southampton Airport. All pilot training is done on the basis of two pilots, one to fly and one doing the emergency drill, but Alistair was alone, with a crew he didn't know and relying entirely on memory, because all the manuals and charts had blown away. He asked for a runway of 2,500 metres (8,200 feet) because he was worried that the plane was so heavy with fuel, a tyre would burst or it would go off the runway, but was told that he could only have one of 1,800 metres (5,905 feet). Incredibly, Alistair completed a completely smooth landing, stopping the aircraft only three-quarters of the way down the runway. The time from the explosion to the landing had been eighteen minutes.

Despite the violent ejection, and enduring 15-knot winds at sub-freezing temperatures for twenty minutes, Lancaster survived the incident. Luckily, he had been in a coma throughout the ordeal, his body having simply shut down. He was hospitalised for a few days and treated for frostbite, and a broken arm and wrists, but suffered no permanent injuries. Within five months he was flying again. Ogden was left with a dislocated shoulder, a frostbitten face and some frostbite damage to his left eye. No one else on board the aeroplane was hurt.

In 1992, a report into the accident was published. It turned out that a BA engineer had fitted a new windscreen with bolts that were too small. These smaller bolts led to the failure of the windshield.

After nine years fighting for compensation, Ogden took early retirement and is now a night watchman in a Salvation Army Hostel.

CUBA LIBRE!

CUBA 1992

Lorenzo Perez, a former pilot in the Cuban Air Force, made headlines in 1991 when he defected to the United States by flying a MiG jet to Florida. Though he had gained his freedom, Lorenzo purchased it at the cost of his family – his wife Victoria, and their two sons – whom he had been forced to leave behind.

Soon after his arrival in the United States, Lorenzo started a campaign to win his family back, but the Cuban government refused to allow them to leave the country. He realised he would somehow have to get them himself.

Using either helicopters or speedboats was ruled out as both were too expensive. The only way he could get to Cuba and back again was with a light aeroplane. He started taking flying lessons because, though he had flown over a thousand hours in high-performance jet aircraft, he had never flown anything smaller.

A few months later he was ready to mount his rescue operation. Some time around 4 a.m. on 19 December 1992, he checked into the Seaward Motel on Florida's Marathon Key. The next morning he walked back to the airport to check his Cessna and refuelled the two wingtip tanks for what he hoped would be a 200-mile round trip.

Several hours before this, he had talked to his wife and, in a carefully planned code, told her when he would be arriving. He would start his flight around sunset, arrive with the last rays of the sun, and get out under a descending curtain of darkness.

On the appointed day, he climbed into the cockpit wearing a running suit, an early Christmas present from friends, who had asked him to wear it on the flight. After one more run-through of his checklist, he started to taxi slowly to the runway. At exactly 5.07 p.m. he radioed local air traffic: 'Cessna 5819. Departing runway 07.'

On his left knee Lorenzo had his flight plan. On his right knee he had strapped his calculator. He had also brought a camera, but nothing else except for some soft drinks and a box of chocolates. To protect himself in the event of being caught, he had left all identification cards at home.

The key to Lorenzo's plan was the clumsy Cuban military chain of command that would be initiated when his plane was spotted. An alert would require a time-consuming series of phone calls up the command hierarchy, from a company to a battalion to a brigade to a division. That would buy him much-needed time as he got closer to his destination.

In fact, Lorenzo was less concerned that the Cuban air defence system would catch him than that his wife, Victoria and children wouldn't make it to the rendezvous point.

He had arranged to meet her on a new highway that ran along the coast to a new airport. The only problem was that the site was located near four anti-aircraft missile complexes. But Lorenzo knew that authorities would need Castro's personal permission before shooting down an aeroplane.

Before long, Lorenzo saw his destination, Matanzas, materialise on the horizon. His wife was supposed to be waiting about a mile east of a bridge where the road curved around a hill. Lorenzo was flying so low, however, that the hill blocked his view of the rendezvous site. He banked around the hill at about 20 feet and finally spotted the rendezvous spot. But he still couldn't see his family. He had only a single chance to land, so he reduced speed and dropped the landing gear.

As he was approaching the two-lane highway, he saw his wife on his left. As he had instructed, she and the children were wearing brightly coloured clothes – fluorescent orange T-shirts and cap – so that he could spot them quickly.

Below him, a small car was moving in the same direction as

the aeroplane. Several hundred yards ahead of it a truck was approaching. Behind that, a bus was trying to pass! Lorenzo planned to fly over the car and land in the highway between the car and the oncoming truck. He didn't have room for a proper landing, but he knew there wasn't time for a second approach. He overflew the car and touched down. When the Cessna came to a stop, Lorenzo found himself staring directly at the truck's driver, who sat clutching his steering wheel, his eyes wide and mouth open.

Victoria didn't see her husband until the aeroplane was almost on the ground. She now gripped her sons' hands and they ran toward the aeroplane. While his family was running towards him, Lorenzo turned the Cessna around, frantically ushered them into the plane and ordered them to keep quiet and sit in the seats behind him. He then twice tried to close the door – but failed each time! On the third try, he finally succeeded.

With the aeroplane's flaps set for a short field take-off, Lorenzo began to accelerate down the highway. As the airspeed indicator showed 60 miles per hour – still not fast enough to take off – Lorenzo could see the highway's curve approaching. He pulled the yoke back slowly and the aeroplane continued gaining speed. He took off at the last possible moment.

As he left Cuba, Lorenzo flew over the sea as low as he could. No moon or stars were shining that night, but soon he and his family saw the lights of the Florida Keys and US Highway 1 with the lights of cars extending north. He called air-traffic control and they assigned him an altitude of 7,000 feet. At 6.45 p.m. he was back on the ground.

From start to finish the rescue flight had taken less than a hundred minutes. And the Cessna had flown so low that it was now covered with salt!

BLADDER BOMB

FORT LAUDERDALE, USA 1993

In 1993, Johann Peter Grzeganek – a German student who spoke little English – was a passenger on a charter flight from Fort Lauderdale to Hanover, Germany.

Even before the commencement of the flight he was very drunk on beer and, shortly after take-off, he moved to the middle of the plane. There, according to one of the stewardesses, 'He acted as if he thought he was in the toilet.'

He was actually trying to make it to the bathroom, but the stewardess would not let him because passengers are not allowed to use it within the first ten minutes of take-off.

When stopped by flight attendants, Grzeganek announced, 'the roof was going to go'. He then made a broad sweeping gesture, which the attendants thought indicated an explosion would occur. He became unruly, and the plane returned to Fort Lauderdale because of fear that he had brought a bomb aboard. A search of Grzeganek's hand luggage, conducted before turning back to Fort Lauderdale, yielded a camera, a jar of cold cream and clothing, but nothing resembling a bomb.

Grzeganek was arrested after the plane landed. As a result, the flight missed its connection in Gander, Newfoundland, forcing the company to divert the plane to New York City and pay for overnight lodging and meals for its passengers.

Later, at his hearing, Grzeganek claimed he had been trying to tell the air hostess that if she did not let him go to the bathroom, his bladder would explode – not the plane! His gesture, he said, was, 'to show that his bladder was going to explode and not the roof of the aircraft', though he went on to elaborate, 'Well, if my bladder explodes, then also the roof would go.' He added that, although he had spoken to one flight attendant in German, she soon left the mid-ship's area and went to the front of the plane, and then only English-speaking personnel were with him.

Herr Grzeganek was subsequently sent to prison for making a bomb threat. Nine months into his sentence, a federal judge released him and he was fined $200, although a written court opinion questioned whether he should have been prosecuted at all.

ATTACK ON THE WHITE HOUSE

WASHINGTON, DC, USA 1994

On Sunday, 11 September 1994, after spending an evening with his brother consuming alcohol and smoking crack cocaine, Frank Eugene Corder asked his sibling to drop him off in the vicinity of Aldino Airport in Churchville, Maryland. Corder walked to the airport and found the keys to a Cessna 150L aeroplane that had been returned to the airport earlier that day after having been rented by another flyer.

Although Corder was not a licensed pilot, he had taken several lessons in the aircraft and had flown it several times during the summer of 1993. According to the aeroplane's Hobbs meter, which records the engine's total running time, Corder started the plane's engine at 1.55 p.m. FAA radar at the Baltimore/Washington International Airport first detected the aeroplane in the vicinity of York, Pennsylvania, at 1.06 a.m.

He flew south for a short distance and then west. At 1.44 a.m., the National Airport tower began receiving transmissions that showed that Corder was approximately 6½ miles north of the White House, flying at an altitude of 2,700 feet. The aircraft descended approximately 1,000 feet over the next three minutes.

At 1.47 a.m., the aeroplane turned directly south, passed over Washington Circle and entered the prohibited airspace that surrounds the White House at 1.48 a.m. (The protected airspace, designated as P-56, is a no-fly zone that generally encompasses the White House and the Mall from the Lincoln Memorial to the Capitol.) The plane flew toward the Mall, descending rapidly.

282

Corder then passed over the Ellipse or the President's Park South, a circular park of some 52 acres, and dived directly toward the White House at a steep angle of descent. His plane crashed onto the White House lawn just south of the Executive Mansion at 1.49 a.m. The aircraft skidded across the ground, knocked some branches off the magnolia tree planted by President Andrew Jackson just west of the South Portico steps, and hit the southwest corner of the first floor of the mansion.

The president and first family were in fact residing at Blair House at the time of the crash, as the White House was undergoing renovations. There was minimal damage to the Mansion but Corder died from multiple, massive blunt-force injuries.

It was the first known deliberate air attack on a major building in America. Corder had no obvious motive for the crime, and although his wife had died some weeks before from cancer, he was said to be getting on with life 'as best he could'. He was building a small kit aircraft of his own at the same airport the Cessna 150L was stolen from, and frequently worked alone at night on his pet project.

Various outlandish suggestions were floated soon afterwards. Although Corder's badly mangled body was recovered from the wreckage, there was no forensic way of establishing whether he had died in the crash itself, or several hours earlier. No one witnessed Frank Corder board or steal the Cessna in Maryland, and at no time did he make radio contact with the control tower or anyone else. Frank Corder behaved in all respects like a ghost, and some have suggested that he may well have been dead before the Cessna left the ground in Maryland.

Immediately after the crash, intelligence sources concurred that the flight was most probably flown as a 'Proof of Concept', designed to thoroughly test Washington's air defences and expose possible flaws. If the Cessna 150L had managed to strike the White House wall directly, the concept would be considered proven, perhaps paving the way for later attacks using heavier aircraft loaded with munitions. In this respect the flight was a complete success.

However, the official judgement was less sinister. Corder, by crashing onto the White House lawn, was attempting to fulfil an ambition he had expressed to friends – to kill himself 'in a big way' by flying an aeroplane either into the White House, or into the dome of the Capitol.

In the wake of Corder's crash and the resulting publicity, the White House became the focus of a cluster of attacks. On 29 October 1994, Francisco Martin Duran, a convicted felon, pulled a semiautomatic rifle from under his trench coat and fired at least 29 shots as he ran down the south sidewalk of Pennsylvania Avenue, spraying the front of the White House with bullets.

In December 1994 there were no less than five incidents, four involving breaches of the mansion's grounds and ranging from fence jumping, and threats of a car bomb, to a homeless man waving a knife on a sidewalk outside the White House – he was shot and killed by police.

Although the White House was reportedly rigged with surface-to-air missiles at the time of the Corder crash, none fired.

GHOST PLANES

LONGDENDALE, ENGLAND 1995

Howden Moors in the Peak District of Derbyshire are scattered with the wreckage of many World War II aircraft. It can be no coincidence, therefore, that Longendale Valley below has been haunted for years by the 'Phantom Bombers of the High Peak'. A local farmer has even set up a study group to monitor events and is regularly contacted by people who have seen ghost planes in the area.

In April 1995, for instance, retired postman Tony Ingle was walking his dog when he saw the sun blocked out by the shadow of a plane overhead – he could see the propellers going round but there was no sound. It banked and appeared to ditch into a nearby field. He ran to the field, but found nothing. His dog now refuses to go into that field.

Many more people have reported seeing low-flying aircraft in the area that eventually just disappear. The most recent sighting was in March 1997, when two friends ventured up onto the moors in the evening to view the Hale-Bopp comet in the clear night sky. What they saw instead was a low-flying plane. It was also seen by a farmer who instinctively ducked, so convinced was he that the apparition was real!

Most extraordinary of all, a local couple also reported hearing the sound of a loud crash and seeing a bright orange glow light up the sky. Another couple also reported the 'explosion'. For fifteen hours, hundreds of emergency service personnel, tracker dogs and two helicopters searched the moorland for the stricken aircraft. No trace of it was ever found.

FROM SEA TO SHINING SEA

PESCADERO, USA 1996

At just 4 feet 2 inches, needing extenders for her feet to reach the plane's rudder pedals and a cushion to see over the instrument panel, seven-year-old Jessica Dubroff was eager to fulfil her quest to become the youngest person to fly across America. Although her father and flight instructor were to accompany her for the eight-day, 6,900-mile flight across the United States and back, Jessica planned to do all the flying. The trio were to start the trip eastwards on the morning of Wednesday, 11 April 1996 from Half Moon Bay, California. They planned to arrive Friday in Falmouth, Massachusetts, after refuelling stops in Cheyenne and Fort Wayne, Indiana.

Jessica Dubroff grew up in a somewhat unconventional family that had only recently emerged from serious financial hardship. Three years before, in 1993, Jessica, then four, was a squatter with her mother, Lisa Blair Hathaway, in an abandoned house in Falmouth, Massachusetts.

At about the same time, Jessica's father, Lloyd Dubroff, who never married Hathaway but was the sole support of their three children, filed for bankruptcy in California, citing debts of more than $150,000. Dubroff at that time was living in Palo Alto with his current wife, and their young daughter. His computer consulting business, according to court records, was foundering and he was facing eviction.

By late 1995, however, Dubroff had apparently recovered sufficiently from his financial problems to be able to pay for Jessica's flying lessons. He had hatched a plan for her to fly across the country and back with himself and her flying instructor as passengers and was footing the $15,000 bill for the venture. The cross-country flight, he told reporters, 'was my idea, but presented to Jessica for her choice. Out of the blue it occurred to me that Jessica could do this.'

He contacted the *Guinness Book of Records* and arranged with ABC News to install a camera in the plane. Even President Clinton was invited on a plane ride when they got to Washington. The family had baseball caps and T-shirts made bearing the logo, 'From Sea to Shining Sea, April 1996' to distribute as souvenirs along the route.

At the same time, Lisa Blair Hathaway solicited contributions to help underwrite the flight and gave out a post-office box number to which donors could send money. She talked of holding a 'Meet the Pilot' day at Half Moon Bay Airport the Saturday before the flight and asked the *Examiner* newspaper to report that the family was seeking 'financial contributions'. She also made it clear that she would like people to bring health food to Jessica's stops along the route because she was a vegetarian. 'She's not going to want to go around for an hour looking for a health-food store,' Hathaway explained.

The great day came and a crowd gathered to wave goodbye. Wearing a baseball cap that said 'Women fly', Jessica was apparently at the controls of the Cessna Cardinal 177 four-seat plane when it took off from the Half Moon Bay Airport on the first leg of her journey. They arrived safely at Cheyenne Airport, where they stopped for refuelling. Jessica was again at the controls at 8.25 a.m. when, in stormy weather, they took off. It was then that disaster struck. They were barely off the ground when, after just missing a house by some 25 feet, the plane nose-dived into a driveway in a residential area about a mile from the airport. Jessica was killed along with her father, Lloyd Dubroff, and flight instructor Joe Reid.

Her mother had described herself as a writer, an artist and a healing consultant, and claimed that she had once considered writing a book on parenting. 'People tend to be very parental with children,' she said. '[Children's] natural state is a state of

THE EXPLODING TOILET

It was 11 p.m. and an old DC-8 freighter loaded with 50,000 pounds of pineapples was somewhere over the Bermuda Triangle, bound from San Juan, Puerto Rico, to Cincinnati. The crew of three were tired, as this would be their last leg in a week's rotation that had sent them from New York to Belgium and back again, onward to Mexico, and then to the Caribbean.

The 34-year-old second officer from Massachusetts was sitting at his station in a sideways-turned chair with his back to the captain and first officer. Feeling like a drink, he stood up and walked out of the cockpit, closing the door behind him. Reaching the small vestibule adjacent to the main cabin door containing a life raft, an oven, a cooler, some storage space and the lavatory, he found that the Diet Cokes were in a cardboard box on the floor, in a six-pack strapped together in clear plastic.

Having pulled out a can, he decided to put the remaining cans in the cooler to chill. The cooler, a red lift-top, stood in front of the lavatory and was packed with bags of ice. The pilot dropped the cans inside, but found that the cooler wouldn't close. There appeared to be too much ice in the cooler and he decided that one of the bags would have to go.

He removed one and shut the cooler lid. Wondering what to do with the extra, sopping-wet bag of ice, he decided to dump it down the toilet, something he had done many times before.

This time, though, when he ripped open the plastic bag, he found that there were no cubes; or, more correctly, there was just one huge cube – greenish and slightly opaque. It slid out weighing probably two pounds or so and clattered off the rim and splashed into the bowl. The caustic blue liquid used in aeroplane toilets washed over the ice as he pressed the flush lever and it disappeared into the hole and out of sight.

He turned, clutching the empty bag, but immediately heard a deep and powerful burble, which then repeated itself; it seemed to emanate from somewhere in the bowels of the plane. The noise grew louder, followed by a rumble, a vibration that passed up through his feet. From behind him came a loud swishing noise.

He turned and looked at the toilet but it had, for all practical purposes, disappeared, and in its place there now roared a fluorescent blue waterfall, a huge, heaving cascade of toilet fluid that shot waist-high into the air, splashing all four corners of the lavatory compartment! What appeared to be smoke from a factory chimney now poured out, rapidly creating a steam-like pall over everything.

The fountain grew taller, and the pilot now saw that the toilet was not actually spraying, but bubbling – it was a geyser of boiling, lathering blue foam topped with a thick white fog. He suddenly realised what had happened. It was not a block of ice that he'd fed to the toilet. It was a block of dry ice. In fact, two pounds of solid carbon dioxide was now mixing with a tank of acid to initiate the turbulent, unstoppable, chemical reaction he now witnessed!

Within seconds, a wide blue river began to flow out of the lavatory and across the floor, where a series of tracks, panels, and gullies promptly split it into several smaller rivers, each leading away to a different region beneath the main deck of the DC-8. The liquid moved rapidly along these paths, spilling off into the corners and crevices. Dribbling between the floor seams of the aeroplane, which was now cruising at 33,000 feet; dribbling down into the entrails of the plane, to freeze itself around cables or short-circuit bundles of vital wiring!

The pilot knew that this cataract was not going to stop until either the carbon dioxide was entirely evaporated or the tank of blue chemical was entirely drained. Meanwhile, the white steam, the evaporating carbon dioxide, was filling the cabin. He decided to call the captain, Jens, who unbuckled his belt and moved quickly toward the cockpit door. But as he entered the gangway, he was greeted by a psychedelic fantasy of colour and smoke, a wall of white fog and a fuming blue cauldron, the outfall from which now covered the entire floor from the entrance of the cockpit to the enormous nylon safety net that separated the crew from its load of pineapples.

'Call flight control,' commanded Jens. 'Get maintenance and explain what happened.'

The pilot rushed back to the cockpit to call the company's maintenance staff. 'You say the toilet exploded?' maintenance replied, incredulous but not particularly helpful, suggesting that they simply 'press on'.

Meanwhile, Jens had grabbed the extension wand for the fire extinguisher – a hollow metal pole the length of a harpoon – and shoved it into the bowl to try to agitate the mixture to stop. Several minutes had now passed, and a good ten gallons had streamed its way onto the floor and beyond.

Up front, the first officer had no idea what was going on. Looking behind him, his view mostly blocked by the circuit-breaker panels and cockpit door, he could just see a haze of white odourless smoke, and his captain, helpless with laughter, thrusting at something with a long metal pole.

The battle went on until the aeroplane eventually touched down safely, its plumbing finally at rest, but not before each and every employee at the cargo centre, informed by the amused mechanics who had received the distress call, knew that some idiot had poured dry ice into the toilet!

There was, amazingly, little permanent damage – it was restricted mainly to the pilot's socks and his hundred-dollar Rockport shoes – while the cargo net, walls, panels and placards aboard aircraft 806 were forever dyed a heavenly azure.

As the pilots stepped aboard the crew bus, the driver looked up and said excitedly, 'So which one of you did it?'

PAYNE STEWART

FLORIDA, USA 1999

In 1999, the colourful American golfer Payne Stewart was in the prime of a brilliant career. He was the defending US Open champion and had played a vital part of the recent American Ryder Cup victory in Boston. He was also, because of his unique clothing (old-school plaid pants and knickers), the most recognisable golfer in the world.

On 25 October, Stewart was expected in Houston for practice rounds for the Tour Championship, the Professional Golfer's Association Tour's final tournament of the year for the top thirty players.

His aircraft, a Lear jet 35, left Orlando, Florida, at about 9.20 a.m., bound for Dallas, Texas. The last communication came when the plane was over Gainesville, Florida. When the crew did not respond to repeated inquiries from air-traffic controllers, an Air Force F-16 fighter jet from Tyndall, Florida, was diverted from a routine training flight to investigate.

As the Lear 35 eerily raced across half a dozen states, various fighter jets took it in turns to monitor its progress and try and make contact. Not long after the last attempt at communication, an F-16 from Elgin Air Force Base in northwest Florida flew close to the aircraft and observed what appeared to be icy condensation on the windshield. This indicated that the normal airflow to the cabin – which includes a steady flow of warm air to defrost the windshield – had ceased. The inside of the plane seemed dark and the fighter pilot could see no movement in the cockpit.

Air Force Captain Chris Hamilton could only watch helplessly as he flew alongside the Lear over Memphis. The 32-year-old air-force pilot had been flying his F-16 Fighting Falcon, nicknamed 'Bullet One', on a training mission over the Gulf of Mexico when he was sent to try to find out what was wrong with the jet. 'It's a very helpless feeling to pull up alongside another aircraft and realise the people inside that aircraft potentially are unconscious or in some other way incapacitated,' Hamilton admitted later. 'And there's nothing I can do physically from my aircraft – even though I'm fifty to a hundred feet away – to help them at all. That's very disheartening.'

As the Lear travelled on its 1,500-mile journey, Payne Stewart's Australian-born wife Tracey, following the drama on CNN television with millions of others, tried to reach her husband on his cellular phone. According to her brother Mike Ferguson, a golf professional, 'She was trying to ring him on his mobile and couldn't raise him. It was just really bad for my sister to be watching it on CNN, knowing that it was her husband on board.'

Finally, three hours after it took off, the plane veered off its steady course and began a steep descent. The descent turned into a spin, and the plane, travelling at more than 600 miles per hour, slammed nose first into a grassy field near Aberdeen, South Dakota. Stewart, the pilot and co-pilot, and three other passengers were all killed.

A report on the accident determined that the probable cause was 'incapacitation of the flight crew members as a result of their failure to receive oxygen following a loss of cabin pressurisation, for undetermined reasons. When this sort of thing happens (which is very rare) above 30,000 feet, the time of useful consciousness begins to get very short for everybody on board.'

A couple of days after Payne's death, British golfer Ian Woosnam left Jersey in the Channel Islands in his private plane for Jerez in Spain, where he was playing in the Volvo Masters. Twenty minutes after take-off, oxygen masks dropped down, indicating cabin depressurisation. As Woosnam and his caddie

'A VERY NASTY MAN HAS JUST TRIED TO KILL US ALL'

GATWICK, ENGLAND 2000

Bryan Ferry, former lead singer of the pop group Roxy Music, was seated next to the cockpit in the upper section of a British Airways jumbo jet flying from Gatwick to Nairobi, with his wife Lucy and three of his sons, when one of them noticed a tall, muscular Kenyan walk from the economy section into the business-class cabin holding a prayer book, talking to himself. He appeared to be delirious as he walked up the aisle towards the cockpit.

Seconds later, the man entered the cockpit through an unlocked door and threw himself at the plane's controls in a crazed suicide attempt. As the struggle between the man and the crew spilled out of the cockpit and into the upper club-class section, the plane dived, then lurched, then dived again.

Alerted to the drama, the captain – William Hagan, who had been resting in the area towards the rear of the plane – ran back to the cockpit to find the man wrestling with the first officer, who was himself trying to gain control of the plane. Somehow in the struggle, the autopilot had been disabled. As Hagan grappled with the Kenyan, the airliner, with 398 people on board, nose-dived two miles from 35,000 feet!

The cabin lights cut out and screaming passengers were thrown against the walls and ceiling. The crew managed to pull the plane out of the dive, and it lurched back up again, the engines making a horrendous shrieking noise. Suddenly there was a violent stall and the whole plane shuddered before it went into another dive.

Emergency alarms were ringing and seatbelt signs were going on and off as the plane lurched to the left. Passengers saw the ground coming up steeply as everything – people, luggage, food and drink – poured down to the front of the plane. One of the stewardesses smashed her ankle as she fell almost the length of the plane. The oxygen masks had dropped. The plane gave another lurch, like a roller coaster, but miraculously pulled itself back up and, within seconds, they were above the clouds once more and on an even keel.

The pilot came on to the Tannoy, completely out of breath, to announce, 'A very nasty man has just tried to kill us all, but the plane is all right now'. With the help of three passengers the crew had overpowered the Kenyan and tied him to a seat. During the struggle the captain received bite wounds to his ear and one of his fingers.

Later, Mrs Jemima Khan, who'd been on the plane, said: 'It was terrifying. The plane stalled, went down 10,000 feet and then after pulling up it went down again. I thought, "Oh God, don't prolong it." I have always been afraid of flying and, I thought, this is it, my worst nightmare, this is the death I fear most.'

THE DA VINCI CONE

MPUMALANGA, SOUTH AFRICA 2000

On 12 March 1999, wearing a specially adapted wing-suit, with webbing between the arms and torso and between the legs, Adrian Nicholas established new world records for the longest skydive and the farthest human flight. Although the exhaust valve in his oxygen mask froze solid, nearly choking him to death, he flew for 4 minutes 55 seconds and covered ten miles. 'I don't think of myself as a nutter but I believe I can fly,' he said afterwards. 'I'm a real-life Peter Pan.'

A year later, he decided to demonstrate the viability of Leonardo da Vinci's famous parachute design. In 1485, Da Vinci had scribbled a simple sketch of a four-sided pyramid covered in linen. Alongside, he had written: 'If a man is provided with a length of gummed linen cloth with a length of twelve yards on each side and twelve yards high, he can jump from any great height whatsoever without injury.'

With advice from Professor Martin Kemp of Oxford University, Nicholas and his Swedish girlfriend, Katarina Ollikainen, constructed a parachute according to Leonardo's design. Ms Ollikainen used only tools and materials that would have been available in Da Vinci's time, apart from some thick balloon tapes to stop the canvas tearing.

On 25 June 2000, Nicholas prepared to launch himself from a hot-air balloon over Mpumalanga, South Africa, where there are wide-open fields and weather ideal for skydiving.

Strapped into a harness attached by four thick ropes to a 70-

foot-square frame of nine pine poles covered in canvas, he was hoisted to 10,000 feet above ground level.

'It was time to go,' Nicholas reflected later, describing the moment before he jumped. 'And I'm thinking, "All right Mr Da Vinci. You promised me it would be safe. I'm trusting you." And we cut it away. And it was very gentle. I was suspended there, hanging in space.'

The balloon dropped altitude for a few seconds, to enable the parachute to fill with air, and the harness was released, allowing the parachute to float free.

Surrounded by two helicopters and two parachutists, Nicholas parachuted for five minutes as a black-box recorder measured his descent. Although aeronautical experts had predicted that it would tip over, fall apart or spin uncontrollably, Leonardo's parachute made such a smooth and slow descent that the two jumpers accompanying Nicholas had to brake twice to stay level with him.

Nicholas said afterwards:

All the experts agreed it wouldn't work – it would tip over or fall apart or spin around and make you sick – but Leonardo was right all along. It's just that no one else has ever bothered trying to build it before. There was no oscillation, no rotation or gyration or anything. And I flew for ages and ages and ages.

The whole experience was incredibly moving, like one of those great English boy's-own adventures. I had a feeling of gentle elation and celebration. It was like floating under a balloon. I was able to stare out at the river below, with the wind rattling through my ears. From my perspective, I just saw this canvas material billowing in the wind like the sails of an ancient sailing boat. And I just hung there in space. You could see people in the fields all around waving and shouting. It was wonderful. Absolutely wonderful.

When Nicholas got within 600 metres of the ground, he cut himself away from Da Vinci's parachute and opened a traditional parachute to take him safely to the ground. 'You don't want to try and land something like that because you can't steer it and there's things about you,' he says. 'Da Vinci never promised that he wouldn't land me in a tree but as I landed, I thanked Leonardo for a wonderful ride.'

Despite its lack of a steering mechanism, Da Vinci's parachute landed close to Nicholas, so gently that all the data equipment was still intact. Nicholas commented, 'It took one of the greatest minds who ever lived to design it, but it took five hundred years to find a man with a brain small enough to actually go and fly it.'

'I'll die skydiving,' Nicholas predicted. 'It will happen. We all die skydiving, eventually. But it will be worth it.' In September 2005 his prediction came true when he was killed in a skydiving accident in Holland.

A WARM WELCOME

GANDER, CANADA 2001

In the 1930s, Gander in Newfoundland, Canada, was the world's largest airport, boasting one square mile of tarmac. Throughout the 'Jet Age' of the fifties and sixties, virtually every transatlantic flight required a refuelling stop at Gander. The airport terminal became a rest stop for the rich and famous, from the Hollywood celebrities to kings and presidents, and 'star-gazing' was a popular local pastime. Today, Gander International Airport is a full-service international airport, providing services on a 24-hour basis with the capabilities and infrastructure to handle the world's largest aircraft.

When the terrorist attacks occurred on the Twin Towers in New York in September 2001, hundreds of planes in the airways over the North Atlantic were diverted. Many were ordered to land elsewhere and 38 commercial airliners carrying over 6,000 passengers were forced, as a precautionary measure, to land in Gander.

After spending the night sleeping on the planes, the passengers were informed that the Red Cross were going to process everyone. When they eventually disembarked, they found themselves in an isolated Canadian island town with a population of 10,400 people marked by hardiness, desolation and high unemployment.

However, almost overnight, Gander and the surrounding small communities within a 47 mile radius had been transformed into a massive reception centre and the bewildered passengers were to spend four days there before being allowed to continue on their way. It would be quite an experience.

All the high schools, meeting halls, lodges and any other large gathering place had been closed and converted into mass lodging areas. Some had cots set up, some had mats with sleeping bags and pillows while every high school student had volunteered to assist in taking care of the 'guests'.

If any woman wanted to be in a women-only facility, it was arranged. Families were kept together and all elderly passengers were taken to private homes. Pregnant women were put up in private homes. There were doctors on call and nurses on call who stayed with the passengers for the duration. Phone calls and emails to the US and Europe were available for everyone once a day.

Countless small gestures of kindness were performed. Oz Fudge, the town constable, searched all over Gander for one particular flight-crew member so that he could give her a hug as a favour to her sister, a fellow law-enforcement officer who managed to reach him by phone. Eithne Smith, an elementary-school teacher, helped the passengers staying at her school to put together letters to family members all over the world, which she then faxed. Bonnie Harris, Vi Tucker and Linda Humby, members of a local animal protection agency, crawled into the jets' cargo holds to feed and care for all of the animals on the flights. Hundreds of people put their names on a list to take passengers into their homes and give them a chance to get cleaned up and relax.

Among the planeloads were a group from DELTA 15, bound for Atlanta. The DELTA planeload of 218 passengers ended up in a town called Lewisporte, about 28 miles from Gander. There they were put in a high school. They were then given tokens to go to the local laundromat to wash their clothes since their luggage was still on the aircraft. During the days, the passengers were given a choice of 'excursion' trips. Some people went on boat cruises of the lakes and harbours. Some went to see the local forests. Local bakeries stayed open to make fresh bread for the 'guests'. Food was prepared by local residents and brought to the school for those who elected to stay put. Others were driven to the restaurant of their choice and fed. After all that, they were delivered to the airport right on time and without a single person missing or late.

When the DELTA passengers came back on board, it was as if they had been on a cruise. The flight back to Atlanta took on the air of a party flight. They swapped stories of their stay, impressing each other with who had the better time. The passengers had bonded and were calling each other by their first names, exchanging phone numbers, postal addresses and email addresses.

And then a strange thing happened. A business-class passenger approached a stewardess and asked if he could speak over the PA to his fellow passengers, something normally never allowed. He picked up the PA and reminded everyone about what they had just gone through and of the hospitality they had received at the hands of total strangers. He said he wanted to do something in return for the good people of the town of Lewisporte and announced that he was going to set up a trust fund under the name of DELTA 15, the purpose of the fund being to provide a scholarship for Lewisporte high-school students. He requested donations of any amount from the other travellers. When the paper bag with donations got back with the amounts, names, phone numbers and addresses, it totalled $14,500. The passenger who had started it all off then promised to match the donations and to begin the administrative work on the scholarship. He added that he would forward this proposal to the Delta Corporation and ask them to donate as well. Today, the Scholarship Fund is up and running. The Gander Connection (www.theganderconnection.org), a website devoted to the incident, is also still going strong.

And all just because some people in faraway places were kind to some strangers who happened to literally drop in among them.

NOW THE DRUGS DON'T WORK...

TAMPA, USA 2002

Charles Bishop did not have an ideal life. His parents divorced before he was a year old. His father eventually dropped out of the picture altogether as Charles and his mother went from state to state – nine moves in his fifteen years. He went to four different middle schools and had recently entered the even more socially challenging world of high school. His teachers say he was bright and involved in normal school activities. However, his classmates – the peers he would most likely look to for friendship – described him as a loner.

On 5 January 2002, he was dropped off for a flying lesson by his grandmother at the St Petersburg-Clearwater Airport, about twenty miles from Tampa. Strangely, he told her not to invite any of his enemies to his funeral should anything happen to him.

Bishop had been learning to fly for some time, but was not authorised to fly alone – the minimum age for a solo pilot in the US being sixteen. However, he boarded a single-engine Cessna and took off alone when the instructor walked away after telling him to do a pre-flight check.

The airport immediately notified the Coast Guard, which sent a helicopter to intercept him. The helicopter attempted to give the pilot visual signals to land at a small airport, but Bishop failed to respond. The plane continued to downtown Tampa where, shortly after five o'clock, it slammed into the Bank of America building at around the 28th floor. A witness reported that the aircraft appeared to have struck the building without making any attempt to avoid it.

Following the crash the tail of the light aircraft could be seen dangling from the western side of the office building, which, fortunately, was nearly empty at the time. No one else was injured apart from Bishop, who died instantly. Although on a completely different scale, the incident clearly echoed the 11 September attacks in New York and Washington, which had taken place a few months previously.

This was dramatically confirmed when a suicide note was found in Bishop's pocket in which he claimed that Osama bin Laden was absolutely justified in the terror he had caused and that he had 'brought a mighty nation to its knees!' He blessed those who had committed the 9/11 atrocity and said the United States would 'have to face the consequences for its horrific actions against the Palestinian people and Iraqis by its allegiance with the monstrous Israelis – who want nothing short of world domination!' Claiming that Al Qaeda had tried to enlist him but that he had carried out the operation alone, he declared that Bin Laden was planning to blow up the Super Bowl with an antiquated nuclear bomb left over from the 1967 Israeli-Syrian war.

Charles Bishop was clearly a troubled young man. His family, however, thought they knew the real reason why. Bishop's mother and grandmother ultimately filed a $70 million law suit against Roche Laboratories, makers of the acne medicine Accutane that Bishop was thought to have been using. The drug is thought by some to have serious side effects. The label on the medicine does acknowledge the possibility of 'depression, psychosis and, rarely, suicidal ideation, suicide attempts and suicide'. It goes on to state, 'Discontinuation of Accutane therapy may be insufficient; further evaluation may be necessary.' The *New York Times* reported that in 2002, doctors reported 94 suicides in the US by Accutane users or recent users and another 257 who were hospitalised with extreme depression or attempted suicide.

By way of a dark postscript, it was later revealed that Bishop's mother and father had made joint suicide attempts years before, though they dismissed these as, 'just the result of drug and alcohol use when we were young'.

FOSSETT HANGS UP HIS BALLOON

YAMMA YAMMA, AUSTRALIA 2002

On 3 July 2002, adventurer Steve Fossett brought his balloon, the *Bud Light Spirit of Freedom*, in to land near Lake Yamma Yamma, some 700 miles northwest of Sydney. He had just completed a successful 14-day, 19-hour-and-51-minute circumnavigation to fulfil a 10-year dream: to complete the first solo round-the-world balloon flight. It had been a long and winding road.

When, in January 1996, Fossett took off from Rapid City, South Dakota, on his first attempt to make the dream a reality, many balloonists thought he was mad. A nonstop solo flight around the world was thought impossible and, when Fossett crashed the next day, it seemed the sceptics were right. But the next year Fossett was back, this time setting a duration and distance record, flying from St Louis in the United States to Sultanpur in India in seven days. He emerged exhausted – the sleep deprivation having brought on hallucinations – but convinced that his low-tech, low-altitude approach would eventually succeed.

Fossett made two more solo attempts in 1998, the latter in the Southern Hemisphere so that he could fly in August and avoid needing permission to fly over China. Both failed.

That winter, when five teams announced attempts on the record, Fossett hitched a ride with Richard Branson and Per Lindstrand. That flight, too, ended short of the finishing line.

In March 1999, news broke that appeared once and for all to have made Fossett's quest redundant. An Englishman, Brian

Jones, and his Swiss captain, Bertrand Piccard, had used a pressurised capsule to catch high-altitude jet-stream winds that catapulted them around the world in nineteen days and beat Fossett to the glory.

But Fossett still wanted to become the first person to make the journey solo, and he now adopted the high-altitude pressurised capsule approach of his rivals. After another failure in 2001, when he crashed in Brazil, he took off from Australia on 18 June 2002 determined to have one last try.

Ironically, it would be the landing that would present him with the toughest part of the trip. Indeed, his final night would be one of the most harrowing of the whole trip. 'I'd completed the round-the-world flight and here I was flying an additional night just to find a good landing spot,' he later recalled, 'and I was just very fearful that things could go wrong.' His fears came true when the balloon was buffeted by severe turbulence, then a propane fire broke out on board.

Despite forecasts of calm conditions, Fossett was forced to make the landing in 20-knot winds, and took a fifteen-minute battering inside the capsule after the balloon's deflation system failed. 'I was skipping along and dragging for the better part of three miles. So the landing itself was epic.' Fossett suffered a few bruises, strained muscles and a cut mouth during a landing he described as 'terrible'.

But it was the end of the seventh and final chapter in a quest that had lasted more than a decade and cost the owner of a Chicago stock-options company tens of millions of pounds. In a press conference scarcely fifteen minutes after he emerged from his capsule, he told reporters, 'This was my most important objective in ballooning. I feel a tremendous sense of satisfaction. This is the reason I took up ballooning.' He added, 'I could probably do with a shower. After that I'll be heading home. I think my wife will be happy to see me and I think she'll be doubly thrilled that I don't have to make any more balloon trips.'

The balloon's envelope was shredded in the landing, but the capsule survived. It was taken to the Smithsonian Institution in Washington, and will hang next to Charles Lindbergh's *Spirit of St Louis*, which made the first solo Atlantic crossing in 1927.

GLACIER GIRL

GREENLAND 2002

When a Lockheed P-38 Lightning lifted off the runway at Middlesboro, KY, USA on 26 October 2002, it was the first time the aeroplane had been in the air since 15 July 1942, the day it skidded to a stop on the icecap of Greenland.

The P-38 Lightning was developed in the late 1930s and first delivered to the US Army Air Corps in 1941. In its time, it was the fastest aircraft in the American military, with a top speed of more than 400 miles per hour. It is also visually quite remarkable, with its twin engines and twin tail booms earning it the nickname 'Fork-tailed Devil' among enemy forces in the Pacific theatre of war. Of more than 10,000 P-38s built, only six remain airworthy today.

One particular P-38 was originally part of 'Operation Bolero', a massive build-up of US warplanes in Great Britain in 1942. On 15 July of that year, six P-38Fs and two B-17Es were flying from Greenland to Iceland en route to Britain when they ran into a blizzard. They turned back to Greenland but the base was snowed in, and they were forced to make an emergency landing on the Greenland icecap. One P-38 flipped over on landing but no one was seriously injured. In fact, the aircraft suffered very little damage. The aircrew were dropped survival gear and rations and were eventually hauled out by dogsled ten days later. One pilot threw the keys of his P-38 onto the fighter's seat for anyone who wanted to recover it later.

By the early 1980s, several people had considered rescuing at least one of the ditched aircraft, but simply finding the aeroplanes under the massive ice build-up proved daunting. Two American aircraft enthusiasts, Patrick Epps and Richard Taylor, mounted a number of exploratory expeditions, finally locating the planes in 1988 using ice-penetrating radar.

Epps had known they would be buried in ice, but everyone was astounded when they found the aircraft had drifted 1½ miles and been buried at a depth of well over 86 metres (268 feet)! This was more than Epps and Taylor expected and ultimately the project was passed on to a Kentucky businessman named J Roy Shoffner. As a boy in Middlesboro, Kentucky, Roy Shoffner had become enamoured of the aircraft, vowing to own one some day.

A series of expeditions using a hot-water drill eventually enabled the recovery crew to reach a B-17, which turned out to have been crushed by the weight of the ice. When they tried one of the P-38s, however, they found it in excellent condition, so they melted out a cavern around it, dismantled it, and brought it to the surface in August 1992. It was a strange moment for one of the team in particular – he had been part of the original rescue mission to bring back the pilots in 1942.

The P-38F was transported back to the United States and, although the airframe had suffered some damage under the ice, about 80 per cent of it was still usable. The plane was then brought back up to operational trim after fifty years in the deep freeze and named, appropriately, *Glacier Girl*.

The end of the expensive and lengthy restoration came when Steve Hinton, one of only a handful of active pilots with experience flying a P-38, climbed in and took off for a few circuits of the airport that included a couple of low passes for photos by the more than 20,000 people who were there to witness the event, among them Brad McManus, one of the pilots who landed on the ice in 1942. 'I loved it,' Hinton said after landing. 'It was perfect.'

Even before this epic event, *Glacier Girl* had become a main attraction in Middlesboro, drawing close on 3,500 people a month to the Lost Squadron Museum to watch the restoration. 'People cannot believe we went down to the icecap, disassembled the aeroplane, brought it up one piece at a time and now have put it back together' said Roy. Asked by one reporter how much the restoration had cost, Roy declined to state an exact figure, though when the reporter commented that he heard the figure of $3 million, Roy acknowledged, 'That's not far off.'

Glacier Girl went on to win three major aviation trophies and is still located at the Lost Squadron Museum in Middlesboro, KY, when it is not on tour as one of the world's six flight-worthy P-38s.

A DEDICATED GHOST

RANDOLPH AIR BASE, USA 2003

It was a hot day in July 2003. Mr Robredo and two other mechanics at the Randolph Air Base in Texas had been working inside a T43 training jet. Just before locking the plane up for the night, Robredo went to the back to check all lights were out. Halfway there, a blast of cold air hit him and he felt a strange chill. The air-conditioning had been turned off – what could it be?

Then he noticed a shadowy figure staring at him. He sensed something very unusual; the hairs stood up on the back of his neck. The figure became clearer. He was in uniform, sitting with his legs crossed – perfectly relaxed. Robredo felt faint and dashed to the exit.

He almost collapsed when he saw one of the other mechanics, his friend Mike Monsalvo. Robredo told him what he had seen and discovered that it was Monsalvo who'd first seen the 'visitor'. He'd walked through the plane – whose tail number, 1154, was the same as Robredo's identification number – while it was still parked in the hangar and had seen a tall figure standing at a training station, staring at him. Monsalvo blamed fatigue for what he'd seen and hadn't told his pal of his experience, thinking Robredo would consider him crazy.

The next day, Robredo went to order a part for the plane and the man who ordered the parts, Allen Kirsh, sensed something was amiss. He asked the normally talkative mechanic what was wrong. Robredo told him of his encounter. By coincidence,

Kirsh had a friend at Buckley Air Force Base, Colorado, who'd worked on the same plane and so, without telling Robredo, he emailed his pal to relay the story and ask him if anything strange had happened on the plane. The friend replied that, in 1982, a crew chief had died of a heart attack on the plane while on a training flight.

The news stunned Robredo, who was certain that it was the crew chief he'd seen. Was the plane haunted? Was it something evil? Robredo concluded that the airman was a benign phantom who watches over aircrews – or, 'Just a dedicated crew chief who's still on the job,' as he put it.

LUCKY SKYDIVER

JOHANNESBURG, SOUTH AFRICA 2004

Christine McKenzie was an experienced skydiver with the Johannesburg Skydiving Club at the Carletonville airfield on the West Rand. On 24 August 2004, she made her 112th jump. Leaving the aircraft at 11,000 feet, she began hurtling towards the ground at 99 miles per hour, but when, after about 45 seconds, she pulled her parachute cord ready for the gentle descent to the ground, the chute didn't open. She tugged at her reserve, but it opened so forcefully that some of the lines snapped and became tangled.

As McKenzie began spinning towards the ground, she tried to untangle the lines but there was nothing she could do. 'I was in a spiral heading to the ground,' she remembered. 'They told me later that if I had fiddled with [the parachute lines] I would have been in trouble. It appears that a lot more lines had snapped and the tangle was keeping the parachute in place.'

She remembered fearing that she was going to die but, incredibly, she bounced into power lines, which broke her fall. 'If it wasn't for the lines, I would have died,' she said. 'It all happened so fast. I hit the ground really hard and I was kinda waiting to die. Then the pain set in. I knew I was alive but I wasn't sure how badly I had been injured.'

Later, speaking from her bed at Milpark Hospital in Johannesburg, McKenzie told the *Johannesburg Star* newspaper that she was dehydrated, and felt slightly dizzy. However, doctors discovered that, despite falling from such a height, she had sustained only a fracture in her pelvic bone. She had no other injuries apart from some bruises. 'I think it was a mere accident . . . I have only one broken bone,' McKenzie said, 'but I'll jump again.'

Vana Gulliver, an instructor at the club, added that a malfunctioning reserve parachute was 'incredibly rare'. 'We have never heard of that before. I wouldn't say she is lucky to be alive, but she's lucky she did not break many more bones.'

UNLUCKY SKYDIVER

VOLOGDA, RUSSIA 2005

Sixteen-year-old Russian Vika Obvalenicheva was an active girl who enjoyed outdoor sports of all kinds. In March 2005, she joined a local skydiving club in the Russian city of Vologda. Club instructors made it clear to new members that they could only commence the sport if they had their parents' permission. Vika's headmaster assured the club that she had the necessary permission – though later, her mother and stepfather denied that they'd ever agreed to their daughter taking up the sport.

After a short period of training, Vika and three other apprentice skydivers were taken up in a small aircraft to an altitude of about a mile and a half. Everyone then jumped, but Vika – perhaps in fear – appears not to have pulled the ring of her main parachute; her reserve parachute opened, but the inexperienced girl failed to control it. Her parachute cords then became snarled in the wires of a high-voltage power line and she suffered massive electric shocks.

Immediately after landing the plane, the leader of the skydiving unit and two doctors boarded an Mi-2 helicopter and headed for the site where the young skydivers had landed. They managed to free Vika from the power lines and set off for the nearest hospital.

Incredibly, nearing the hospital, the helicopter then crashed. In a hurry, and aware that every minute was precious, the pilot failed to spot aluminium wires stretched between the twelve-storey building of the hospital and an adjacent five-storey building. The helicopter hit the wires and veered out of control, coming down less than 100 feet from the hospital. Patients and doctors watched aghast as its propeller blades were scattered as it disintegrated, killing all on board.

Doctors originally thought that Vika had not lived through the earlier accident. Tragically, two days later, forensic experts concluded from her internal injuries that, having survived a botched skydive and massive electric shocks, she'd ultimately died at the hands of those who had come to rescue her.

DUMPED UPON FROM A GREAT HEIGHT

LEOMINSTER, USA 2005

Nina Gambone, 31, of Leominster, Massachusetts, had just arrived home from a trip to the grocery store at around 7 p.m. when she heard what she later called 'an explosion. The entire house shook.' Gambone said she thought the impact had been caused by a bomb – until she saw an icy lump the size of a beach ball in her car. The roof was bowed inward and the windshield was smashed. The car, to use her phrase, was 'totalled'. 'The car's done,' Lt Raymond Booth of Leominster Police added. 'That thing's not going anywhere. If it (the object) had hit somebody, it would have killed them.'

Leominster lies along a flight path towards Boston's Logan Airport and Federal Aviation Administration officials later confirmed the 'bomb' was of the bathroom variety and cautioned Gambone not to touch the ice, which was most likely human waste.

'They said don't touch it, it's very likely waste. She said if you have come in contact with it, wash your hands,' said Michael Pinder, who lived at the house. However, Gambone's son, Nathan, had already picked up the ice, using his sweatshirt to shield his hands. 'I've got to clean my sweatshirt now,' he said after hearing the advice from the FAA.

The FAA told the police that the dense, white ice that struck Gambone's car most likely fell from a European flight. 'If it's from a domestic flight, the ice is blue,' Lt Booth said, adding that the FAA would try to find out which plane had dropped the ice by looking at the time of the incident, although it could be hard to determine which aircraft was responsible.

Later, an FAA spokesman, Jim Peters, said the waste was most likely dropped by a commercial overseas flight headed into Logan International Airport. 'We pulled the radar tracks and narrowed it down to about five possible carriers,' Peters said. 'Sometimes we do have success, but we were unable to do it this time.'

Mrs Gambone was shocked when told by the FAA that no one from the organisation was coming out to document the incident and that they could give no advice as to what to do next.

'After we explained what we thought was a pretty big deal and that out of state news stations had responded to the scene more quickly, he told us that it must have been a slow news day. He had no answers on the waste – now partially melted in the car. He said the fire department should have cleaned it up. The Fire Chief came out the next day at noon and said they had no intention of cleaning out the material in the car driveway. They came to collect the two chunks I had in my freezer and put them back into the car. They couldn't remove the glob because it is classified as hazardous waste.'

Gambone told reporters, 'My grandmother loved the car. She loved her little Toyota and when she passed away last year she left it to me. It was a 91 and it only has 71,000 miles on it. Luckily, I work at UndercoverWear, a lingerie home party company. Immediately following the incident UndercoverWear gracious donated a rental car to me for two weeks.'

SOMEONE JUST DROPPED IN

LONG ISLAND, USA 2005

At 7 a.m on 5 June 2005, Pam Hearne heard 'a very loud bang' outside her family's New York Long Island house, but thought little of it and went to work. It wasn't until she got back home at 10.30 a.m. that she noticed something bizarre out her window.

'There was a human body part back there,' she said. 'It was rather large.'

A man's severed leg – with a white Adidas sneaker still attached – had plummeted from the sky onto her garage roof and bounced into the backyard.

What's more, on closer inspection, there was also part of the spine and a hip.

A US customs inspector later discovered the rest of the man's body in the wheel well of a South African Airways passenger plane Flight 203, which landed at John F. Kennedy International Airport in New York.

A South African Airways spokeswoman said it appeared to have been a stowaway attempt that had gone disastrously wrong. She said the plane from Johannesburg, had stopped in Dakar, Senegal, on its way to New York.

The pilot reported feeling vibrations at take-off but conducted a check and found nothing amiss, said Nassau County, New York, police detective Kevin Smith.

During the flight, Smith said the pilot felt more 'vibrating sensations and heard pounding, but nothing appeared wrong with the plane.'

DINNER AND DIVE

BATH, ENGLAND 2005

David Hempleman-Adams, Bear Grylls and Lieutenant Commander Alan Veal had all previously been involved in dangerous and daunting challenges. In 1996, Hempleman-Adams became the first Briton to walk solo and unsupported to the South Pole and in 2000 he was the first man to fly a balloon over the North Pole. Mr Grylls, a former member of the British SAS, became one of the youngest climbers to reach the summit of Mount Everest and return alive in 1997, aged 22.
the first man to fly a balloon over the North Pole.

However, in June 2005, they tried something a little different. To honour fifty years of the Duke of Edinburgh's Award, the three adventurers set out to break a world record previously held by adventurer Henry Shelford, who had conducted a dinner party 22,326ft (6805 metres) up a Tibetan mountain in 2004!

Clad in formal evening wear, the three ascended to 24,262 feet above Bath in southwest England. Grylls and Veal then climbed forty feet down to a platform with a formally laid dinner table, where they dined on asparagus spears followed by poached salmon and a terrine of summer fruits, all served in specially designed warm boxes. Temperatures reached −45°C as the adventurers enjoyed duck a l'orange on plastic plates.

After the meal, they saluted the Queen before skydiving to earth.

'It was fantastic to nail that record but it was a dangerous stunt,' Grylls told reporters. 'The scariest moment was when my oxygen mask slipped off when I was hanging upside down from the table, but we pulled it together in the end.'

Mr Hempleman-Adams said: 'Without doubt, this is the strangest record I have ever attempted. It was a fun stunt but was at the same time very dangerous. There were potentially a lot of things that could have gone wrong. The only drawback about the stunt was the other two members of the team ate all the food so there was nothing left when I landed.'